# BACH

*Series edited by Stanley Sadie*

# THE MASTER MUSICIANS

## Titles Available in Paperback

*Berlioz* · Hugh Macdonald

*Brahms* · Malcolm MacDonald

*Britten* · Michael Kennedy

*Bruckner* · Derek Watson

*Chopin* · Jim Samson

*Grieg* · John Horton

*Handel* · Donald Burrows

*Liszt* · Derek Watson

*Mahler* · Michael Kennedy

*Mendelssohn* · Philip Radcliffe

*Monteverdi* · Denis Arnold

*Purcell* · J. A. Westrup

*Rachmaninoff* · Geoffrey Norris

*Schoenberg* · Malcolm MacDonald

*Schubert* · John Reed

*Sibelius* · Robert Layton

*Richard Strauss* · Michael Kennedy

*Tchaikovsky* · Edward Garden

*Vaughan Williams* · James Day

*Verdi* · Julian Budden

*Vivaldi* · Michael Talbot

## Titles Available in Hardcover

*Bach* · Malcolm Boyd

*Beethoven* · Barry Cooper

*Chopin* · Jim Samson

*Elgar* · Robert Anderson

*Handel* · Donald Burrows

*Schumann* · Eric Frederick Jensen

*Schütz* · Basil Smallman

*Richard Strauss* · Michael Kennedy

*Stravinsky* · Paul Griffiths

## Titles In Preparation

*Bartók* · Malcolm Gillies

*Dvořák* · Jan Smaczny

*Musorgsky* · David Brown

*Puccini* · Julian Budden

*Tchaikovsky* · R. John Wiley

THE MASTER MUSICIANS

# BACH

*Malcolm Boyd*

OXFORD
UNIVERSITY PRESS

# OXFORD
### UNIVERSITY PRESS

Oxford   New York
Athens   Auckland   Bangkok   Bogatá   Buenos Aires   Calcutta
Cape Town   Chennai   Dar es Salaam   Delhi   Florence   Hong Kong   Istanbul
Karachi   Kuala Lumpur   Madrid   Melbourne   Mexico City   Mumbai
Nairobi   Paris   São Paulo   Singapore   Taipei   Tokyo   Toronto   Warsaw

*and associated companies in*
Berlin   Ibadan

Copyright © 2000 by Malcolm Boyd
First published 1983 by J. M. Dent & Sons Ltd.
First paperback edition 1986 by J. M. Dent & Sons Ltd.
Second edition 1990
Reprinted with corrections 1995 by Oxford University Press
American edition 1997 by Schirmer Books
Third edition 2000

Published by Oxford University Press, Inc.
198 Madison Avenue, New York, New York 10016

Library of Congress Cataloging-in-Publication Data
Boyd, Malcolm.
Bach / Malcolm Boyd. — 3rd ed.
p. cm. — (The master musicians)
Includes bibliographical references and index.

ISBN 978-0-19-514222-8 (cloth)
ISBN 978-0-19-530771-9 (pbk)

1. Bach, Johann Sebastian, 1685–1750.
2. Composers—Germany—Biography.
I. Title.
II. Master musicians series.
ML410.B1 B73 2000
780'.92—dc21   [B]   00-033976

*Series designed by Carla Bolte*

3 5 7 9 8 6 4

Printed in the United States of America
on acid free paper

## TO COLIN AND DELYTH

*O holder Tag, erwünschte Zeit . . .*

# Contents

# Preface

I T IS NOT TO EXCUSE ANY SHORTCOMINGS IN THE PRESENT VOLUME if I say that the task of writing about J. S. Bach is a more formidable one in the 1980s than it was in 1900 or 1947, when my predecessors in the Master Musicians series published their studies of the composer. At that time the image of Bach as a devout Lutheran, his art and life wholly directed towards the improvement of church music, was well established, and seemingly on the firmest foundations. After all, hadn't Philipp Spitta thoroughly researched archival sources for his exhaustive book on the composer published in 1873–80? Hadn't he established a chronology for Bach's works based on the most rigorous scientific methods, including the study of paper types, watermarks, and calligraphy? And didn't the monumental edition of the music published by the Bach-Gesellschaft in 1851–99 provide as complete and accurate a text as any scholar could wish for?

What might be called the Spitta image of Bach survived until the 1950s, when the new chronology, affecting particularly the Leipzig cantatas, was proposed by Alfred Dürr at Göttingen and Georg von Dadelsen at Tübingen; the cantatas were now seen to occupy only the early years of Bach's cantorate. The wider implications of this discovery were expounded by Friedrich Blume in an essay, presented at the 1962 *Bachfest* in Mainz, which was regarded, indeed intended, as an earthquake, with the chronology of Dürr and Dadelsen at its epicentre. Despite recent attempts, notably by Piero Buscaroli, to bring the new Bach image into focus, it will not be seen clearly until the tremors set up by that earthquake have subsided. Meanwhile, other issues have also claimed the attention of Bach scholars in the wake of the new collected edition (*Neue Bach-Ausgabe*) initiated in 1950: questions of textual criticism and attribution, the evaluation of different versions and adaptations, and the relevance to Bach's music of *Affektenlehre, Figurenlehre*, numerology,

Lutheranism, and the *Aufklärung*, not to mention the multifarious aspects of performing practice.

It is not my purpose in this brief introductory volume to come to grips with the many problems that preoccupy Bach scholars today, but rather to present as coherent an account as possible of Bach's life and works in the light of current knowledge. To this end I have avoided the life/works dichotomy that operates so well in other Master Musicians volumes and organized the book in a way which will, I hope, serve to show the unique connection that exists between Bach's music and the circumstances in which it was written. The first two chapters are mainly biographical, the last mainly exegetical; the others alternate between biography and discussion of the music. As far as the latter is concerned, chronology is at times relaxed in order to organize the discussion in broad categories (organ music, church music etc.), but where it has been found desirable to divide a particular genre between different chapters the reader will be guided to related sections by cross-references within the text and by the book's index.

I am grateful to Stanley Sadie for persuading me to embark on the writing of this book, and for encouraging me to finish it. Visits to East Germany were made possible by financial help from University College, Cardiff, and pleasurable by the warm hospitality of Heinz and Gertrud Sawade in Mühlhausen and Charlotte Bemmann in Leipzig. For assistance of various kinds I am deeply indebted to David Humphreys, David Wyn Jones, Charles Langmaid, Ruth Thackeray and, not least, my wife Beryl and son Jeremy. Without their help the book would have been the poorer. The difficulty of writing anything on Bach remotely worthy of its subject remains.

*Cardiff, 1983*                                                    M.B

### Note on the third edition

For this new edition, marking the 250th anniversary of Bach's death in 1750, the test has been thoroughly revised to take into account recent findings and fresh perspectives on the music. While the basic shape of the book remains the same, with discussion of the music interleaved between the biographical chapters to which it relates, due reference has been made to the chronological refinements that have challenged, without yet invalidating, this structure. The opportunity has also been taken to revise the list of Bach's works, to reorganize and expand the bibliography, and to provide a new map. For several of the revisions I am indebted to my reviewers and colleagues, among whom I would mention in particular Peter Williams, Don Franklin, and Stephen Crist. I would also like to thank Julia Kellerman, who saw the book through its earlier revisions at J. M. Dent & Sons and then at OUP, and Ursula Payne, whose careful editorial work helped to shape the present edition.

*Cardiff, 1999*                                                     *M.B*

# Illustrations

*Integrated Illustrations*

# Bibliographical References

Brief references only are given in text and footnotes to items included in the Select Bibliography (Appendix D). Some standard works frequently referred to are cited by the author's name or an abbreviation. They are:

BC      Schulze, Hans-Joachim, and Wolff, Christoph, *Bach Compendium: Analytisch-bibliographisches Repertorium der Werke Johann Sebastian Bachs* (Leipzig, 1985–)

BG      *J. S. Bach: Werke* [collected edition of the Bach-Gesellschaft] (Leipzig, 1851–99)

BWV      Schmieder, Wolfgang, *Thematisch-systematisches Verzeichnis der musikalischen Werke Johann Sebastian Bachs: Bach-Werke-Verzeichnis* (Leipzig, 1950; 2nd ed., 1990); *Kleine Ausgabe*, ed. A. Dürr, Y. Kobayashi, and K. Beisswenger (Wiesbaden, 1998)

NBA      *Neue Bach-Ausgabe* [collected edition of the Johann-Sebastian-Bach-Institut, Göttingen, and the Bach-Archiv, Leipzig] (Kassel and Basle, 1954–)

Schweitzer      Schweitzer, Albert, *J. S. Bach* (London, 1911; German version, 1908; French original, 1905)

Spitta      Spitta, Philipp, *Johann Sebastian Bach* (London, 1884–5; German original, 1873–80)

Terry      Terry, Charles Sanford, *Bach: a Biography* (London, 1928; 6th ed., 1967)

NBR      David, Hans T., and Mendel, Arthur: *The Bach Reader* (New York and London, 1945; 2nd ed., 1966); revised and enlarged by C. Wolff as *The New Bach Reader* (New York, 1998)

## A note on currency

12 pfennig = 1 groschen; 21 groschen = 1 florin (or gulden); 24 groschen = 1 thaler. Bach's salary in 1714 was 250 florins; in 1718 it was 400 thalers, and in 1730 about 700 thalers. These figures do not include payments in kind.

A pound of raw meat could be bought for about 2 groschen and a pound of butter for about 35 pfennig (although it might cost twice that in winter); coffee was relatively expensive at about 12 groschen a pound, and tea was even dearer. Clothing was also expensive, but a good clavichord could be purchased for about 20 thalers, less than seven times the published price of Bach's *Clavier-Übung* III.

NORTH
SEA

Lübeck ○

Hamburg ○

Lüneburg □
(1700-1702)

*R. Weser*

*R. Elbe*

BRANDENBURG

*R. Havel*

Berlin ○

Potsdam ○

• Celle

• Hanover

• Bückeburg

*R. Spree*

○ Zerbst

□ Cöthen (1717-1723)

Göttingen
•

Sangerhausen ○

Mülhausen □
(1707-1708)

Cassel ○

*R. Unstrut*

*R. Saale*

○ Halle

□ Leipzig (1723-1750)

Dresden ○

Weissenfels ○

○ Zeitz

SAXONY

*R. Elbe*

Eisenach (1685-1695) □

□ Weimar (1703, 1708-1717)

Ohrdruf (1695-1700) □ □ Arnstadt (1703-1707)

THURINGIA

*R. Werra*

○ Schleitz

*R. Elster*

Carlsbad ○

□ Places where Bach lived
○ Places visited by Bach
• Other places

0    20    40    60    80 Miles

0   20   40   60   80 Kilometers

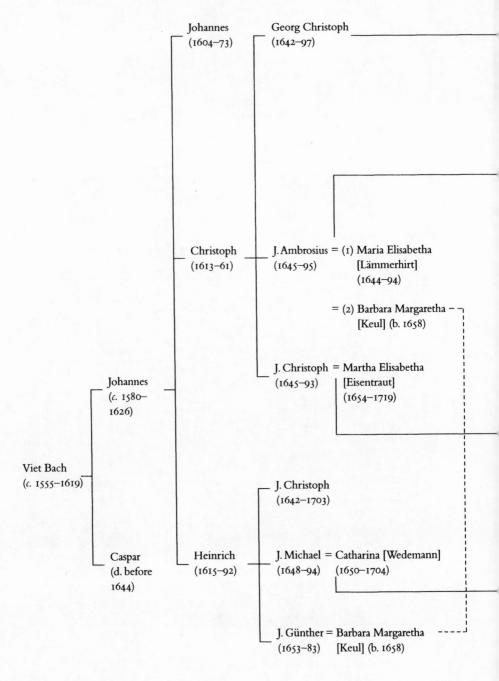

[maiden names are shown in square brackets]

2 A Bach Family Tree

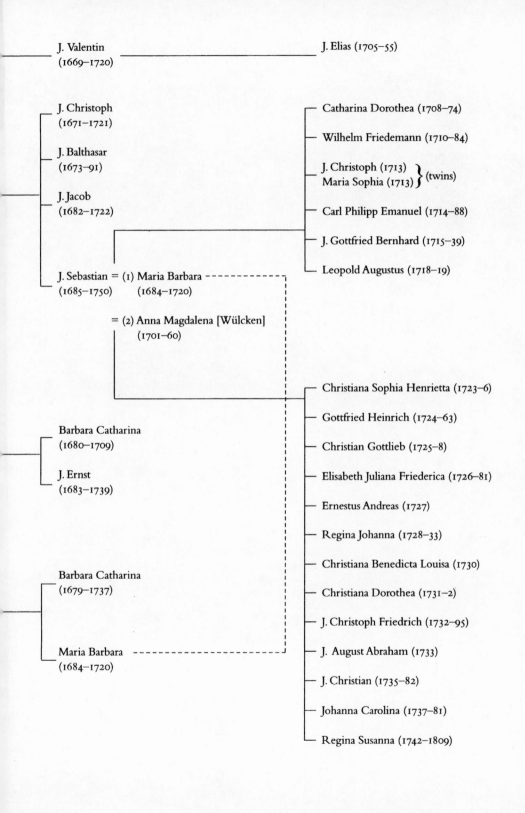

J. Valentin
(1669–1720)

J. Elias (1705–55)

J. Christoph
(1671–1721)

J. Balthasar
(1673–91)

J. Jacob
(1682–1722)

Catharina Dorothea (1708–74)

Wilhelm Friedemann (1710–84)

J. Christoph (1713)
Maria Sophia (1713) } (twins)

Carl Philipp Emanuel (1714–88)

J. Gottfried Bernhard (1715–39)

Leopold Augustus (1718–19)

J. Sebastian = (1) Maria Barbara
(1685–1750)      (1684–1720)

= (2) Anna Magdalena [Wülcken]
        (1701–60)

Barbara Catharina
(1680–1709)

J. Ernst
(1683–1739)

Christiana Sophia Henrietta (1723–6)

Gottfried Heinrich (1724–63)

Christian Gottlieb (1725–8)

Elisabeth Juliana Friederica (1726–81)

Ernestus Andreas (1727)

Regina Johanna (1728–33)

Christiana Benedicta Louisa (1730)

Barbara Catharina
(1679–1737)

Maria Barbara
(1684–1720)

Christiana Dorothea (1731–2)

J. Christoph Friedrich (1732–95)

J. August Abraham (1733)

J. Christian (1735–82)

Johanna Carolina (1737–81)

Regina Susanna (1742–1809)

# BACH

# CHAPTER 1

# Background and Early Years

## (1685–1703)

THE LANDSCAPE OF THURINGIA, THAT REGION OF CENTRAL Germany lying just south of the Harz Mountains, has altered little since Bach's time. Even today it is known as the 'green heart' of Germany. Its wooded slopes and gently rolling fields, in the folds of which red-tiled roofs cluster round the modest spire of a village church, continue to please the eye of the visitor and to provide a setting in which mankind and nature can exist harmoniously together. Most of the villages (and, one is tempted to add, the roads that connect them) seem also to have changed little since the eighteenth century, although the churches no longer offer the possibility of employment to organists, organ builders, tuners, and repairers to the extent they once did. Even in Bach's day it was to the larger towns and the free imperial cities of Thuringia and neighbouring regions that musicians looked for a professional career. The need there was for church organists, for Kantors to teach in the schools and to organize a town's musical activities, and for *Stadtpfeifer* to provide music for municipal and civic functions and to augment the churches' instrumental resources when called upon to do so. Music was not studied as an independent university discipline, but teachers and students in university towns such as Erfurt, Halle, Jena, and Leipzig involved themselves in the musical life of the community, principally through the church and the secular *collegium musicum*.

Other, and perhaps more lucrative, employment could be found at the princely courts that proliferated at the time in central Germany.

While exercising little or no military and political influence, these petty principalities and dukedoms, altering in size and number as dynasties flourished and declined, vied with each other in intellectual and cultural pursuits; most of them maintained a *Kapelle*, a body of singers and instrumentalists who provided music for the court chapel and for such secular enterprises as the prince or duke was interested in encouraging. Even such minor courts as Weimar and Cöthen, where Bach was employed, offered musicians a better chance of advancement than all but the largest churches and the most generous municipalities. The payment of salaries at court may have been irregular at times, but other things compensated for this, and an appointment as *Konzertmeister* or *Kapellmeister* brought the ambitious musician a measure of prestige not easily to be won in an ecclesiastical or municipal post.

Opera was the only important sphere of professional music-making in which Thuringia was unable to compete with other parts of Germany in the early eighteenth century. Some courts in the region did support opera sporadically and on a modest scale; at the Weissenfels court, for example, with which Bach enjoyed close contact, German operas were performed most years between 1680 and 1736, and from 1696 to 1709 touring opera troupes appeared regularly at the Weimar court. In Leipzig, too, opera gained a precarious foothold between 1693 and 1720, first under Nicolaus Adam Strungk (1640–1700) and then under Telemann. But the main operatic centres in Germany lay further afield, and composers eager to realize their gifts in the theatre would travel east to Dresden, south to Munich, or north to Brunswick, Hanover, and Hamburg. A case in point is Reinhard Keiser, a native of Thuringia and a pupil at the Thomasschule in Leipzig, who pursued his career as an opera composer first in Brunswick and then in Hamburg, where in 1705 Handel produced his first operas, *Almira* and *Nero*.

One reason for Thuringia's resistance to opera, and to the overwhelming penetration of Italian musical styles that usually accompanied it, was the presence of a strong Lutheran tradition. Martin Luther was born at Eisleben, in the northern part of Thuringia, in 1483, and died there in 1546. He went to the Lateinschule in Eisenach (the same that Bach was to attend two centuries later) and to the university of Erfurt, and it was at the Wartburg Castle, overlooking Eisenach, that he found refuge after being excommunicated and outlawed by the Diet of

Worms. The spiritual presence of one for whom music was 'a gift from God' and 'next in importance to theology' remained strong throughout Thuringia. Luther had been knowledgeable enough in the art to be able to admire the works of Josquin Desprez, Heinrich Isaac, and Ludwig Senfl, and practised enough in it to derive enjoyment from singing and playing the lute and the flute. His achievement in establishing the German hymn, or chorale, was of fundamental importance to the formation and preservation of a distinctively German musical style, especially in church music, during the Italian-dominated Baroque period. The conception of music as 'sounding number' received its most powerful expression in the music (particularly the late music) of Bach.

The social, political, and religious climate of Thuringia tended to produce a particular type of musician: traditional, conservative, slow to be influenced by wider European developments. Contact with foreign ideas and innovations in musical style came mainly through the courts, as Bach was to find at Weimar and later at Dresden, while in the towns (and to some extent in the courts as well) local traditions were perpetuated by a system of guilds and by the handing on of employment from father to son (or in some cases from father to son-in-law). The Baroque aesthetic placed craftsmanship above originality (or at any rate regarded craftsmanship as a prerequisite of originality), and this was conducive to the establishing of musical families, of which the Scarlattis in Italy, the Couperins in France, and the Purcells in England were outstanding examples. The family (or clan, as it has with some justification been called) into which Johann Sebastian Bach was born in 1685 had furnished Thuringia with some of its best musicians for three or four generations, and the name 'Bach' had become so common in musical circles that (if it did not in fact mean by derivation 'musician'[1]) it had become synonymous with 'musician' in many places. J. S. Bach's awareness of this family tradition, and the pride he took in it, can be judged from the valuable Genealogy (the *Ursprung der musikalisch-Bachischen Familie*) which he compiled in 1735. Brought up to date in 1774–5 by his son Carl Philipp Emanuel, this traces musical members of the family back through six generations to a certain Veit (or Vitus) Bach, a native of

---

[1] See G. Kraft, 'Neue Beiträge zur Bach-Genealogie', *Beiträge zur Musikwissenschaft*, i (1959), 29–61.

'Ungarn', which included parts of Moravia and Slovakia as well as Hungary. A baker by trade, he left home with his son Johannes because of religious persecution and settled in the Thuringian village of Wechmar, near Gotha, in the 1590s. According to the Genealogy, Veit enjoyed playing the cittern, 'which he even took with him to the mill and played while the grinding was going on'. (This Veit, who died in 1619, has frequently been confused with another Veit Bach, possibly not a family member, who died before 1578.)

Veit Bach had two further sons: the second has not been identified, but the youngest, Caspar, was active as a musician in Gotha and later in Arnstadt. It was, however, from Johannes (*c.* 1580–1626), a baker like his father and a town musician, that J. S. Bach descended, the succession proceeding to Christoph (1613–61, court and town musician at Weimar, Erfurt, and Arnstadt) and then to Johann Ambrosius (1645–95), Sebastian's father. Ambrosius and his brother Johann Christoph (1645–93) were the first of a number of twins among the Bachs, and they resembled each other so much in manner and appearance that, as C. P. E. Bach noted in the Genealogy, 'even their wives were unable to tell them apart'. After living closely together for over twenty-five years, sharing the loss of both parents in 1661 and enduring the siege of Erfurt by troops of Archbishop Johann Philipp of Mainz three years later, they finally separated in 1671 when Christoph became a court musician at Arnstadt and Ambrosius a *Hausmann* (town musician) at Eisenach.

What no doubt helped Ambrosius to secure the Eisenach appointment was the presence there of his cousin, another Johann Christoph (1642–1703), who for six years had been organist at the important Georgenkirche and was also organist and harpsichordist to the Duke of Eisenach, Johann Georg I. Christoph was highly thought of for his practical and creative gifts, and was in fact the most talented composer among the Bachs before Johann Sebastian himself, in whose early development he may have played an important role. But an intractable disposition earned him many enemies, and as a musician Ambrosius seems to have enjoyed greater esteem among the townspeople, and certainly among the town councillors. Ambrosius's duties as *Hausmann* included twice-daily performances of chorales from the tower of the town hall, at which he would have played the trumpet, and assistance as violinist or viola player in concerted music at church on Sundays and feast days; to these duties were added others when, in 1677, he was made a member of the court orchestra. He was evidently a musician of some ability, and in 1684, when he sought to take up a new appointment at Erfurt, the authorities refused to release him.

In 1668, three years before settling in Eisenach, Ambrosius had married Maria Elisabetha Lämmerhirt (or Lemmerhirt), who came from a family already tenuously connected by marriage to the Bachs (her half-sister Hedwig was the second wife of Ambrosius's uncle, Johannes Bach [1604–73], town musician and organist at Erfurt). Before the couple left Erfurt for Eisenach they had buried one son and christened a second, Johann Christoph. Six more children were born to them at Eisenach, the last being Johann Sebastian on 21 March (old style) 1685; he was christened two days later at the font of the historic Georgenkirche. The name Sebastian was given to him by one of his godparents, Sebastian Nagel, *Hausmann* at Gotha. His first name was that of his other god-father, Johann Georg Koch, a forester at Eisenach, but Johann was an exceedingly common name in Germany at the time, and nowhere more so than among the Bachs: Ambrosius's six sons were all called Johann, as were the four sons of his twin brother Christoph, and there were numerous other Johanns and Johannas elsewhere in the family.

Nothing is known for certain about Sebastian's early years until 1693, when, at the age of eight, he was listed forty-seventh in the fifth class (Quinta) of the Lateinschule at Eisenach. He was by no means the first of the Bachs to be educated there. A distant uncle, Jacob (1655–1718), from the Meiningen branch of the family, had entered the school in 1669 (he was expelled for theft two years later) and the names of four brothers and four cousins also appear in the school records. Religious instruction and Latin grammar formed the basis of the curriculum, which included also some arithmetic and history, and in the higher forms Greek, Hebrew, philosophy, logic, and rhetoric. Sebastian probably enrolled in the school on or shortly after his seventh birthday in 1692, and he remained there until 1695. The bare facts of his scholastic progress are recorded in the annual school lists, and can be summarized as follows:

| Date | Class | Number in class | Position | Absences |
|------|-------|-----------------|----------|----------|
| 1692–3 | Quinta | 90 | 47 | 96 |
| 1693–4 | Quinta | 90 | 14 | 59 |
| 1694–5 | Quarta | 64 | 23 | 103 |

It was customary to spend two years in each class, but promotion depended upon achievement rather than age, and so the number of boys in a class tended to decrease further up the school. Sebastian's final position of twenty-third after one year in the Quarta compares favourably with that of his brother Johann Jacob, who came twenty-fifth in the same class despite being three years older and having fewer absences.

The nature and extent of Sebastian's musical training during these years remain matters for conjecture. His father presumably taught him to play the violin, and probably introduced him to the rudiments of music theory as well. What, if anything, his father's cousin Christoph contributed to his musical education at Eisenach is difficult to guess. Karl Geiringer has suggested that the two families may not have been very close,[2] and both Mizler's Obituary[3] and Bach's first biographer, Johann Nikolaus Forkel, tell us that Sebastian's first lessons in keyboard playing came later, at Ohrdruf, from his elder brother Johann Christoph. But even if the cousin gave him no formal instruction, the boy would certainly have come into contact with him at the Georgenkirche, and he may even at this early stage have been aware of the special qualities of the music of this 'profound composer', as he later called him. Undoubtedly Sebastian would have learnt, too, from Andreas Christian Dedekind, Kantor at the Lateinschule. He was in charge of the *chorus symphoniacus* that sang at the Georgenkirche, and Sebastian's 'uncommonly fine treble voice' (as the Obituary described it) must have been in demand for this and for the *Schulkurrende*, when singers from the school serenaded the neighbourhood to raise money.

School was held from 6 a.m. until 9 a.m. (from 7 a.m until 10 a.m.

[2] *The Bach Family*, 74.
[3] Written by C. P. E. Bach and J. F. Agricola in 1750 and published in the final issue of L. C. Mizler's *Musikalische Bibliothek* (1754). An English translation is in *NBR*, pp. 297–307.

during the winter) and from 1 p.m. until 3 p.m., Wednesdays and Saturdays being half-holidays. Reckoned in hours (one hour being the length of a lesson; the German word *Stunde* serves for both) the total of 103 absences recorded for Sebastian during 1694–5 would represent four whole weeks away from school; reckoned in half-days it would indicate longer periods of absence. In either case the figure perhaps reflects the tragic domestic events of that year. Sebastian's father, already saddened by the early death in 1691 of his second surviving son, Johann Balthasar, and by the death at Arnstadt in 1693 of his much-loved twin brother, Johann Christoph, had to suffer in May 1694 the loss of his wife Elisabetha. Ambrosius was left with three children to look after (the eldest having by then left for Ohrdruf), and he resolved to provide for them by marrying again.

When Barbara Margaretha Bartholomaei (née Keul) entered into matrimony with Ambrosius Bach on 27 November 1694 it was not the first time in her thirty-six years that she had married into the Bach family. Her late husband had been deacon at Arnstadt, but before that she had been the wife of Ambrosius's cousin Johann Günther (1653–83), described in the Genealogy as 'a good musician and a skilful maker of various newly invented instruments'. Possibly Ambrosius's decision to remarry was strengthened by a sense of family obligation towards Barbara Margaretha and her nine-year-old daughter Christina Maria—and still more towards Günther's daughter Catharina Margaretha (born six months after her father's death, in October 1683), if she was still living. In any event, the match was ill-fated. Günther had died only four months after his marriage to Barbara Margaretha, and Jacob Bartholomaei after about four-and-a-half years. On 20 February 1695, less than three months after her marriage to Ambrosius, the unlucky lady was widowed for a third time, and Sebastian made an orphan.

After appealing unsuccessfully to the council for permission to carry on her late husband's duties with the help of assistants and apprentices, as the widow of his twin brother had been allowed to do at Arnstadt, Barbara Margaretha was forced to look for someone to take care of the two orphaned sons, Jacob and Sebastian, now aged thirteen and ten respectively. The relative best able to do this was their elder brother Johann Christoph, who since 1690 had been organist at the Michaeliskirche at Ohrdruf and had married there in October 1694. Christoph's house stood in what is now the Bachstrasse, not far from the church itself, and it was there that Jacob and Sebastian came to live in March 1695. With their own first child already expected (he was born on 21 July), this must have stretched the modest resources of Christoph and his new wife quite considerably; Jacob returned to Eisenach after his fifteenth birthday in 1697, but by then a second child was on the way. Sebastian also remained at Ohrdruf until he was fifteen, and we may suppose that his musical training during these years came mainly from his elder brother. Christoph had studied at Erfurt under Johann Pachelbel, the most important organ composer of the central German school, and his library of keyboard music, which Sebastian would certainly have known, included works by Pachelbel, Froberger, Kerll, and other German masters.

It was under Christoph's guidance, according to Mizler's Obituary, that Sebastian 'laid the foundations of his keyboard technique', and it is therefore unfortunate, and almost certainly unjust, that Christoph has been remembered chiefly for what must seem today an act of unkindness towards his younger brother. It appears that Sebastian had for some reason been denied access to a book of keyboard pieces belonging to Christoph, and to obtain it had practised what the Obituary calls 'the following innocent deceit':

> The book was kept in a cupboard secured only by lattice doors. He [Sebastian] was therefore able to reach through the lattice with his small hands and roll up the book, which had only a paper cover; in this way he was able to remove it at night, while everyone else was in bed, and to copy it by moonlight, since he had no other light. After six months he was delighted to have this musical treasure in his hands, and tried secretly and with unusual zeal to profit from it until, to his deep dismay, his brother got to know of it and was harsh enough to confiscate the music he had taken such pains to copy.

We are insufficiently informed about Christoph's character to be able to judge his motives in this affair (or, for that matter, the veracity of the story itself), but we know enough about his younger brother to recognize here an early example of Sebastian's determination to seek out every possible opportunity for developing and perfecting his art, even at the risk of incurring the displeasure of others. There were soon to be further examples of this single-mindedness.

Christoph did not neglect his brother's general education. On Sebastian's arrival in Ohrdruf he was sent to the old Klosterschule, where the progressive educational reforms of Comenius Jan Ámos Komenský) had been adopted, and which attracted pupils from as far away as Cassel and Jena. Latin grammar and theology remained at the basis of the curriculum, but geography, history, arithmetic, and natural science were also taught, and music (Luther's handmaid to theology) was prominent in the timetable; four hours a week were devoted to it in the third and fourth classes, five in the first and second. As at Eisenach, there was also a *Kurrende* choir from which Sebastian, and no doubt Johann Christoph, derived much-needed financial benefit. Sebastian seems to have found the curriculum more agreeable (or perhaps the competition of his classmates less formidable) than at Eisenach, and his school record is impressive. Entering the fourth class in March 1695 (or so one presumes; the register contains no entries for 1694–5), he was evidently promoted to the third (Tertia) in July. In 1696 he was fourth and the following year first in the class, gaining promotion to the Secunda. Similar progress, from fifth in 1698 to second in 1699, earned him a place in the top class, but after a few months in the Prima his school career at Ohrdruf was cut short. A week or two before his fifteenth birthday he left the town and set out for Lüneburg in northern Germany.

The reason for Sebastian's departure from Ohrdruf is conveyed in the phrase 'ob defectum hospitiorum' found against his name in the school register (see p. 10), but it is uncertain whether we should infer from this a shortage of space in Christoph's house or, as seems more likely, the lack of a free place at the school. Konrad Küster has shown that the top class, the Prima, was overcrowded in 1700, and that this possibly coupled with Bach's change of voice, may have been the reason for his leaving.[4] Why he should have transferred to a place some 200 miles away, where there were no family connections and where the Bachs had never exercised their profession, also requires explanation,

[4] K. Küster, *Der junge Bach*, 97–109.

3 Class list (1699) of the Klosterschule, Ohrdruf, recording Bach's
departure 'ob defectum hospitiorum'

and this is to be found in events that had taken place at the Klosterschule during the preceding two or three years. The Kantor and master in charge of the Tertia there was a certain Johann Heinrich Arnold, known and feared for his severity. In fact, so intolerable was the discipline he exacted that in 1697 he was dismissed and replaced by Elias Herda, a young man from Leina, near Gotha, only a few miles north of Ohrdruf. Herda had studied theology at the university of Jena, but before that he had attended the Michaelisschule at Lüneburg, and it was probably on his recommendation that Bach secured a place there. It has been suggested that Herda may have persuaded Bach, with his outstanding scholastic record, to aim eventually for a university education, and this would help to explain why he did not immediately look for musical employment in Thuringia, as his brother Jacob had done.[5] On the other hand, the Lüneburg organist George Böhm could also have been the magnet that attracted Bach's steps to the north, as we shall see. What is certain is that the Michaelisschule offered free board and tuition to children and youths with good voices, and it presented an immediate solution to the problem of an indigent boy forced to make his way in the world 'ob defectum hospitiorum'.

Bach was not the only pupil from Ohrdruf to make the journey to Lüneburg in March 1700, for Herda had secured a place also for one of his schoolfellows, Georg Erdmann. Their names appear together in the lists of the Lüneburg *Mettenchor* (Mattins choir) for April and May 1700 (see p. 12). This was composed of about fifteen singers selected from the larger and less specialized *chorus symphoniacus*, but restricted to poor children who were paid a nominal sum for their services. The lists show that in 1700 Bach and Erdmann each received 12 groschen for April and the same sum for May, and they doubtless benefited also from monies raised by the *chorus symphoniacus* at weddings, funerals, and the usual *Kurrenden*. Unfortunately the payment lists after May 1700 have not survived, so we cannot be certain how long Bach remained a member of the *Mettenchor*. Most biographers follow Spitta, who stated that Bach's voice broke shortly after he went to Lüneburg and conjectured that he then earned his place in the school by playing the violin and

[5] A. Basso, *Frau Musika: la vita e le opere di J. S. Bach*, i, p. 226.

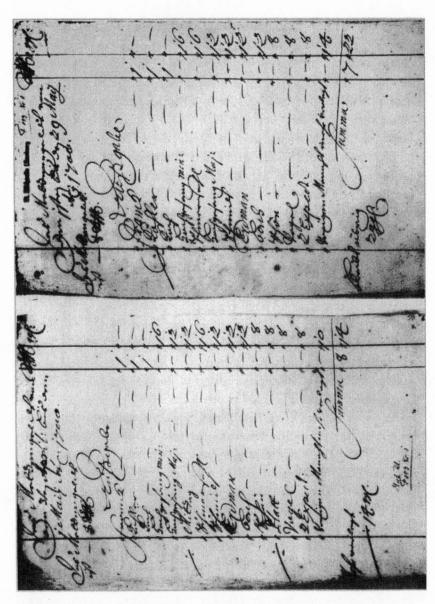

4 Record of payments to the *Mettenchor*, Lüneburg, April–May 1700

harpsichord. Forkel, however, is imprecise on this point, and the Obituary, from which Spitta took his information, states merely that Bach's voice broke 'some time' ('einige Zeit') after his arrival in Lüneburg. A school regulation of about 1736 stated categorically that scholars receiving free board and remuneration 'must be children of poor people and have good treble voices'.[6] This, however, was over thirty years after Bach was admitted to the school, and Küster has produced evidence that suggests that both he and Erdmann entered the *Mettenchor* as bass singers.[7] It was, apparently, quite common for Lüneburg choirs to recruit their tenors and basses from central Germany.

The repertory of the *Mettenchor* was drawn from an unusually fine music library begun in 1555 by the first Lutheran Kantor[8] and subsequently enlarged, notably by Friedrich Emanuel Praetorius (1623–95). By 1696, when August Braun succeeded Praetorius as Kantor and a catalogue of the library was drawn up, the collection had grown to some 1,100 manuscript volumes by at least 175 different composers, as well as a large number of printed works. What personal use Bach, as a mere choirboy, was allowed to make of this library we do not know, but he must have known something of its contents. It included Latin polyphony by Lassus, Monteverdi, Carissimi, Rovetta, and others, and sacred works by the greatest German masters of the seventeenth century: Buxtehude, Hammerschmidt, Kerll, Scheidt, Schein, Schütz, Tunder etc. Bach might also have been aware of the inclusion of pieces by his great-uncle Heinrich (1615–92) and by his father's cousin Johann Christoph, still living then at Eisenach.

Also represented in this precious library (unfortunately destroyed by fire in about 1800) was Georg Böhm, organist at the Johanniskirche in Lüneburg from 1698 until his death in 1733 and a composer of keyboard and church music. Whether Bach actually studied the organ with Böhm is uncertain (the poor state of the Johanniskirche instrument at the time perhaps argues against it), but we have it on C. P. E. Bach's authority that he 'loved and studied the works of the Lüneburg organist Böhm',

---

[6] Terry, 35, n. 3.

[7] K. Küster, op. cit. pp. 85–97.

[8] Published in M. Seiffert, 'Die Chorbibliothek der St. Michaelisschule in Lüneburg zu Seb. Bach's Zeit', *Sammelbände der Internationalen Musik-Gesellschaft*, ix (1908), 593–621.

and it seems likely that the two were personally acquainted. Böhm was a native of Thuringia, born and brought up near Ohrdruf, and he had been a schoolfellow of Johann Bernard Vonhof, father-in-law of Bach's elder brother Johann Christoph. Quite possibly Bach had left Ohrdruf with at least one letter of introduction to the Lüneburg organist, and the fact that Böhm later acted as agent in north Germany for printed editions of the Bach Partitas suggests that they knew each other well.

Before moving to Lüneburg Böhm had spent five or more years in Hamburg, where he had heard, and perhaps studied with, the renowned Johann Adam Reincken, organist at the Catharinenkirche since 1663. It was perhaps in Böhm's company, or at least at his instigation, that Bach more than once made the 30-mile journey from Lüneburg to hear Reincken, who was considered one of the finest organists in Germany. A further reason for visiting Hamburg was the presence there of his cousin Johann Ernst (1683–1739), who had been at school with him at Ohrdruf before continuing his musical training in Hamburg (he later succeeded Sebastian as organist at Arnstadt). No doubt Ernst also introduced his cousin to other musical attractions in the Hanseatic city, including perhaps opera performances under Reinhard Keiser which were soon to bring the young Handel to Hamburg. The cultural life offered by a prosperous port and commercial centre must have made a strong impression on a youth who had lived until then in small provincial towns, and the possibility of making a career in Hamburg remained in Bach's mind, as we shall see, some twenty years later.

There were, however, in Lüneburg itself other sources of musical stimulus for Bach. Adjoining the Michaelisschule was the Ritter-academie, an educational establishment for the sons of noblemen where French was spoken as the language of *politesse*, and where the essentially French arts of fencing and dancing were cultivated. The dancing master there was a certain Thomas de la Selle, who was also employed, possibly as a violinist, in the *Kapelle* maintained by the francophile Duke Georg Wilhelm of Brunswick-Lüneburg, whose court, modelled on Versailles, was situated at Celle, some 50 miles south of Lüneburg. The Obituary tells us that the young Bach 'had the opportunity to go and listen to a then-famous band kept by the Duke of Celle, consisting for the most part of Frenchmen; thus he acquired a thorough grounding in the French taste, which, in those regions, was at the time something quite new' (*NBR*, 300). It has usually been assumed from this that Bach made fairly frequent journeys to Celle in the company of De la Selle, but, as Christoph Wolff pointed out,[9] the Obituary nowhere states that he actually went there, and indeed it is unlikely that he could have raised the money or obtained permission from the Michaelisschule to do so. In 1700 the duchess, Eléonore Desmier d'Olbreuse, chose her dower house in Lüneburg, and it is probable that Bach heard the Celle orchestra there or elsewhere in the town. Precisely what music Bach would have heard them play we do not know, but it would presumably have included orchestral suites and chamber music by the fashionable French composers of the day and by frenchified Germans such as J. S. Kusser (in fact of Hungarian origin), Georg Muffatt, and J. C. F. Fischer. The court was Calvinist, and so, even if he did travel to Celle, Bach would not have heard any French sacred music for voices, though he did at some stage become familiar with liturgical organ pieces by François Couperin, Raison, and Grigny, whose *Premier livre d'orgue* he later copied out in his own hand.

The date of Bach's departure from Lüneburg is unknown, but at Easter 1702 he would have completed the usual two years in the top class of the Michaelisschule and we may suppose that, not wishing to proceed to university or lacking the funds to do so, he began to look for openings in the profession of music. The first to come along seems to have been at the Jacobikirche in Sangerhausen, near Halle, where a successor was needed to Gottfried Christoph Gräffenhayn, who had died early in July 1702. Bach submitted to the customary *Probe* (examination), which normally included the performance of a piece of concerted music by the applicant, and despite his youth and lack of experience he was immediately offered the post. But the reigning duke, Johann Georg of Saxe-Weissenfels, had other ideas, and intervened to secure the appointment of his own candidate, Johann Augustin Kobelius, remembered now as a composer of operas for the Weissenfels court. Bach's immediate reaction to this example of ducal partiality is not recorded; that he regarded it as an injustice is suggested by his letter of 18 November 1736 to burgomaster Klemm, recommending his son Johann Gottfried Bernhard for a similar post at Sangerhausen, in which

[9] C. Wolff, *Bach: Essays on his Life and Music*, 62.

he calls on the council to fulfill their promise of 'nearly thirty years ago' (in fact thirty-four years).

Bach's movements during the months that followed cannot now be traced, but by March 1703 we find him employed as a 'lackey' at the minor Weimar court of Duke Johann Ernst. Terry (p. 56) suggested that the Duke of Weissenfels, who maintained close relations with the Weimar court, may have secured this appointment for Bach to compensate him for the loss of the Sangerhausen post; but the presence at Weimar of another lackey-musician by the name of David Hoffmann, possibly a member of the Hoffmann family closely related by marriage to the Bachs, may also have helped. It is impossible to be specific about Bach's duties, or even about his actual position, at the Weimar court. In the Genealogy he is described as 'HoffMusicus' (court musician) and according to Forkel he was 'engaged to play the violin', but in an Arnstadt document of 13 July 1703 he is mentioned as 'HoffOrganiste' (court organist) at Weimar. This last may be technically an error, but it probably reflects the truth about Bach's activities during these months. That he was by then an organist of quite exceptional ability is evident from the readiness of the Sangerhausen authorities to appoint him, and there is every reason to suppose that at Weimar he was frequently called upon to substitute for the titular organist, Johann Effler, who was advanced in years and in poor health. In any event, it seems that the Weimar position was little more than a stop-gap in Bach's search for an organist's post—a search that was soon to come to an end at Arnstadt.

# CHAPTER 2

# Arnstadt, Mühlhausen

## (1703–8)

ITUATED SOME TWENTY MILES SOUTH-WEST OF WEIMAR, ARN-
stadt was the principal town in the territory of Schwarzburg-
Arnstadt, ruled since 1681 by Count Anton Günther II (1653–1716).[1]
When Bach went there in 1703 his family name was already familiar to
many of its 3,800 inhabitants, and had been since about 1620, when
Caspar Bach (d. before 1644) and four of his sons, Caspar, Johannes,
Melchior and Nicolaus, found employment in the town. They were
followed by a long line of Bachs, including Johann Sebastian's father
and his uncle Johann Christoph; Ambrosius had lived and worked there
between 1654 and 1667, and his twin brother had served Count Ludwig
Günther and his successor as *Hofmusicus* (court musician) from 1671
until 1693. Still remembered also would have been old Heinrich Bach,
who for over fifty years was organist at the town's two principal
churches, the Liebfrauenkirche and the Oberkirche; he died in 1692,
aged almost seventy-seven.

Nowhere among the Bachs at Arnstadt do we find a predecessor for
Sebastian as organist of the town's third church, the Bonifatiuskirche,
for the very good reason that this building, along with the municipal
offices and over 400 dwelling houses, had been destroyed by fire in
1581. It was not until nearly 100 years later, in 1676, that the money
was found to rebuild the Bonifatiuskirche, which on its completion in

[1] He was elevated to the rank of prince in 1697, but did not use the title until 1707.

1683 became known as the Neue Kirche (new church), and even then it remained without an organ until one was commissioned in 1699 from Johann Friedrich Wender, one of the most reputable Thuringian builders. Wender's contract stipulated that the work should be completed by 24 June 1701, but it was not until two years after this that the instrument was ready. Meanwhile an organist had been appointed in the person of Andreas Börner (1673–1728), the son-in-law of Christoph Herthum (1651–1710), Heinrich Bach's successor at the two principal churches.

It may seem surprising that when the time came in July 1703 to test and exhibit Wender's new organ, it was not Börner, nor even Herthum, who was chosen to carry out these functions, but the young and as yet little-known Johann Sebastian Bach. The decision to call upon the services of an eighteen-year-old from another town cannot be explained solely by reason of Bach's early mastery of organ technique, even in a region where such mastery was appreciated and respected; we must look also at the family connections that so often secured advancement for the musical Bachs in Thuringia. Bach had at least two such connections in Arnstadt in 1703, not counting his stepmother Barbara Margaretha, who had presumably returned to Arnstadt with her daughter after being widowed in 1695. One was the organist Christoph Herthum, who had married a daughter of Heinrich Bach, Maria Catharina, in 1668, when both he and his bride were only seventeen. The other was the burgomaster Martin Feldhaus, whose wife's sisters, Maria Elisabetha and Catharina Wedemann, had both married relatives of Sebastian, respectively Johann Christoph of Eisenach and Johann Michael (1648–94), organist at Gehren, about 15 miles south of Arnstadt, from 1673 until his death. Bach was not short of influential contacts at Arnstadt.

Where Bach had acquired the expertise that, from this time onwards, was in such demand when there was a new or rebuilt organ to be tested and assessed is something of a mystery. A keen ear for the acoustical properties of an instrument or a building seems to have been a natural endowment, but the technical knowledge required to adjudicate on such matters as wind pressure, voicing, and the thickness and quality of pipe metal could have come only from close study and observation. It is worth recalling that during Bach's early years at Eisenach the organ at the Georgenkirche frequently needed attention; work on its rebuilding started the year after he left. Moreover, his brother Christoph's organ at Ohrdruf, which Pachelbel had tested in 1693, was extensively rebuilt between 1696 and 1713 (and so partly during Bach's years there). Again, at Lüneburg the Michaeliskirche organ had undergone extensive repairs when Bach was at school there, and Böhm's organ in the Johanniskirche also needed a good deal of attention at that time. There had been many opportunities for Bach to observe organ builders and craftsmen at work, and, knowing what we do about his curiosity over other musical matters, we may safely assume that he took every possible chance to learn from them.

It was, however, Bach's gifts as a performer, rather than his expert evaluation of the instrument itself, that impressed the consistory and citizens of Arnstadt in July 1703—so much so, indeed, that he was immediately offered the post of organist at the Neue Kirche in preference to Börner, who was compensated by a transfer to the Liebfrauenkirche (technically a promotion, since this was the more important church). As the chronology of Bach's first contacts with Arnstadt has been frequently confused, it may be useful to set it out here:

?3 July 1703: Wender is granted his certificate after a successful
  inspection of the new organ by Bach and at least one other assessor
8 July (Sunday): Bach gives a public recital on the new organ
13 July: he receives his fee and expenses (8 florins 13 groschen)
9 August: his contract as organist of the Neue Kirche is drawn up
14 August: he enters upon his duties at the Neue Kirche

Under the terms of his contract Bach was expected to accompany the services at the Neue Kirche on Sundays, feast days, and other occasions of public worship, to maintain the organ in good order, and to report any faults that might develop in it. In return he was to be paid an annual salary of 84 florins 6 groschen, which compared very favourably with what other Arnstadt musicians received. In view of subsequent events it is worth remarking that Bach's contract made no mention of any obligation to provide the church with 'figural' music (that is, more advanced choral music, usually with instruments). Indeed, performance of any vocal music more complex than chorales and simple motets was virtually ruled out by the poor quality of the Gymnasium students allotted to him, and the situation was aggravated by Bach's inability to maintain good discipline among them. From what we know about the

Arnstadt students this would have been a difficult enough task for an experienced choirmaster; it was doubly so for someone no older than many of the choristers themselves.

Bach's duties left him with ample free time, much of which he presumably spent perfecting his organ technique and making his first essays in composition. It is also likely, although there is no evidence to prove it, that his services were required for musical entertainments at Neideck Castle, where Count Anton Günther drew from time to time on the resources of the town to augment his permanent *Kapelle*. At court Bach would have come into contact with Paul Gleitsmann, who had succeeded Adam Drese as *Kapellmeister* in 1701, and he would have heard something, too, of the poet Salomo Franck, with whom he was later to collaborate at Weimar. Franck had served as *Regierungs-Sekräter* (administrative secretary) to the count from 1689 to 1697, when he left for Jena, and in 1700 he had written the text for a secular cantata, or serenata, to inaugurate (on 23 August) the Augustenburg, the country seat that the countess, Augusta Dorothea, had had built in the vicinity of Arnstadt.

It was after a visit to Neideck Castle on 4 August 1705 that an incident occurred which provides the earliest evidence we have of the difficulties that Bach had to face at Arnstadt. Returning home late that evening in the company of his cousin Barbara Catharina,[2] he was approached in the market-place by a pupil from the Gymnasium, a certain Johann Heinrich Geyersbach, three years Bach's senior, and five companions. Geyersbach, a bassoonist, threatened Bach with a stick, saying that he had insulted him and his instrument, whereupon Bach drew his sword to defend himself. After a scuffle the disputants were separated, but they were later summoned before the consistory to explain their conduct, and evidence was taken also from

[2] Probably the third daughter (b. 13 December 1679) of Johann Michael Bach of Gehren, and elder sister of Sebastian's future wife, Maria Barbara. Another slightly younger cousin, also called Barbara Catharina Bach (b. May 1680), was living at Arnstadt at the same time; she was the daughter of Sebastian's late uncle Johann Christoph. Karl Müller (*Arnstadter Bachbuch* [Arnstadt, 2nd ed., 1957], 105) stated that it was this younger cousin who was with Bach on the evening in question, but this seems unlikely in view of the fact that in the Arnstadt burial register (ibid., 155) she is said to have been bedridden for over four years before her death in January 1709.

Barbara Catharina and two of the other students, Hoffmann and Schüttwürfel. Bach had to admit that he had called Geyersbach a 'Zippel Fagottist'. This is usually translated in English text as 'nanny-goat bassoonist' and taken to refer to Geyersbach's imperfect mastery of his instrument, but Konrad Küster has drawn attention to the derivation of *Zippel* from *Zippeler*, a German form of the Latin *discipulus* (pupil).[3] According to this interpretation Bach would have been drawing an invidious social distinction between himself, a twenty-year-old professional organist, and Geyersbach, a twenty-three-year-old schoolboy. Whatever the nature of the insult, the consistory's reprimand did not rest there, but referred also to Bach's inability to get on with the students and his unwillingness to rehearse them in figural music. Bach, in his reply, pointed out the need for a *director musices* to train the choir.

Bach was soon in further trouble with the consistory. Some two months after the brush with Geyersbach he was granted leave of absence for four weeks to visit the northern city of Lübeck, a journey of some 260 miles which he is said to have made on foot. The purpose of the visit was to hear and learn from Dietrich Buxtehude; but another reason for going (perhaps even the main one) might have been to explore the possibility of succeeding this famous sixty-eight-year-old organist, who had at his command at the Marienkirche a splendid three-manual instrument with fifty-four speaking stops. Two years earlier Handel and his friend Johann Mattheson had journeyed to Lübeck from Hamburg for the same reason, but they had been unwilling to accept the main condition imposed upon any successor: that he should marry Buxtehude's daughter. Bach also let pass the chance to become the great man's son-in-law (Anna Margaretha Buxtehude was ten years his senior and of unprepossessing appearance), but he found other things to detain him in Lübeck, including the *Abendmusiken*, a series of evening concerts of spiritual, oratorio-like music which Buxtehude arranged annually in the Marienkirche on the last two Sundays after Trinity and the second, third, and fourth Sundays of Advent. In 1705 two additional 'extraordinaire' *Abendmusiken* were given on 2 and 3 December, at which Buxtehude's *Castrum doloris* and *Templum honoris* were performed, the first

[3] K. Küster, *Der junge Bach*, 136.

to commemorate the late emperor, Leopold I, and the second to hail his successor, Joseph I.

Bach was presumably present at these and the other *Abendmusiken* of 1705, details of which have unfortunately not survived. How he occupied the rest of his time in north Germany we do not know—possibly he renewed friendships he had made some years previously in Hamburg and Lüneburg—but he was back in Arnstadt by 7 February 1706, when he took communion, and a fortnight later he was trying to satisfy an angry consistory as to why an absence of four weeks had grown into one of four months. The old complaints, that he failed to get on with the students and neglected to rehearse them in figural music, were renewed, and a further charge was added: that of introducing sundry curious embellishments ('viele wunderliche *variationes*') and many strange notes ('viele frembde Thone') into the hymns, to the confusion of the congregation. Whether Bach was attempting to put into practice what he had heard at Lübeck is not entirely clear.

Bach's refusal to rehearse the students in concerted music remained the main bone of contention between him and the consistory, and it doubtless lay behind other criticisms of his conduct, including that made on 11 November 1706, when he was accused of having breached regulations by admitting to the choir loft a 'frembde Jungfer' (usually translated as 'stranger maiden'). Most writers since Spitta have identified the young lady in question as Bach's cousin and future wife, Maria Barbara. She was born on 20 October 1684 at Gehren, where her father, Johann Michael Bach, was organist, and the supposition is that she came to live with her uncle, the burgomaster Martin Feldhaus, after her mother's death in October 1704 and that Bach was also living under the same roof. The consistory's use of the word 'frembde' in referring to a niece of the burgomaster who had lived in the town for over two years is puzzling, until one realizes that it ought probably to be translated as 'unauthorized' rather than as 'stranger'.

One indisputable fact to emerge from the consistory minutes is that Bach was not getting along at all well with either the students or his superiors, and the fault seems to have been chiefly Bach's. As someone scarcely out of his teens, he must have appeared intolerably arrogant and self-willed, and, whatever posterity might think, the consistory had every right to question whether what Bach did for the Neue Kirche merited the salary they paid him. At the same time, it must be said that his actions stemmed from a perfect understanding of the musical situation at Arnstadt. He knew that with the available resources he could never achieve what he was soon to refer to as his aim for a 'well-regulated church music', and he was not prepared to strive for anything short of this. The only way he could resolve an increasingly irksome situation was to look elsewhere. Fortunately an opportunity soon presented itself at Mühlhausen.

Mühlhausen, about 36 miles north-west of Arnstadt, was an imperial free city governed by an elected council of six aldermen and forty-two councillors. One of its two principal churches was the Blasiuskirche (see Plate 6), a building of cathedral proportions dating from the thirteenth to fourteenth centuries and scarcely altered since then. It owed its musical reputation to a long line of fine organists, of whom Johann Rudolf Ahle (1625–73) was the most important. A native of Mühlhausen, Ahle composed in both sacred and secular genres and enriched the repertory of congregational hymns; in his last year he served the city as burgomaster. He was succeeded at the Blasiuskirche by his son Johann Georg, who won fame as both poet and musician. Father and son between them served the Blasiuskirche as organists for over fifty years.

The younger Ahle died on 2 December 1706 at the age of fifty-five. Among those who were invited to compete for the post was Johann Gottfried Walther, a relative of Bach and organist at the Thomaskirche in Erfurt. Walther declined the invitation to make the customary *Probe*, and instead went to Weimar as organist of the Stadtkirche, where he later came into close contact with Bach. There were presumably other attempts to fill the vacancy before Bach was invited to Mühlhausen for his *Probe* the following Easter. Mühlhausen was one of the few important towns in Thuringia not already 'colonized' by the Bachs, but it is not surprising to find some family connection linking Sebastian with the place. One of the councillors responsible for choosing a new organist there was Johann Hermann Bellstedt, whose brother, Johann Gottfried, lived at Arnstadt and was married to Susanna Barbara Wedemann, a maternal aunt of Maria Barbara and a sister-in-law of Martin Feldhaus. It was quite possibly J. H. Bellstedt who proposed Bach's candidature for the Blasiuskirche post, and it was he whom the parish council asked to work out a 'favourable agreement' with Bach a month after his successful *Probe*. The delay in offering Bach the post perhaps reflects reservations about appointing someone whose relations with his previous employers had been far from cordial, but the council was evidently well satisfied at securing someone of Bach's reputation as a musician, and when he appeared before them on 14 June 1707 he was asked to state his terms. He requested, and was granted, the salary he had been paid at Arnstadt (85 gulden—about 20 gulden more than Ahle had been paid), together with the same perquisites of grain, wood, and faggots that his predecessor had received and a wagon to convey his belongings from Arnstadt. On 29 June Bach requested his dismissal from the Arnstadt consistory and assigned the last quarter of his salary to his cousin Johann Ernst, who succeeded him (with a much smaller salary) at the Neue Kirche.

Once established at Mühlhausen with what must have seemed good prospects, Bach found himself in a position to make Maria Barbara his wife. (They were second cousins, and so their relationship did not infringe the laws of consanguinity.) At the opportune moment came a legacy of 50 gulden (more than half a year's salary) from his maternal uncle, Tobias Lämmerhirt, who had died at Erfurt on 10 August 1707, and the couple were married in the village church at Dornheim, a mile or two outside Arnstadt, on 17 October. The choice of Dornheim for the ceremony no doubt resulted from their friendship with the pastor there, Johann Lorenz Stauber. Stauber's first wife had died the previous June, and in June 1708 he was to marry Regina Wedemann, Maria Barbara's aunt.

While Bach's marriage to Maria Barbara must have been the source of much personal happiness, he was soon to find that his appointment at Mühlhausen could offer him little professional satisfaction. His relations with his employers, who evidently recognized his outstanding ability, were amicable, but opportunities for the composition and performance of concerted music were again very restricted. Most (probably all) of the church cantatas he wrote at Mühlhausen had no connection at all with the Blasiuskirche, where it seems that opposition was strong to any kind of church music more advanced in style than that of the Ahles. Spitta (i, 358–61) suggested as the main reason for this the Pietist leanings of Johann Adolf Frohne, the church's pastor and superintendent. Philipp Jakob Spener, whose *Pia desideria* (1675) had signalled the rise of the Pietist movement, had died only two years previously (in 1705), and his crusade for an undogmatic, subjective, and devotional Christianity which stressed the moral responsibility of the individual had by then found wide support among Lutherans. In some ways akin to Puritanism, Pietism tended to frown on the use in church of any music more elaborate than hymns and simple motets.

Opposed to Frohne in the controversy that had divided congregations in Mühlhausen for almost a decade before Bach's arrival was the pastor of the Marienkirche, Georg Christian Eilmar, a strictly orthodox Lutheran. The researches of Martin Petzoldt, however, have shown that Frohne's religious convictions did not, in fact, incline towards Pietism, and that the dispute between the two pastors was more to do with their personal temperaments and their interpretations of the scriptures.[4] The long-established practice at Mühlhausen for the two pastors to alternate weekly between the two main churches must have allowed the controversy to impinge strongly on their congregations. We may doubt whether Bach allowed himself to be caught up in it, but he and Eilmar do seem to have formed close professional and personal ties. Eilmar almost certainly furnished the texts for some of Bach's early cantatas, and on 29 December 1708 he stood godfather at Weimar to Bach's first child, Catharina Dorothea. Two years later Eilmar's daughter, Anna Dorothea, was godmother to Bach's eldest son, Wilhelm Friedemann.

When Spitta first drew attention to the religious squabbles at Mühlhausen he did not, as has been said, suggest that it was to these that Bach alluded when he complained, in his letter of resignation to the parish council, of the 'Wiedrigkeit' (hindrance) and 'Verdriesslichkeit' (vexation) he had experienced during his year as organist of the Blasiuskirche.[5] In fact, Spitta stated quite clearly that in Bach's use of these words

> We must understand in the first place the disposition of a portion of the municipality of Mühlhausen which clung to old fashions and customs, and neither could nor would follow Bach's bold flights, and even looked askance

[4] M. Petzoldt, *Bachstätten aufsuchen* (Leipzig, 1992), 133–4.

[5] See F. Blume, 'J. S Bach's Youth', *Musical Quarterly*, liv (1968), 1–30; also H. Serwer, ' "Wiedrigkeit" and "Verdriesslichkeit" in Mühlhausen', *Musical Quarterly*, lv (1969), 20–30.

at the stranger who conducted himself so despotically in a position which, as far back as the memory of man extended, had always been filled by a native of the city, and for its sole honour and glory.[6]

It was indeed this 'clinging to old fashions and customs' that caused Bach to experience hindrances and vexations at Mühlhausen. Heinrich Nicolaus Gerber, later a pupil of Bach, complained about the town in 1717–21 as a place where, as far as music was concerned, darkness covered the earth, and even as late as 1762 Johann Lorenz Albrecht, Kantor and organist at the Marienkirche, severely criticized Mühlhausen for its entrenched conservatism, its resistance to new ideas and musical styles, and its archaic system of organizing the available vocal and instrumental resources.[7]

Bach had attempted against impossible odds to improve the condition of church music not only in Mühlhausen itself but also in the neighbouring villages, where, as he said in his letter of resignation, 'the music is often better than the *harmonie* produced here'. He had secured for the benefit of the parish a 'good collection of the finest church compositions' (which, we may be sure, he had few opportunities to perform), and had complied with the terms of his contract by reporting on the repairs needed to the Blasiuskirche organ. Indeed, in this last particular he had gone further and drawn up a detailed project for rebuilding the organ which was put to the parish council on 21 February 1708, and agreed to. The work included the addition of a third manual, and it was entrusted to Wender, who had constructed the Neue Kirche organ at Arnstadt. By the time it was finished Bach was installed in his new post at Weimar.

Despite the 'Wiedrigkeit' and 'Verdriesslichkeit' of Mühlhausen, Bach remained on good terms with his employers and parted from them amicably. It is clear from his letter of resignation that 'the most gracious *entrée* to the *Kapelle* and Chamber Music of His Serene Highness of Saxe-Weimar' had come unexpectedly; as he explained to the council, it offered him an immediate increase in salary and the prospect of achieving his goal of a 'well-regulated church music'. Efforts were no

[6] Spitta, i, 357.

[7] F. W. Marpurg, ed., *Historisch-kritische Beyträge zur Aufnahme der Musik*, v (1762), 381–409; see Serwer, loc. cit.

doubt made to persuade him to remain at the Blasiuskirche, but on 26 June 1708 the council agreed to his dismissal, 'since he could not be made to stay', requesting only that he should supervise the rebuilding of the organ. This he most probably did, and it is likely that he also composed the organ chorale *Ein' feste Burg* (BWV720) to inaugurate the restored organ in 1709, as Spitta suggested. Certainly he kept in close touch with Mühlhausen for a time, and in 1709 (and perhaps in 1710 also) he returned to direct a new cantata for the annual change of town council, the cantata *Gott ist mein König* (BWV71) having been a conspicuous success on the same occasion in 1708.

Bach was succeeded at the Blasiuskirche by his cousin Johann Friedrich (*c.* 1682–1730), who remained there until he died. In 1735 Bach's third son, Johann Gottfried Bernhard, became organist at the Marienkirche. Another Thuringian town had been 'colonized'.

### Early Works

Bach was no youthful prodigy as far as composition was concerned. Except for two or three cantatas, very few of the works he wrote before leaving Mühlhausen at the age of twenty-three would be regularly performed today if they had been composed by anyone else. As might be expected, they are mainly for organ or clavier (a generic term used here for any keyboard instrument other than the organ); all but one of the few surviving cantatas are occasional pieces, not composed for the regular church services at Arnstadt or Mühlhausen.

Many of the early clavier pieces included in *BG* and listed by Schmieder are now known to be spurious, or at best of doubtful authenticity. Perhaps the earliest of those that remain is the Capriccio in E major (BWV993), a single fugal movement written *in honorem Johann Christoph Bachii Ohrdrufiensis*, as its title states. It shows how well Bach had profited from the instruction of his elder brother at Ohrdruf, and also how much he still had to learn about organizing fugal pieces on a large scale. The *Capriccio sopra la lontananza del fratello dilettissimo* BWV992 (known under its English title as 'Capriccio on the departure of his most loved brother') is more familiar, mainly on account of its naive programmatic content: it is said to depict the feelings of family and friends when Bach's brother Johann Jacob left Eisenach to enlist in the service of Charles XII of Sweden. The last two movements include the call of the posthorn. The piece is usually dated *c.* 1704, the time of Jacob's departure; but it could have been written later, and it is worth pointing out that the word *lontananza* in the title should be translated as 'absence' rather than 'departure'. The title itself, like that of the last movement of the roughly contemporaneous Sonata in D major (BWV963), *Thema all'imitatio gallina cuccu* (Theme in imitation of the hen and the cuckoo), suggests Italian influence, but Bach probably found his models nearer home in pieces by Poglietti, Kerll, and Kuhnau.

Also thought to date from the Arnstadt-Mühlhausen or early Weimar periods are four toccatas for clavier (BWV912–15), multi-sectional works like the organ toccatas, incorporating fugal movements. Perhaps the best known is the E minor Toccata (BWV914), described by Spitta (i, 441) as 'one of those pieces steeped in melancholy which Bach alone could write'. Its final fugal section, however, is apparently a reworking of a piece by an Italian composer not yet identified;[8] possibly it dates from the same period as similar *rifacimenti* of Legrenzi and Corelli pieces (BWV574 and 579) and the fugues on themes from Albinoni's trio sonatas Op. 1 (BWV946, 950–1).

The dangers of relying on stylistic analysis alone in determining authorship or chronology are no less acute when studying the early organ music, and since other evidence is again scanty the general picture must remain largely conjectural. The only organ piece from the period to survive complete in what is probably Bach's own hand (see Plate 3) is the cantus firmus setting of the Advent hymn *Wie schön leuchtet der Morgenstern* (BWV739); if authentic, it dates from about 1705. The type of chorale setting more readily associated with the Arnstadt years, however (indeed, often referred to simply as the 'Arnstadt type'), is one in which each line of a straightforward chordal harmonization is separated from the next by a brief improvisatory flourish. The harmonies are typically adventurous and often chromatic, as in Ex. 1.1, *Gelobet seist du, Jesu Christ* (BWV722).

Although this piece, like most other surviving examples of the type (e.g. BWV715, 726, and 732), is now thought to date from the Weimar years, and although we cannot be sure that Bach used it to accompany

---

[8] G. Pestelli, 'Un'altra rielaborazione bachiana: la fuga della toccata BWV914', *Rivista italiana di musicologia*, xvi (1981), 40–4.

**Ex. 1.1**

BWV722, bars 1–5

a congregation, it does seem that it was this kind of harmonization to which the consistory at Arnstadt took exception when they reproved their organist in 1706 'for having hitherto introduced sundry curious embellishments in the chorales and mingled many strange notes in them, with the result that the congregation has been confused'.

Some of Bach's earliest organ chorales are included in a manuscript volume now in Yale University Library (MS LM 4708), which was brought to scholarly attention independently, and almost simultaneously, by Christoph Wolff and Wilhelm Krumbach in 1985.[9] It was compiled some time after 1790 by Johann Gottfried Neumeister (1757–1849), a pupil of Bach's friend and colleague Georg Andreas Sorge, and includes in all eighty-two chorale preludes, of which thirty-eight are attributed to J. S. Bach and twenty-eight to other members of the Bach family.

[9] C. Wolff, 'Bach's Organ Music: Studies and Discoveries', *Musical Times*, cxxvi (1985), 149–52; W. Krumbach: 'Sechzig unbekannte Orgelwerke von Johann Sebastian Bach: ein vorläufiger Fundbericht', *Neue Zeitschrift für Musik*, cxlvi/3 (1985), 4–12.

The pieces are arranged, like those in Bach's *Orgel-Büchlein* (see p. 53), in the order of the liturgical year, and indeed two of them (BWV601 and 639) were included in the *Orgel-Büchlein* (Little Organ Book); three others (BWV719, 737, and 742) appear in other sources in the form in which they are found in the Neumeister volume, and a further two (BWV714 and 957) were previously known in shorter versions. One prelude, on *Christe, der du bist Tag and Licht*, to which the BWV number 1096 was originally attached, has been shown to be by Johann Pachelbel.

Several of the remaining thirty pieces can be shown, on stylistic grounds, to belong to Bach's earliest years as a composer. The titles of most of the hymns were entered in the *Orgel-Büchlein* for subsequent composition, but, except possibly for *Als Jesus Christus in der Nacht* (BWV1108, a title not entered in the *Orgel-Büchlein*), none of the versions in the Neumeister collection would have been appropriate for inclusion in the other volume, since they lack both the concision and the motivic integrity of the *Orgel-Büchlein* chorales and only a few of them specify use of the pedals. They show a tendency to treat each line of the hymn separately, in half-a-dozen cases even changing the metre (and by implication the tempo and possibly the registration) more than once, perhaps in response to a particular text. The Neumeister collection nevertheless represents a valuable addition to the canon of Bach's organ works, and an interesting one in the way that certain features, for example the often fragmented figuration and a penchant for echoes marked *p,* reflect the style of the early cantatas.

Among the other chorale-based pieces of the early period are three sets of variations (*partite diverse*, BWV766–8), models for which—if they date from the Lüneburg years, as Spitta first suggested—Bach could have found to hand in the chorale *partite* of Georg Böhm (although the music itself suggests other influences as well). Böhm's *partite* were probably designed as clavier music for use in the home, and there is much in the style of Bach's pieces that suggests the same purpose. Pedals are not obligatory at all in the first two sets, and are required in only five of the eleven variations on *Sei gegrüsset, Jesu gütig* (BWV768). This is unquestionably the most interesting of the three works. The number of variations and the order in which they appear vary considerably from one source to another, and the lack of a definitive shape, together with

the variable quality of the music itself, suggests that BWV768 was probably composed over a fairly lengthy period; the earliest source dates
from Bach's Weimar years (1708–17).

To arrive at even a tentative chronology for the early organ pieces
not based on chorales is, if anything, more difficult still. All that can be
done here is to point to certain stylistic features of the preludes (or
toccatas) and fugues that others have assigned to the Arnstadt-
Mühlhausen period, bearing in mind that many of those features continue to appear in the Weimar works up to about 1712. One thing to
notice, then, is that most of the pieces, despite being called 'prelude
and fugue' or 'toccata and fugue' in modern editions, and even in the
sources, are multi-sectional works of a type referred to by north
German organists simply as 'praeambulum' or 'praeludium'.[10] A good
example is the Prelude and Fugue in E major (BWV566), printed in *BG*
and listed by Schmieder as 'Toccata' (it exists also in a C major version,
generally thought to be earlier). This is in four quite separate sections,
the second and fourth being fugues on contrasted but thematically related subjects—a feature, too, of Buxtehude's preludes and toccatas. In
other works, such as the so-called Prelude and Fugue in A minor
(BWV551), the music is more continuous. BWV551 has five sections, the
second fugue being followed by a coda obviously designed to regain
the brilliant bravura style of the opening, and so to provide a climactic
ending. Most other preludes and fugues of this period are similar in
style and construction, but with only three sections, the fugue occupying a central position.

Among other features of the early organ preludes are their impressive
and sometimes quite lengthy (but not difficult) pedal solos, their chordal
'trills' (fully notated), much rushing about over the keyboard in semiquaver and demisemiquaver runs, and generally speaking a loose construction which suggests a recalled improvisation. The fugues, on the
other hand, despite relying heavily on sequence and often remaining
unadventurously in tonic and dominant keys, are surprisingly well organized (i.e. thematic), even though their subjects are typically long and
'garrulous' (Ex. 1.2). It is not surprising to find that pedal entries are
usually long-delayed and sometimes modified.

[10] P. Williams, *The Organ Music of J. S. Bach*, i, 222.

Ex. 1.2

(a)                                                                    BWV531/ii, bars 1–3

(b) Allegro                                                            BWV535a/ii, bars 1–5

(c)                                                                    BWV578, bars 1–5

Works representative of this early style and usually thought to date
from the Arnstadt-Mühlhausen years include (in addition to those already mentioned) the Preludes and Fugues in C (BWV531), G minor
(535a, an early and incomplete version of 535), and G major (550), the
Prelude (only) in G (BWV568), the Fugue (only) in G minor (BWV578),
and the Fantasia in G (BWV572); the 'Little' E minor Prelude and Fugue
(BWV533) is less flamboyant, more tightly organized, and without the
usual toccata-like flourish at the end of the fugue. It is ironic that the
famous Toccata in D minor (BWV565), in which the rhetoric of the
prelude–fugue–postlude combination is at its most exuberant and dramatic, should show features that put Bach's authorship in doubt, at least
in the form in which we know it today.[11] The difficulty in establishing
tight stylistic norms for the music of the early period must, however,
leave the question of its authenticity open.

The situation is somewhat clearer with the early cantatas, the background to which is sketched in a later chapter (see pp. 123 ff.). These
all date from Bach's period as organist of the Blasiuskirche, Mühlhausen,

[11] See R. Bullivant, *Fugue* (London, 1971), 161, and P. Williams, 'BWV565: a toccata in D
minor for organ by J. S. Bach?', *Early Music*, ix (1981), 330–7.

although they were not written for performance there. The earliest is probably *Aus der Tiefen rufe ich* (BWV131), a penitential work which Terry (81) connected with the disastrous fire that destroyed part of Mühlhausen in 1707. Its text may have been compiled by G. C. Eilmar, pastor of the Marienkirche, who was probably responsible also for that of *Gott ist mein König* (BWV71), written for the service marking the town council election on 4 February 1708 and printed at the council's expense. *Gottes Zeit ist die allerbeste Zeit* (BWV106) was for a funeral, *Der Herr denket an uns* (BWV196) for a wedding (perhaps that of Maria Barbara's aunt, Regina Wedemann, to the pastor Johann Lorenz Stauber). With these works belongs also Cantata 150, *Nach dir, Herr, verlanget mich*, which is thought to date from Bach's first year at Weimar (1708–9).

The occasional nature of these cantatas helps to explain the diversity of their texts, structures, and instrumentation, which in no two cases are the same. But they also share certain features in common. Like some of the clavier and organ works, they fall into several short sections without any very sharp distinction between one section and another, or even between solo and tutti items. The texts, untouched by the reforms that Erdmann Neumeister brought to the cantata, never invite the use of recitative, and da capo arias, too, are almost entirely absent. Phrase lengths are short and the range of keys very restricted. Motet style, with instruments doubling the voices, predominates in the choruses. The cantatas thus reflect the conservatism that permeated church music at Mühlhausen, and the only one that Bach felt able to revive at Leipzig later on was *Christ lag in Todes Banden* (BWV4), a chorale cantata on the Easter hymn, which he added to his second annual cycle in 1725.

For all their immaturity and dependence on parochial models, these early cantatas have achieved a degree of popularity in modern times which is out of proportion to that accorded (in live performance, at least) to Bach's later and finer examples of the genre. The reason is no doubt that the early works have a larger numbers of four-part (SATB) sections and therefore commend themselves to choral societies more readily than the later ones, most of which have (apart from simple chorales) only one four-part movement, and sometimes none at all. Probably the best known of all the pre-Weimar cantatas is No. 106,

*Gottes Zeit ist die allerbeste Zeit,* also known as the 'Actus tragicus'. It may have been composed for the funeral of Bach's uncle Tobias Lämmerhirt, who died on 10 August 1707, but there is no certain evidence for this; the earliest source is a copy dating from after Bach's death, and it is there that the title 'Actus tragicus' is found. The work opens with an instrumental Sonatina which, despite its major key, takes a sombre colouring from the scoring—for two recorders, two bass viols, and continuo—and from the prevalence of drooping 'sigh' motifs. The rest of the work is built around three choruses: the first, in three sections, is somewhat in motet style, the instruments for the most part doubling the voices; the last in an elaborate working-out of the seventh strophe of Adam Reusser's chorale *In dich habe ich gehoffet, Herr,* with the last line set as a fugue. The remarkable central chorus again combines three distinct elements: a fugal setting of a verse from Ecclesiasticus, 'Es ist der alte Bund', a soprano arioso from Revelation, 'Ja komm, Herr Jesu', and (in the instrumental accompaniment) the chorale melody *Ich hab mein Sach Gott heimgestellt.* On each side of the central chorus there are two sections for solo voices, resulting in the kind of symmetrical layout that can be observed in many of Bach's later works:

Sonatina—Chorus—Tenor—Bass—Chorus—Alto—Bass + Alto—Chorus

The early cantatas as a whole reveal a youthful exuberance and an almost Romantic approach which Bach was rarely to recapture in his later years. This goes, by and large, for the clavier and organ music as well. Something was inevitably lost in acquiring the control, technique, and sense of proportion that were to make possible the masterpieces of the future. But it is doubtful whether Bach could ever have developed from a gifted but minor German composer into an artist of international importance within the narrow confines of Arnstadt and Mühlhausen. He needed a window opening on wider musical horizons, and a catalyst to help form his mature musical style. Weimar was to provide that window, Vivaldi and the modern Italian concerto the catalyst.

# *Weimar*

## [1708–17]

THE MODERN VISITOR TO WEIMAR MAY HAVE TO LOOK HARD for evidence of Bach's connection with the place. Weimar's most glittering period as a centre for the arts, particularly literature and music, came during the century after Bach's death, when Wieland, Goethe, Schiller, Hummel, and Liszt all lived and worked there. The houses of these great men, and the monuments, libraries, and museums dedicated to their memory, today draw hundreds of visitors to the town. The buildings in which Bach lived and worked, on the other hand, have for the most part disappeared. The palace, built by Duke Wilhelm IV in 1650–64 and known as the 'Wilhelmsburg' (see Plate 7), was destroyed by fire in 1774, and with it the ducal chapel (the 'Himmelsburg'; see Plate 9) where Bach's earliest mature cantatas were heard and where he officiated at the two-manual organ reconstructed shortly before his arrival by Johann Conrad Weishaupt. Gone, too, is the house where Bach and his growing family lived, until 1713 at least; it stood next to the famous Elephant Hotel in the market-place, but it had already been much altered before it was bombed in February 1945.

The building of most interest to the Bach pilgrim today is the Stadt-kirche, dedicated to Saints Peter and Paul but now called the Herder-kirche after the theologian and poet Johann Gottfried Herder, who was its pastor from 1776 until his death in 1803. Visitors go there today to admire the altarpiece by Lucas Cranach the elder, which even in Bach's time was the church's most cherished ornament. Bach held no official position at the Stadtkirche, but he certainly made use of the organ there while his own instrument at the castle was under repair. The permanent organist was Bach's kinsman Johann Gottfried Walther,[1] who had secured the post after declining the Mühlhausen invitation in 1707. On his arrival in Weimar he had been put in charge of the musical education of the young and talented Prince Johann Ernst, a nephew of the reigning duke. There will be occasion to speak further about the friendship and collaboration between Weimar's two principal organists and about its effect on Bach's creative development.

It was at the Stadtkirche that the six children born to Maria Barbara at Weimar were christened. The first was a girl, Catharina Dorothea, born at Christmastide 1708 and baptized on 29 December. Two years later, on St Cecilia's Day (22 November) 1710, came Wilhelm Friedemann, considered by many as the most musically gifted of all Bach's offspring. Neither of the twins, Maria Sophia and Johann Christoph. (b. 23 February 1713), survived the first crucial month of life, but two further sons, Carl Philipp Emanuel (b. 8 March 1714) and Johann Gottfried Bernhard (b. 11 May 1715) lived to continue in the musical traditions of the family. Emanuel became an important composer in his own right, as well as a trustworthy custodian of his father's patrimony; Bernhard was to bring his father much concern and disappointment before his early death in 1739. There will be more to say about both of them in later chapters.

The names of those who acted as godparents are recorded in the baptismal registers at Weimar, providing interesting clues to the social circle in which the Bachs moved at this time. Among those named there are of course a number of relatives, showing that the couple kept in touch with their families at Eisenach, Arnstadt, and Ohrdruf. From Mühlhausen came Pastor Eilmar, his married daughter Anna Dorothea, and Paul Friedemann Meckbach, son of the burgomaster Conrad Meckbach. Weimar colleagues include the Kantor Georg Theodor Reineccius and a court musician, Adam Immanuel Weldig, owner of the house in the market-place where the Bach family lodged. In March 1714 Georg Philipp Telemann, with whom Bach was evidently in close

---

[1] Bach's maternal grandfather, Valentin Lämmerhirt (1585–1665), was also the paternal grandfather, by a previous marriage, of Walther's mother.

contact during Telemann's years as *Konzertmeister* at Eisenach (1708–12), came from Frankfurt to be godfather to Carl Philipp Emanuel. It is perhaps worth remarking that no member of the ruling house at Weimar, and only one quite unimportant courtier, the young Baron von Lyncker, is to be found among the godparents.

During Bach's short time at the Weimar court in 1703 he had been employed as a violinist by Duke Johann Ernst (1664–1707), who, under a family law of 1629, reigned jointly with his elder brother Duke Wilhelm Ernst (1662–1728). In 1709 Ernst August (1688–1748), elder son of Duke Johann Ernst, attained his majority and became co-regent, but it was his uncle, Wilhelm Ernst, who became Bach's new employer in 1708. No member of this august family better deserved the name 'Ernst' than the serious-minded Wilhelm. After studying theology at the university of Jena he devoted most of his time and resources to religious observances, in which he involved the entire Weimar court. An orthodox Lutheran by persuasion, he nevertheless showed a leaning towards Pietism; he re-instituted the practice of confirmation and attached particular importance to the moral efficacy of the sermon, even testing his servants on the attention and understanding they brought to the sermons preached in the ducal chapel. He imposed a puritanical regime at the Wilhelmsburg, forbidding the dances that had previously marked the celebrations of certain feast days and imposing a 'lights-out' at 9 p.m. in summer and 8 p.m. in winter. But while he took it upon himself to look after the salvation of his subjects' souls with a zeal bordering on bigotry, Duke Wilhelm also felt an obligation to provide for their cultural welfare. He founded a fine library and collection of coins, in charge of which was Salomo Franck, Bach's cantata librettist at Weimar, and he set up an orphanage and a seminary. The court *Kapelle*, which the first Duke Johann Ernst (1627–83) had disbanded, was reconstituted. The musicians served not only to adorn the chapel services; dressed in hussar liveries, they enlivened the sober life of the court with performances of French and Italian music. In 1696 Duke Wilhelm had even introduced opera performances (of a moralistic kind), for which music was probably supplied by the vice-*Kapellmeister* Georg Christoph Strattner, but these came to an end shortly after Bach's appointment.

Strattner had been appointed in 1695 to assist the *Kapellmeister* Johann Samuel Drese, who suffered ill health and became increasingly unable to carry out his duties. Strattner was succeeded as vice-*Kapellmeister* by Drese's son, Johann Wilhelm. The constitution of the *Kapelle* when Bach joined it in 1708 is not known, but it probably changed little before 1714, when it numbered twenty-one musicians as well as Bach and the Dreses. Nine of these were listed as singers and twelve as instrumentalists (four string players, six trumpeters, a timpanist, and a bassoonist); there were in addition six choirboys. This unbalanced ensemble must no doubt have been shuffled about, perhaps with the help of players from outside, to produce the forces needed for the cantatas Bach wrote at Weimar. Singers frequently doubled as instrumentalists (the tenor Johann Döbernitz, for example, also played bassoon) and the trumpeters were no doubt competent as horn and trombone players, and probably as violinists, too.

Bach's position was at first that of *Hoforganist*, in which capacity he succeeded the aged and infirm Johann Effler, for whom he had frequently deputized in 1703. But the documents also mention him as *Cammermusicus*, so he would have been expected to don a hussar costume and play violin or viola in the court orchestra. These duties left him time for other activities, and as his fame as an organist spread he became increasingly in demand as a teacher. Johann Martin Schubart, who had been his pupil in Mühlhausen, continued to study with him in Weimar and succeeded him as *Hoforganist* there. Schubart was, in his turn, succeeded in 1721 by another Bach pupil, Johann Caspar Vogler. Other Weimar pupils included Johann Tobias Krebs and two members of the Bach family: Johann Lorenz (1695–1773) from Schweinfurt, who became Kantor at Lahm, midway between Coburg and Bamberg in Franconia, and Johann Bernhard (1700–43) from Ohrdruf, who followed Bach to Cöthen and was employed as a copyist there before succeeding his father at the Michaeliskirche in Ohrdruf. Bach continued to be in demand also as a specialist in organ design and construction, and he seems to have collaborated on several occasions with the organ builder Heinrich Nicolaus Trebs, whom he had known previously at Mühlhausen. Trebs's first commission at Weimar was probably for an organ in the new church at Taubach, a village nearby; Bach himself drew up the specification and tested the instrument. Between 1712 and 1714 Trebs also carried out repairs and extensions to Bach's organ in the Himmelsburg. In a testimonial of 1711 Bach referred to him as 'a reasonable and conscientious man', and in November 1713 he acted as godfather to Trebs's son, Johann Gottfried.

A month after the infant Trebs's baptism Bach began to take a particular interest, though not at first a professional one, in the organ of the Liebfrauenkirche at Halle, which Christoph Cuncius had been commissioned to enlarge to three manuals, with sixty-three speaking stops. Handel's teacher, Friedrich Wilhelm Zachow, had been organist there from 1684 until his death in August 1712, and Bach must have found tempting the possibility of succeeding him at a fine new instrument in a university town, with all the resources needed to perform ambitious church music. The church authorities, for their part, had failed to agree on a successor and were eager to find a well-qualified candidate for the post. Bach seems not to have made a formal application, but he visited Halle in December 1713 and was persuaded by the pastor, Johann Michael Heineccius, to make the customary *Probe* and to perform a cantata (possibly an early version of No. 21, *Ich hatte viel Bekümmernis*, or, more likely, No. 63, *Christen, ätzet diesen Tag*). On 13 December Bach was made a verbal offer of the organistship which he accepted, and the following day a detailed contract was drawn up (it even specified the stops to be used in accompanying the congregation) and two copies were sent to Weimar for Bach's signature. The salary was to be in all 171 thaler 12 groschen, plus 1 thaler for each wedding and the same for each piece of 'Catechissmus *Musique*'.

At this point, however, Bach seems to have had second thoughts. He was particularly concerned about the *Accidentien*—the incidental emoluments which then (as now) made up a substantial proportion of an organist's salary—and in his reply dated 14 January 1714 he promised to furnish details of certain changes he would like to see 'in respect of the *salarium* as well as of the duties'. The church committee considered these on 1 February but felt it impossible to increase their offer, and it was pointed out to Bach that while the duties were similar to those at Weimar he could expect a much larger income from the *Accidentien*. He was given two days to make up his mind. Whether or not he reached a decision within the time limit we do not know; neither can we be certain if there was any direct connection between his declining the Halle post and Duke Wilhelm's directive of 25 February increasing his salary at Weimar from 215 to 250 florins. Less than a week later, on

2 March 1714, he was promoted 'at his most humble request' to the rank of *Konzertmeister*. If Bach had used the Halle offer to secure advancement at Weimar he would merely have been following a practice that, if not explicitly condoned, was widely accepted. But in fact in a letter to the lawyer August Becker, who had negotiated with him on behalf of the Liebfrauenkirche, he denied that he had dealt unfairly with the Halle authorities:

Most distinguished, learned, and honoured Sir,

That the worshipful church *Collegium* is surprised that I have turned down the post of organist which (as they believe) I aspired to, does not surprise me at all, since I see how little they have understood the matter. They imagine that I sought the post of organist, but I am not aware of any such thing. As I see it, I allowed my name to go forward and the worshipful *Collegium* approached me; for after presenting myself I was quite ready to leave, and would have done so had not Dr Heineccius courteously insisted that I should remain to compose the *Stuck* [cantata] you know of. Besides, no-one can be expected to move to a place where he will be worse off, and yet this is something that cannot be ascertained in two or three weeks. Indeed, in my firm opinion not even after several years, let alone fourteen days, can one evaluate the salary of a position in which the *Accidentia* must be taken into account. This was partly the reason why I accepted the appointment and then requested that I might withdraw. However, it should not be concluded from all this that I have deceived the worshipful *Collegium* so as to persuade my gracious Master to increase my salary; he already holds my service and my art in such regard that there is no need for me to travel to Halle in order to improve my salary here. I am sorry, then, that what the worshipful *Collegium* was so certain of has turned out so uncertainly, but I would add the following: even were I to earn as much in Halle as I do here in Weimar, should I not still prefer my present office to the other? You, as a lawyer, may best judge of that, and if you will be so kind as to convey this explanation of my conduct to the praiseworthy Collegium I will remain, for my part, your Honour's obedient

Joh: Seb: Bach

Weimar, 19 March 1714                      Concertmeister and Hofforg.

Bach's letter evidently satisfied the appointing committee; in April 1716 he was invited back to Halle, along with Johann Kuhnau from Leipzig and Christian Friedrich Rolle from Quedlinburg, to test and inaugurate Cuncius's new organ, and was lavishly entertained. Meanwhile the post of organist at the Liebfrauenkirche had gone to one of the original candidates, Gottfried Kirchhoff, a former pupil of Zachow and a good enough composer for two of his keyboard pieces (BWV907–8) to be ascribed at one time to Bach.

During his first two years as *Konzertmeister* Bach seems to have enjoyed a life of happy domesticity at home and peaceful creativity at the Wilhelmsburg. Duke Wilhelm showed his satisfaction by ordering, on 20 March 1715, that Bach should henceforth receive a *Kapellmeister's* share of the perquisites and honoraria earned by the *Kapelle*—recognition, perhaps, that he was already doing the job of a *Kapellmeister*. In fact, his salary already exceeded that of *Kapellmeister* Drese. The promotion to *Kapellmeister* carried with it the obligation of composing and performing a cantata each month in the Himmelsburg, and Bach opened his account with one of the most attractive of all his cantatas, *Himmelskönig, sei willkommen* (BWV182) on Palm Sunday 1714. However, if he ever formed the intention of completing an annual cycle of cantatas over a four-year period, his plans must have been thwarted by the months of official mourning after the premature death of Duke Wilhelm's nephew, the musically gifted Prince Johann Ernst (1696–1715). Between 11 August and 3 November 1715 music was not permitted in the Himmelsburg, or in any other church in the dukedom, and Bach's cantata production was brought to a temporary halt.[2] When it was resumed, a new start was evidently made to the rota that Bach shared with the Dreses, and he found himself called upon to provide cantatas in 1716 for the same Sundays in the church's calendar as in 1715. He therefore appears to have repeated some earlier works, resuming the composition of new ones in August 1716 and accelerating his output to one each week in December. As far as can be determined from the present state of research, the chronology of Bach's Weimar cantatas from the time of his appointment as *Konzertmeister* is as follows:

[2] A. Glöckner, 'Zur Chronologie der Weimarer Kantaten Johann Sebastian Bachs', *Bach-Jahrbuch*, lxxi (1985), 159–64.

1714: BWV182, 12, 172, 21*b*, 199*a*, 61, ?63, 152
1715: BWV?18, 54, 31, 165, 185, 163, 132
1716: BWV155, 80*a*, 161, 162, 70*a*, 186*a*, 147*a*.[3]

Meanwhile differences had arisen between Bach and his employer. These seem to have resulted from the former's participation in the household of Duke Wilhelm's nephew and co-regent, Duke Ernst August. Ernst occupied the Rotes Schloss (Red Castle), which communicated with the Wilhelmsburg through a long covered gallery (see Plate 7), and it was there, too, that his brother Prince Johann Ernst had lived until illness forced him to leave Weimar in July 1714. The young prince's passion for Italian music, particularly concertos, profoundly affected the music Bach wrote at this time, as we shall see in Chapter 6. Bach did not instruct Duke Ernst August, as was once thought, but he continued to be associated with music-making at the Red Castle after the death of Johann Ernst in 1715. Resentful of his nephew's quite legitimate participation in the government of the duchy of Saxe-Weimar, and perhaps disapproving of the far from puritanical regime at the Red Castle, Duke Wilhelm began imposing fines of 10 thalers on any member of his household who served there. Such an imposition must have seemed offensive to Bach's sense of justice, and he evidently chose to ignore it. He even went as far as to join in a presentation to Duke Ernst August, perhaps to mark his marriage on 24 January 1716 to Eleonore Wilhelmine, sister of Prince Leopold of Anhalt-Cöthen (Bach's future employer). The following April the same duke's birthday was celebrated with a performance of the secular hunting cantata *Was mir behagt, ist nur die muntre Jagd* (BWV208), originally composed for Duke Christian of Weissenfels, probably in 1713.

After many years of illness Samuel Drese, who had been *Kapellmeister* at Weimar since 1683, died on 1 December 1716. His son Wilhelm, vice-*Kapellmeister* since 1704, seems to have been a mediocre musician, and his promotion to the senior post could not be taken for granted. Bach might with good reason have expected preferment, and his sudden

---

[3] The difficulties surrounding the chronology of Bach's Weimar cantatas have been convincingly confronted, if not entirely resolved, in K. Hofmann, 'Neue Überlegungen zu Bachs Weimarer Kantaten-Kalender', *Bach-Jahrbuch*, lxxix (1993), 9–30. See also R. A. Leaver, 'Cantata', in M. Boyd, ed., *Oxford Composer Companions: J. S. Bach*, 82–9.

spurt of composition after Samuel Drese's demise (producing three new cantatas in as many weeks) may be understood as a bid for the vacant post. Duke Wilhelm, however, first sought the services of Telemann, and when he declined offered the post to the younger Drese, no doubt in consideration of his seniority and of the long service of the Drese family at Weimar.[4] At this point Bach's output of cantatas ceased abruptly, either because Drese assumed responsibility for them or because Bach simply refused to go on supplying them. In either case, Bach must have recognized that he could hope for no further advancement at Weimar and that he would have to look elsewhere for the coveted title of *Kapellmeister*.

A possibility for such advancement soon presented itself at Gotha, a town long associated with the Bachs, where the *Kapellmeister* Christian Friedrich Witt had fallen ill (he died on 3 April 1717). Bach substituted for Witt in presenting the Good Friday Passion in the ducal chapel at Gotha on 26 March 1717,[5] but when it came to choosing Witt's successor the following month Duke Friedrich II, like Duke Wilhelm at Weimar, was interested only in securing Telemann, who declined the post but took advantage of the offer to improve his pay and conditions at Frankfurt. The Gotha vacancy was filled temporarily by Francesco Venturini, who retained his position as *Kapellmeister* at Hanover, and permanently from November 1719 by G. H. Stölzel. In the summer of 1717, however, Bach's ambitions were fulfilled when Prince Leopold of Anhalt-Cöthen, who had doubtless become acquainted with Bach and his outstanding abilities on the occasion of his sister's marriage to Duke Ernst August in January 1716, invited him to replace Augustin Reinhard Stricker as *Kapellmeister* at Cöthen. This princely post carried with it a princely salary of 400 thalers (about a third more than Bach received at Weimar), and in addition Prince Leopold made him a handsome gift of 50 thalers 'as a most gracious recompense on taking up his

[4] The Dreses' association with the Weimar court began in 1652 when Samuel's father, Adam Drese (*c.* 1620–1701), was appointed *Kapellmeister*. He left for Jena after the Weimar *Kapelle* was disbanded by the first Duke Johann Ernst in 1662.

[5] A. Glöckner, 'Neue Spuren zu Bachs Weimarer Passion', in *Passionsmusiken im Umfeld Johann Sebastian Bachs—Bach unter den Diktaturen 1933–1945 und 1945–1989: Bericht über die Wissenschaftliche Konferenz anlässlich des 69. Bach-Festes der Neuen Bachgesellschaft*, ed. H.-J. Schulze, U. Leisinger, and P. Wollny (Hildesheim, 1995), 33–46.

appointment'. But release from employment was not always easily obtained (as Bach's father had found at Eisenach in 1684) and Duke Wilhelm, doubtless displeased that Bach's advancement had been secured through connections at the Red Castle, simply refused to let his *Konzertmeister* go. One can only guess at the diplomatic representations Prince Leopold must have made, presumably with his sister as intermediary, to try to secure Bach's release; but Duke Wilhelm remained intransigent.

Meanwhile Bach's salary at Cöthen was credited to him from 1 August 1717, and Duke Wilhelm seems at first to have allowed him his usual freedom. Some time in the autumn, probably towards the end of September, he visited Dresden, where the French organist and composer Louis Marchand was creating a stir in musical circles and at court. Eighteenth-century society delighted in contests of skill between musical giants—a famous example is the one between Handel and Domenico Scarlatti in Rome—and Bach was prevailed upon by the Dresden *Konzertmeister*, Jean Baptiste Volumier, to send Marchand a letter in which, according to the Obituary, he 'offered to execute extempore any musical task that Marchand might set him, and hoped that Marchand would show similar willingness'. Accounts of what ensued vary a good deal in their details; the earliest and probably the most reliable is that given in 1739 by Johann Abraham Birnbaum, possibly using information supplied by Bach himself. Making the contest sound more like a duel, he wrote:

> The time came for the two virtuosos to match themselves against each other. The *Hofcompositeur* [Bach], together with the judges of this musical contest, waited anxiously for the opponent, but in vain. Eventually it was discovered that he had left Dresden at dawn by the express stagecoach. Obviously the Frenchman, so accustomed to being admired, must have found his ability unequal to the powerful assaults of his skilful and gallant opponent. Otherwise he would not have fled so hastily for safety.

Encouraged, perhaps, by his success in Dresden, Bach returned to Weimar and began to press Duke Wilhelm for his release. The duke, however, persisted in his refusal, and in the end became so enraged at Bach's insistence that on 6 November he had him placed under arrest and held

him prisoner until 2 December, when he at last granted him an ignominious dismissal. Although Duke Wilhelm's actions seem to have been
motivated as much by a true appreciation of his *Konzertmeister's* merits
as by malice, Bach can have felt few regrets as he set out on the 60-
mile journey to Cöthen.

# CHAPTER 4

# Organ Music

ACH'S EMPLOYMENT AS AN ORGANIST SPANNED ONLY THE early part of his career. Most of the organ music we hear today originated during the Weimar years and was no doubt connected in some way with his duties as court organist there. But even after 1717, although he never again held an organist's post, Bach needed organ music for recitals and dedication ceremonies, and he went on composing or revising it until his very last years. The occasional nature of much of the organ music is reflected in the way it has been preserved. Except for the *Orgel-Büchlein* (Little Organ Book), Bach seems to have shown no interest at Weimar in arranging his organ music in sets, as he was soon to do with the clavier and instrumental music at Cöthen. It was not until much later that he bestowed some kind of order on it. The autograph of the six organ sonatas dates from about 1727, and all the published works (*Clavier-Übung* III, the Canonic Variations, and the six 'Schübler' chorales) appeared during the last ten years or so of his life. It was during this decade, too, that he revised and brought together the so-called Eighteen or Leipzig chorales, written during the Weimar years. For the rest, particularly for the works not based on chorales, we must often fall back on miscellaneous copies, some of them late and unreliable, and in view of this it is hardly surprising that the organ music raises more problems of chronology and authenticity than any other section of Bach's oeuvre. Peter Williams has scrutinized all earlier research and brought forward many fresh insights in a study of the organ music to which the present chapter is much indebted;[1] even so, many problems remain that will probably never be solved.

Bach had two organs at his disposal in Weimar, since in addition to the court organ he also used that of his kinsman J. G. Walther in the Stadtkirche. This was a two-manual organ built by Christoph Junge in 1685. Bach's own instrument was in the ducal chapel (the Himmelsburg), sited just beneath the ceiling and high above the altar, as if in heaven itself (see Plate 9). The original instrument was built by Ludwig Compenius in 1657–8: a two-manual organ with thirty-eight stops. It was extensively rebuilt by Johann Conrad Weishaupt in 1707–8, shortly before Bach's arrival, and further substantial repairs and modifications were made by H. N. Trebs in 1712–14. A Glockenspiel stop was added (or perhaps renewed) in 1716, and Trebs did further work on the organ in 1719–20, after Bach had left Weimar. It is uncertain, therefore, how accurately the following specification, dating from 1737, represents the instrument that Bach played, but it probably gives some idea of it. (Wender's organ in the Neue Kirche, Arnstadt, was of about the same size.)

| *Oberwerk* (upper manual) | | *Brustwerk* (lower manual) | |
|---|---|---|---|
| 1. Principal | 8ft | 1. Principal | 8ft |
| 2. Quintaton | 16ft | 2. Viol da gamba | 8ft |
| 3. Gemshorn | 8ft | 3. Gedackt | 8ft |
| 4. Gedackt | 8ft | 4. Trompette | 8ft |
| 5. Quintaton | 4ft | 5. Kleingedackt | 4ft |
| 6. Octave | 4ft | 6. Octave | 4ft |
| 7. Mixture | 6 ranks | 7. Waldflöte | 2ft |
| 8. Cymbel | 3 ranks | 8. Sesquialtera | |
| 9. Glockenspiel | | | |

*Pedal*

| 1. Gross Untersatz | 32ft | 5. Principal | 8ft |
|---|---|---|---|
| 2. Sub-Bass | 16ft | 6. Trompette | 8ft |
| 3. Posaune | 16ft | 7. Cornett | 4ft |
| 4. Violon | 16ft | | |

Also Tremulant, Cymbelstern, and couplers

[1] P. Williams, *The Organ Music of J. S. Bach*.

This was a much smaller organ than the one Bach had left at Mühl-hausen, but the historian G. A. Wette, who documented the specifi-cation above, described its quality as 'incomparable'. While it would not have been adequate for all the organ music Bach wrote, it does suggest that performers of the great Weimar works do well to concen-trate on colour and brilliance in their registrations rather than on sheer weight of sound. Unfortunately Bach's music rarely contains precise indications of registration, so we cannot be certain how often he changed stops during the course of a piece, or even how often he changed manuals or couplers. Obviously the kinds of tonal refinement obtainable only by means of such recent innovations as combination pistons and swell pedals are injurious to the style of the music. On the other hand, an unusually adventurous approach to registration is indi-cated by a passage in one of C. P. E. Bach's letters to Forkel (?1774): 'Organists were often startled at his idiosyncratic choice of stops when he wanted to try out their organs. They thought such a registration could not possibly sound well as he had planned it, but they soon heard an effect which astounded them.'

Some of the organ works that Bach wrote at Arnstadt and Mühl-hausen were mentioned in a previous chapter (see pp. 28–32). Those dating from his early years at Weimar (insofar as they can be separated chronologically from their predecessors) belong to the same German (especially north German) tradition, with its roots in the seventeenth century. The impossibility of determining composition dates for such works as the fugues on themes by Legrenzi (BWV574) and Corelli (BWV579) makes it difficult to estimate the direct impact of Italian mu-sic on Bach's organ style. Three keyboard fugues on themes by Albi-noni (BWV946, 950–1) probably date from the early Weimar years, and in 1714 Bach acquired a copy of Frescobaldi's *Fiori musicali* (Venice, 1635), a collection of liturgical organ pieces including three organ Masses. The following year he (together with one of his pupils) copied four of Bonporti's *Invenzioni* Op. 10 (Bologna, 1712), which may have given him the idea for the title of his own two-part Inventions, writ-ten at Cöthen in the early 1720s.[2] Of still greater importance (not only

[2] M. Talbot, 'Bonporti, Francesco Antonio' in S. Sadie (ed.), *The New Grove Dictionary of Music and Musicians* (London, 1980), iii, 36.

to the development of his organ style) was his encounter with the new Italian concertos, especially Vivaldi's, some of which he arranged for organ and harpsichord (see pp. 80–2), At the same time, his continuing interest in French music should not be overlooked. It was probably in 1713 that he copied Nicolas de Grigny's *Premier livre d'orgue* (Paris, 1699) and Charles Dieupart's *Six suittes de clavessin* (Amsterdam, 1701). These, then, were some of the influences that Bach absorbed in moulding the mature and individual style we recognize first in the organ music of the later Weimar years (from about 1712 onwards).

It is both customary and convenient to divide Bach's organ works into two main groups of more or less equal size: those based on chorale melodies, and 'free' compositions independent of chorales. To do this is not, as might be imagined, to separate the liturgical organ music from the rest. Some of the chorale-based pieces would certainly have served to introduce (and in some cases, perhaps, even to accompany) the congregational singing of a hymn; others may have been played in alternation with choir and congregation, or as communion pieces. But it is evident from Bach's visit to Hamburg in 1720, when he improvised for about half an hour on the tune of *An Wasserflüssen Babylon* to an audience that included Reincken, that chorale settings could serve a non-liturgical purpose as well; and the canonic variations on *Vom Himmel hoch* were certainly not designed for church use. Also, while the 'free' toccatas, fantasias, preludes, and fugues might have been intended primarily as recital or teaching material, there is no reason why some should not also have served as introductory or closing voluntaries in church.

## Chorale Settings

About ninety of Bach's extant chorale settings are contained in the four collections he made during his lifetime: the *Orgel-Büchlein*, *Clavier-Übung* III, the 'Schübler' set, and the 'Leipzig' collection. Some sixty others (mostly copies) are in various manuscripts, the most important being the Neumeister collection at Yale University, described earlier (see pp. 29–30), and the so-called Kirnberger collection, compiled about 1760. The latter is transmitted in two manuscripts now in the Staatsbibliothek zu Berlin and contains twenty-four chorales

(BWV690–713), most of them dating from the early Weimar years. Neither manuscript is actually in the hand of Bach's pupil Johann Philipp Kirnberger, but they were presumably made at his instigation, and perhaps under his supervision, while he was employed in Berlin as curator of the music library of Princess Anna Amalia, sister of Frederick the Great.

The 'Arnstadt' type of chorale prelude described in Chapter 2 is one that Bach soon discarded. Uncertainties about chronology make it impossible to say whether or not it lived on for a time in the well-known *In dulci jubilo* (BWV729) and the more accomplished *Vom Himmel hoch* (BWV738); both preludes show a more developed form than those usually assigned to the Arnstadt-Mühlhausen years, and they were presumably not designed to accompany a congregation. Possibly the last and certainly one of the simplest examples of the type is *Liebster Jesu, wir sind hier* (BWV706). Among the earliest Weimar preludes is *Ein' feste Burg* (BWV720), almost certainly written, as Spitta suggested, to inaugurate the organ of the Blasiuskirche in Mühlhausen after its rebuilding by Wender in 1708–9. While eschewing the fugal treatment that the opening seems to promise, the chorale melody is worked out in a variety of styles, migrating from one voice, and from one registration, to another in a way that seems well calculated to demonstrate the capabilities of a new organ. Frequent rests provide opportunities for drawing stops, including no doubt the Glockenspiel, requested and paid for by the parishioners, at the final pedal entry (Ex. 4.1).

It is unusual to find such variety of treatment in a single continuous chorale setting, but the other miscellaneous chorales show the still wider range of possibilities open to the composer. Representative of older types are *Gelobet seist du, Jesu Christ* (BWV723) and *Allein Gott in der Höh' sei Ehr'* (BWV711). The first follows the pattern established by Pachelbel in which each line of the chorale melody is preceded by motet-like imitation of itself in shorter note-values; the second is a bicinium (a two-part piece suggestive of a teacher–pupil duet) in which the chorale melody in the right hand is accompanied by active cello-like figuration in the left. Neither piece is of any outstanding merit or even particularly idiomatic to the organ, and the authenticity of both has been questioned. Other preludes that treat the chorale melody as a

**Ex. 4.1**

BWV720, bars 49–54

cantus firmus include the trios BWV694 and 710, the fugue on the Magnificat (BWV733, also in the Pachelbel mould) and *Valet will ich dir geben* (BWV736), described by Alberto Basso as 'one of the most majestic and brilliant works of the Weimar period'.[3] (Peter Williams praises it even more highly by suggesting that it might have been written at Leipzig.[4]) In these four works the cantus firmus is in the pedals, but it is worth

[3] *Frau Musika*, i, 469.
[4] Op. cit., ii, 283.

mentioning that the practice, common in Bach's time, of notating organ music on two staves rather than three has led modern editors to specify pedals in other works where they were perhaps not intended. The title-page of the Kirnberger collection specifies 'Choraelen vor 1 und 2 Claviren and Pedal', but among works certainly designed for manuals only are the seven short fughettas on Advent and Christmas hymns (BWV696–9, 701, and 703–4)—neatly turned miniatures that work out the first line only of the chorale.

Also in the Kirnberger collection are two extended chorale fantasias (BWV695 and 713) and three preludes (BWV727 and 730–1) that come close in style to those of the *Orgel-Büchlein* (BWV599–644). The contents of this famous volume were assembled for the most part between 1713 and 1716, but the title-page was written later, after Bach had moved to Cöthen, and should be read in the context of other didactic works (the Inventions, Sinfonias, and *Well-tempered Clavier*) of the Cöthen period: 'Little Organ Book, wherein the incipient organist is given instruction in the various ways of working out a chorale and also practice in the use of the pedals, which are treated in the chorales therein as entirely obbligato.' To this Bach added an inscription in verse which could well serve as a motto for his whole life's work: 'Dem Höchsten Gott allein zu Ehren,/ Dem Nechsten, draus sich zu belehren'.[5] The significance of the diminutive (*Büchlein*) in the title is lost in modern editions; the pages of Bach's manuscript measure 6 × 7½ ins (15.5 × 19 cm)—smaller than the page on which these words are printed.

The *Orgel-Büchlein* was planned as a volume of 164 chorales (counting separately the two similar settings of *Liebster Jesu, wir sind hier*, BWV633–4) and Bach evidently began by writing in the titles. He must, however, even at this stage, have had some idea of the kind of treatment he would give each of the melodies, since he needed to know how much space to allot them. In most cases he allowed a single page, but some, he knew, would require two, and one (*Christ ist erstanden*, in which each verse is given a different treatment) would need three. Most preludes occupy fewer than twenty bars, but Bach underestimated the length of some of them and found it necessary to insert a separate slip of paper or to complete them in tablature at the foot of a page. The

---

[5] 'To the highest God alone to praise Him, and to my neighbour for his self-instruction.'

first fifty-five chorales were to follow the church's calendar, beginning with Advent and ending with Trinity; the remainder, for which various sub-groupings have been suggested, were to illustrate aspects of the Christian life. Bach completed only forty-six of the pieces, the collection being fairly comprehensive for the church year as far as Easter, but only sketchily fulfilling his intentions for the rest.

Included in the volume are a trio (BWV639) in F minor (an unusual key for organ music in Bach's time) and an exuberant New Year fantasia, *In dir ist Freude* (BWV615), whose pedal ostinato seems to suggest bells and might have been accompanied by the Cymbelstern stop of the Weimar castle organ. These pieces, however, are not typical of the *Orgel-Büchlein*, the other preludes all belonging to one or another of three types rarely found outside this particular collection.

1. BWV614, 622, and 641. The chorale melody, elaborately decorated, is played as a solo by the right hand, the left hand and pedals accompanying. The longest and most poignantly expressive of these three pieces (it is one of those occupying two pages in the manuscript) is *O Mensch, bewein' dein' Sünde gross* (O man, bewail thy great sin, BWV622), often quoted on account of the chromaticism of its final line (Ex. 4.2a), but already distinguished by its shapely and memorable coloratura. The C♭ major triad (*) in the penultimate bar, a *locus classicus* of Baroque chromatic harmony, is easily (and often) explained as an approach to the Neapolitan sixth that follows it (F♮ acting as an appoggiatura to F♭), but its effect at that point results from its unexpectedness after the preceding E♭ major triad, to which it is unrelated except by the single note they have in common. If any clue to Bach's expressive intention is needed, it might be provided by the aria 'Mein Jesu, ziehe mich nach dir' in Cantata 22, where exactly the same unusual progression (in the same key) underlines the words 'deinen Leiden' (your suffering) (Ex. 4.2b). The effect might be thought more Romantic than Baroque, and it is interesting to note that, with the C♭ triad spelt enharmonically as B major, this is exactly the progression that separates (and connects) the first two movements of Beethoven's 'Emperor' Concerto.

2. BWV600, 608, 618–20, 624, 629, and 633–4. These are all canons, and were no doubt influenced by the canonic preludes of J. G. Walther, whose example seems to have been important for the conception and

**Ex. 4.2**

([I will] go [to] Jerusalem, to your suffering)

character of the *Orgel-Büchlein* as a whole.[6] In each case it is the chorale melody itself that is treated canonically, but in *In dulci jubilo* (BWV608) the other two parts also proceed in canon independently of the cantus firmus (Ex. 4.3). It is typical of the *Orgel-Büchlein* that for the last two lines of this chorale Bach relaxes the cantus firmus canon for the sake of the harmony by extending the time interval between the two parts, and at the same point he abandons the other canon altogether. Canon, as a symbol for the divine law, may be used to reinforce belief but, in the *Orgel-Büchlein* at least, it never hardens into dogma.

3. The remaining thirty-two chorale preludes belong to a type that, because of its particular association with this collection, is often referred

[6] P. Williams, op. cit., ii, 10, 12.

**Ex. 4.3**

BWV608, bars 1–5

to simply as the '*Orgel-Büchlein* type'. Its essential features (not all of them present in every chorale) are: (a) four-part texture; (b) the chorale melody, mainly in crotchets, clearly placed in the top voice; (c) contrapuntal working-out of accompanimental figures (sometimes derived from the chorale melody) in the middle parts, often maintaining an unbroken semiquaver movement; and (d) a pedal part either independent of the others in its figuration or sharing that of the middle parts. As a rule there are no interludes between the lines of the chorale. The type is well illustrated by one of the best known of all the *Orgel-Büchlein* pieces, *Durch Adams Fall ist ganz verderbt* (BWV637) (Ex. 4.4). The obvious but effective equating of Adam's Fall (sin) with the falling sevenths in the pedals—a musical metaphor, of course, rather than a

**Ex. 4.4**

BWV637, bars 1–3

simile—has frequently been commented on, but what contributes even more to the profoundly disturbing effect of this setting is the vacillation between major and minor thirds (x), which increases as the music proceeds. In this way Bach suggests how human nature has been corrupted ('ganz verderbt') by Adam's transgression.

Musical representation of some image or emotion in the chorale text is the starting-point for most of the *Orgel-Büchlein* preludes, but the figures suggested by the text are then developed for their purely musical possibilities. Bach criticism has by and large moved away from the rather rigid and subjective equations that Schweitzer drew between symbol and musical-rhetorical *figura*, and there are obvious dangers in attaching a general significance to a particular affective response, especially in the case of a composer who was apt to make the same music serve for different texts. As Peter Williams has written, 'both the terms and the resulting "interpretation" of a certain chorale can be expressed in different ways, since music is not a language with a definable or replaceable vocabulary'.[7] Nevertheless, Schweitzer and others were right to recognize the particular painterly and poetic qualities of the *Orgel-Büchlein*.

Despite the claims of its title-page, the *Orgel-Büchlein* exhibits a variety of detail and expression rather than of method. To appreciate Bach's mastery of other types, especially more extended ones, we must turn to the later sets. The contents of *Clavier-Übung* III (1739) as a whole will be the concern of a later chapter (see pp. 193–8). Its twenty-one chorale movements (BWV669–89) begin with nine settings of Lutheran *Missa* plainchants: two each of *Kyrie, Gott Vater in Ewigkeit, Christe, aller Welt Trost* and *Kyrie, Gott heiliger Geist*, and three of the German Gloria, *Allein Gott in der Höh' sei Ehr'*. Then follow six Catechism hymns, each in two settings—a large one with pedals and a smaller one without. Compared with the *Orgel-Büchlein* preludes, these have an austere, almost forbidding quality which may be attributed partly to the plainchant origins of the melodies and, in some of the larger settings (BWV669–71 and 686), to their *stile antico* counterpoint. Even in the *manualiter* preludes, which are mostly more relaxed in style, the emphasis is often

[7] Op. cit., ii, 15.

on contrapuntal artifice rather than on an affective representation of the text. Bach was clearly not concerned to attract a wide market for his first published organ music. He did, however, avail himself of a variety of prelude types. The three settings of *Allein Gott in der Höh'* are all trios, reinforcing the Trinitarian elements in the work; the second setting of *Dies sind die heil'gen zehn Gebot* is a fughetta, its tenfold entry of the subject (based on the first line of the hymn) symbolizing the ten commandments; BWV677 and 681 are also fughettas, 680 and 689 fugues; and BWV688 (among the most attractive of the *Clavier-Übung* III preludes, as well as being one of the most difficult to play) surrounds a pedal cantus firmus with playful imitative figures in a ritornello scheme.

Ritornello structures are to the fore in the six 'Schübler' chorales (BWV645–50), which is only to be expected since at least five of them were arranged from cantata movements that Bach wrote at Leipzig between 1724 and 1731. Printed in 1748–9 by Johann Georg Schübler of Zella, this was evidently more a publishing venture than *Clavier-Übung* III had been. For it Bach chose items from his cantata scores that could be transcribed with little alteration to make up an attractive set of half a dozen pieces in as many different keys:

| BWV | Title | Key | Origin |
|---|---|---|---|
| 645 | Wachet auf, ruft uns die Stimme | E♭ major | Cantata 140 (1731) |
| 646 | Wo soll ich fliehen hin | E minor | —— |
| 647 | Wer nur den lieben Gott lässt walten | C minor | Cantata 93 (1724) |
| 648 | Meine Seele erhebt den Herren | D minor | Cantata 10 (1724) |
| 649 | Ach bleib bei uns, Herr Jesu Christ | B♭ major | Cantata 6 (1725) |
| 650 | Kommst du nun, Jesu, vom Himmel | G major | Cantata 137 (1725) |

Whether or not the selection and order were influenced by other considerations as well is a matter for conjecture.[8] So, too, is the question of whether or not BWV646 is an arrangement, like the others. The

[8] For a summary of various theories regarding the unity and disposition of the set, see P. Williams, op. cit., ii, 104–6.

nature of the left-hand part, which is unlike most continuo lines, seems to indicate an original organ piece. In structure and texture, and to some extent in figuration as well, it recalls the G minor setting of the same chorale in the Kirnberger collection (BWV694). The other 'Schübler' preludes (especially Nos. 1, 5 and 6) exemplify a novel type of organ chorale in which the freely written counterpoint, with a strong melodic character and a rounded phrase structure of its own, rivals the cantus firmus as the main melodic element in the composition. Asked to identify 'the main tune' of the first prelude, one would probably quote not the chorale melody in the left hand but the new line that precedes and accompanies it. For all its suave melodiousness, this is remarkable for its unorthodox use of dissonance, particularly in the way that Bach moves away from dissonant notes by leap rather than by step (Ex. 4.5).

**Ex. 4.5**

BWV645, bars 13–16

At about the same time as he was arranging chorales for Schübler, Bach was also collecting together, revising, and writing out in a fair copy some of the organ chorales he had composed during his years at Weimar. Often referred to as the 'Eighteen', the collection is better described as the 'Seventeen' (BWV651–67), since the final piece, *Vor deinen Thron* (BWV668), is incomplete, separated from the others in the manuscript and in a different hand. (It was perhaps a revision of this version that Bach 'in his blindness dictated extempore to one of his friends', as the *Nachricht* in the first edition of the *Art of Fugue* tells us.) Except that different settings of the same melody are grouped together, the pieces do not seem to follow any particular order, although some commentators have claimed to find one. Length and quality appear to have been the main criteria for inclusion, and if the *Orgel-Büchlein* shows Bach as a poetic miniaturist in chorale writing, the 'Leipzig' collection shows him as a master of chorale settings on the grandest scale. Indicative of the contrast between the two sets is *Komm, Gott Schöpfer, heiliger Geist* (BWV667), an expansion to more than three times its original size of the *Orgel-Büchlein* version (BWV631).

A similar expansion has occurred with *Komm, heiliger Geist,* which opens the collection; in this case the forty-eight bars of what is presumably an earlier version have grown to 106. A second working of the same melody is even longer in actual duration, its pre-imitation of each chorale line extensively and fugally developed, and the soprano cantus firmus decorated in a leisurely way; the spacious design is completed by a climactic coda, a feature of the 'Leipzig' chorales (although some codas are more meditative than climactic). There are striking points of resemblance between the melody of this chorale and that of *An Wasserflüssen Babylon*, and it was probably this that led Bach to place them next to each other in the manuscript and to treat them similarly in matters of key, metre, and melodic decoration. *Schmücke dich, o liebe Seele* (No. 4), which Schumann was moved to call 'as priceless and profound a piece of music as ever sprang from an artist's imagination', recalls the 'Schübler' preludes in its continuo-like bass and in the melodiousness of its accompanying paraphrases; its languid sensuousness is also reminiscent (or prophetic) of the aria 'Schlummert ein' in Cantata 82. The trio *Herr Jesu Christ, dich zu uns wend* (No. 5) displays the tuneful, flowing counterpoint that distinguishes many of the 'Leipzig' chorales. Its motifs are derived from the first line of the melody, which is not heard complete until it appears as a cantus firmus in the pedals at the end. Similar in construction, and perhaps even more original in its use of paraphrase technique, is No. 14, the last of three fine settings of *Allein Gott in der Höh' sei Ehr'*.

Another chorale to receive three different settings is *Nun komm, der Heiden Heiland*. In the first the chorale tune is made into an expressive

coloratura melody in the manner of Böhm and Buxtehude; the treatment is freer than in O Mensch, bewein' dein' Sünde gross (BWV622), for
example, and the design is made more spacious by pre-imitation of the
first line, interludes between succeeding lines, and a meditative coda
over a long-held tonic pedal. The second setting is a trio whose two
lower parts (left hand and pedals) interweave canonically for much of
the time in a low tessitura, producing a texture unique in Bach's organ
music and one that poses registration problems for the performer. The
final setting is an impressive combination of fugue, ritornello, and cantus firmus (pedals) 'in organo pleno'. Despite the fact that all three
settings are in the same key (G minor), there is no firm evidence that
they were conceived as a group. But it is natural to look for some
explanation for three such very different and strongly characterized
treatments of the same chorale; Peter Williams has suggested a portrayal
of Jesus as beatifier, harrower of Hell, and Saviour in Glory.[9]

## Preludes and Fugues

Problems of chronology and attribution are multiplied when we turn
from the chorale settings to the freely composed organ pieces, and there
are in addition other problems, for example that of deciding whether a
prelude and its fugue originally belonged together. Only one prelude
and fugue (in Clavier-Übung III) appeared in print during Bach's lifetime,
and autographs exist for only about half a dozen other works. The
composer seems never to have grouped his preludes and fugues in sets,
as he did the organ chorales, and the impression of a miscellany is
reinforced by the titles as they appear in the sources. The preludes,
toccatas, and fantasias coupled with the fugues are insufficiently differ-
entiated in style or structure to permit any meaningful categorization,
and indeed different titles are sometimes attached to the same composition. In the discussion that follows, therefore, the term 'prelude', unless referring to a particular piece, will be understood to include also
'toccata' and 'fantasia'.

Insofar as their chronology can be determined on stylistic grounds,
the organ works in this category do show a distinct trend towards the
standardization of discrete prelude-and-fugue pairs such as we find in

[9] Op. cit., ii, 156–7.

the *Well-tempered Clavier*. They also show a move towards greater co-
herence and a less improvisatory manner within the component movements, which is paralleled in other, more accurately datable works.
Vestiges of the north German multisectional toccata, familiar from Buxtehude's examples, begin to disappear as Bach at Weimar comes into
close contact with neat Italian structures, and the long straggling fugue
subjects of the early works (see the examples quoted on p. 32) give way
to pithier, more contrapuntally workable themes. However, it would
be foolhardy to propose a precise chronology on the basis of formal and
stylistic analysis alone, and any attempt to do so would be defeated by
the existence of different versions and by the unreliability of some of
the sources. The works discussed in this section have been chosen to
illustrate a trend, not to suggest a chronology in any but the broadest
terms.

Among the preludes and fugues generally thought to date from the
Weimar years, BWV532, 535, 543, 549, and 564 show several features
that connect them stylistically to those of the Arnstadt-Mühlhausen period. The earliest, perhaps, is the C minor Prelude and Fugue (BWV549),
which shares much in common with the Prelude and Fugue in C major
(BWV531) and could even date from the same time. The influence of
Buxtehude and Böhm is still strong in the prelude, with its opening
pedal solo; the fugue entries are restricted to tonic and dominant
pitches, the single pedal entry is long delayed, and counterpoint is abandoned at the end for a coda featuring demisemiquaver scales. Any suggestion that BWV531 and 549 were conceived as a complementary pair
must, however, take account of the fact that BWV549 exists in another,
almost certainly earlier, version in D minor. The G minor Prelude and
Fugue (BWV535) has the same prelude—fugue—coda structure (with
an unusual but unmistakable foreshadowing of the fugue subject in the
pedals during the prelude), and so does the A minor Prelude and Fugue
(BWV543), in which the three sections are more tightly organized and
the pedal part better integrated than in the other two works.

The Prelude and Fugue in D major (BWV532) and the Toccata in C
major (BWV564) are also multi-sectional pieces, the first incorporating
a lengthy passage of Italianate *alla breve* counterpoint within its prelude,
and ending with a fugue whose subject makes something original and
memorable out of simple repetition and sequence (Ex. 4.6). Much of

**Ex. 4.6**

BWV532/ii, bars 1–6

the enjoyment of this lively piece derives from the unpredictability (in pitch and registration rather than in actual substance) of the counter-subject material that comes between the two phrases of the subject. The Toccata in C, with its three quite independent movements, is unique among Bach's works. It begins with brilliant improvisatory solos for manual and pedal separately in the style of the early preludes, but then goes on to work out figures from the pedal solo in a most purposeful and cohesive manner. The skittish fugue theme, like that of BWV532, contains long rests that invite prattling interjections later on. Between these two movements comes an Adagio (A minor) in the style of a violin or oboe sonata with continuo accompaniment.

The similarity of BWV564 to the overall form (fast–slow–fast) of the three-movement Vivaldi concerto has often been observed, but the influence of the Italian concerto is much more prominent in some of the (presumably) later organ works, while the north German toccata tradition is left further behind. Preludes and fugues thought to date from the later Weimar period show some or all of the following characteristics:

1. A prelude which may be virtuoso in style, but in which bravura solos for manuals or pedals (if they occur) are well integrated with the rest of the movement.

2. A pedal part which, in both preludes and fugues, is more continuous and more thematic than in the earlier works.

3. A fugue subject which is more concise, often in long note values, capable of engendering growth and sometimes designed for stretto.

The result of these reforms is a prelude which may complement the fugue or contrast with it, but which has a thematic, fully worked out structure of its own, and a fugue which is cumulative in effect and therefore can (indeed, must) dispense with the bravura coda typical of the earlier works.

A work embodying these developments is the so-called Dorian Toccata and Fugue in D minor (BWV538), one of the few organ pieces for which we have documentary evidence of a performance by Bach himself (he played it at the opening of the rebuilt organ in the Martinskirche, Cassel, in September 1732). A still finer work, and an even severer test for the mettle of an organ, is the Toccata and Fugue in F major (BWV540), written for the Weissenfels organ or for some other instrument with a high pedal *f*. The opening of the toccata might easily have served for a modest two-part invention (it is, in fact, not unlike the opening of the 'Little' Prelude (No. 3) in D minor, BWV935) (Ex. 4.7), but from it Bach constructs a majestic piece which, after a substantial introduction (canonic development of the initial idea over long tonic and dominant pedal points, alternating with imposing pedal

**Ex. 4.7**

BWV540/i, bars 1–5

BWV935, bars 1–5

solos: bars 1–177), is propelled forward by a thrusting ritornello theme and given new charges of energy by unexpected harmonies at crucial cadence points (bars 204–5, 318–19, and 424–5). The *alla breve* fugue, although possibly composed later, complements the toccata perfectly, not in the weight of its material but in the interest and ingenuity of its counterpoint. Its two themes are worked out separately at first, and then together.

Less satisfying is the pairing of fantasia and fugue in the 'Great' G minor (BWV542), and there are even stronger reasons in this case for supposing the two movements to have been written at different times. The fantasia is an astonishing harmonic *tour de force*, exploiting diminished sevenths, enharmonic transitions and unexpected chromatic switches in a piece of musical rhetoric more powerful even than the Chromatic Fantasia in D minor for harpsichord. The organ fugue (separate from the fantasia in most of the contemporary manuscripts) is a comparatively lightweight piece with a subject perhaps based on a Dutch song. Its length makes it an acceptable companion for the fantasia, but a better balance of prelude and fugue is often achieved in lesser works, for example in the unpretentiously attractive A major prelude and its unusually graceful 3/4 fugue (BWV536). Although the sources are inconclusive on this point, both movements seem to be revisions of earlier versions.

Another fugue belonging to this group is notable for an interesting, if not altogether successful, formal innovation. The C minor fugue (BWV537; the one that Elgar orchestrated) begins with an exposition, episode, and counter-exposition in the home key. An imperfect cadence ushers in a second pair of fugue subjects (minims rising chromatically through a perfect fourth and quavers moving sequentially with them) and these are developed in a purposeful manner for forty-eight bars. What follows, however, is not the combination of the two fugues that occurs, for example, in BWV540 (a few moments with paper and pen will reveal that the themes will not combine satisfactorily), but a literal restatement of the first exposition (bars 5–28) with the final bars adapted to accommodate a short dominant pedal and a brief coda. One cannot regret that this unproductive marriage of da capo form and fugue held only a limited appeal for Bach. He employed it in only a few other works: two for lute (BWV997–8), the organ fugue in E minor (BWV548) known as the 'Wedge', and (probably) the incomplete keyboard fugue in C minor (BWV906). These all date from the Leipzig years (after 1723), and possibly BWV537, too, was composed later than is generally thought.

The E minor fugue gets its title from the wedge-like shape of its subject: beginning on the tonic, its intervals gradually widen to an octave on either side of it. After an orderly exposition, some brilliant passagework for the manuals threatens almost to drive out the wedge, but this is nevertheless Bach's most successful attempt at combining fugue and da capo form. His late mastery of the organ prelude and fugue is, however, better demonstrated in three other Leipzig works. The E♭ major Prelude and Fugue that frame Part III of the *Clavier-Übung* will be the subject of later comments (see p. 194). The B minor (BWV544) is another of those works, like the 'Great' G minor, in which the prelude overshadows the fugue in intensity of expression and sheer command of the medium. Spitta (iii, 210) found the prelude 'a labyrinth of romantic harmony, such as has never been constructed by any more modern composer', but there is nothing labyrinthine about its structure; it is one of the most spacious and clearly articulated of all Bach's ritornello movements. The subject of the fugue is, after this, curiously self-effacing in its plain stepwise quavers—so much so, in fact, that several entries are apt to go unnoticed among the continuo-like quaver tread of left hand and pedals.

More classical in its style and proportions, and undeservedly neglected in comparison with some of the works already discussed, is the Prelude and Fugue in C major (BWV547), which is certainly among the finest of all Bach's organ works, and one of the most original too. Fundamental to its many subtleties is a relationship between manuals and pedals in both movements quite unlike that in any other prelude and fugue by Bach (although parallels may be found among the chorale settings). In the prelude the hands work out an initial 'inventio', somewhat in the style of a three-part sinfonia for clavier, while the feet punctuate the movement with a bell-like ostinato. The fugue is close in style to many of the pieces in the *Well-tempered Clavier*, and Peter Williams has observed a quite remarkable resemblance between its exposition and that of the fughetta in A major (for manuals only) on *Allein*

*Gott in der Höh' sei Ehr'* in *Clavier-Übung* III (BWV677).[10] The movement has, however, one unique feature. The fleeting character and agile leaps of the single-bar subject would seem to exclude the pedals, and so they do for two-thirds of the fugue's seventy-two bars. Their entry, however, is as logical as it is unexpected, and the more effective for being so long delayed. They play four statements of the subject at their own speed (i.e. in augmentation), the other parts combining in all kinds of strettos and inversions (Ex. 4.8). Even among Bach's organ fugues it is difficult to find one that surpasses this in contrapuntal resource, or one that is better 'orchestrated' for the instrument.

### Miscellaneous Organ Works

There are several organ works that belong to neither of the above categories. The concerto arrangements, made probably in 1713–14 for

**Ex. 4.8**

BWV547/ii, bars 49–53

S = subject

[10] Op. cit., i, 159–60.

Prince Johann Ernst at Weimar, are discussed in a later chapter (see pp. 81–2), as are the late Canonic Variations on *Vom Himmel hoch* (see pp. 214–15). The Fantasia in C minor (BWV562) is a sombre French-style piece in five parts; what was to have been its companion fugue was also in five parts, but Bach's autograph breaks off at the counter-exposition (in stretto) and the movement was probably never completed. Two Italianate works showing the influence of Frescobaldi and (in the second, at least) Corelli are the Canzona in D minor (BWV588) and the *Alla breve* in D major (BWV589). Also Italianate in style, at least as far as its first movement is concerned, is the Pastorale in F major (BWV590). Although universally known under this title, it is given a slightly different one—that of 'Pastorella'—in the manuscript sources, and thus belongs to a tradition of church compositions for Christmas. It is not clear, however, what part (if any) it played in the Christmas liturgy; it is not even clear whether its four short movements always belonged together. Only in the first of them is the use of the pedals obligatory. This has all the hallmarks of the kind of pastoral Christmas music familiar from Corelli's *Christmas Concerto* (Op. 6 No. 8), Handel's *Messiah* and Bach's own *Christmas Oratorio* (introduction to Part II): a lilting 12/8 metre, long-held bass drones, and mellifluous phrases in parallel thirds and sixths. The second and third sections show no obvious connections with Christmas, but the last one—a kind of fugal dance in binary form—begins with a faintly disguised reference to the Christmas hymn *Resonet in laudibus*, often sung in English-speaking countries to the words 'Joseph dearest, Joseph mine'.

More important are the six sonatas and the Passacaglia in C minor. Bach's autograph of the sonatas (BWV525–30) dates from about 1730, but some of the movements were arranged from earlier works. According to Forkel (101–2) they were compiled by Bach 'for his eldest son William Friedemann, who, by practising them, prepared himself to become the great performer on the organ that he afterwards was'. Their study has since become a standard part of an organist's training. They encourage independence of hands and feet, and require clean playing if their three strands are to be heard as if played by two melody instruments and a bass. The texture of the organ sonatas does in fact recall that of the violin and flute sonatas with harpsichord obbligato, except that their pedal parts are less active than they would be if written for the left hand of a harpsichordist. Their structure, on the other hand, draws less on sonata than on concerto models, both for their three-movement form (fast–slow–fast) and for the ritornello designs of most of the outer movements. The sixth sonata (perhaps the only one originally and completely composed as an organ trio) even opens with unisons like the ritornellos of some Vivaldi and Bach concertos. Not deriving from the concerto, however, is the binary form with repeats found in four of the sonata movements. One of these, the slow movement of the sixth sonata, is a particularly developed example of the form, the second section ending with a complete subdominant recapitulation of the first. The sonatas show occasional touches of the new *galant* style, perhaps in deference to Wilhelm Friedemann's taste for what his father once mentioned as 'the lovely ditties' of the Dresden opera.

It has sometimes been argued, albeit not very convincingly, that the sonatas were intended not for the organ but for harpsichord with pedals. The same claim has been put forward, with better reason, for the Passacaglia and Fugue in C minor (BWV582), whose fourteenth and fifteenth variations especially seem more idiomatic to a stringed keyboard instrument than to the organ. But, whatever Bach's intentions, countless performances have proved the effectiveness of the passacaglia on the organ, and no other instrument can so convincingly achieve the dynamic climaxes that Bach obviously envisaged at the final variation and again at the end of the fugue. Moreover, early manuscript sources clearly indicate that the work is for *organo* (in one case *organo pleno*). It has often been pointed out that the first half of Bach's eight-bar passacaglia theme is identical with the bass of the Christe in the second mass from André Raison's *Livre d'orgue* (Paris, 1688), but despite the fact that Raison's piece is called a 'trio en passacaille', the possibility of a simple coincidence seems very high. Certainly BWV582 owes more to the example of pieces nearer home, notably three chaconnes (in C minor, D minor, and E minor) by Buxtehude. After a solo pedal statement of the theme, Bach writes twenty variations and a fugue. The overall course of the variations is one that proceeds from simplicity to complexity, but within this plan they can be grouped into sets according to where subsidiary points of climax and contrast are seen to occur. In fact, some decision of this kind must be made by any player not content to adopt an *organo pleno* registration for the whole work. Writers and performers differ in their opinions as to how these groupings should best be made, but a division into 12 + 3 + 5 variations is generally favoured.[11] Agreement is more general in seeing the double fugue as the crowning glory of the work, and the success of Bach's wholly original variations-and-fugue design has been confirmed by the many later composers (including Brahms, Reger, Britten, and Rubbra) who have adopted it in works of a very different kind.

[11] For a résumé of various possible groupings see P. Williams, op. cit., i, 263–4.

# CHAPTER 5

# Cöthen

## (1717–23)

HE TOWN OF CÖTHEN (NOW KÖTHEN), ABOUT 60 MILES
north of Weimar, was from 1603 the seat of the princes of
Anhalt-Cöthen, heirs to a territory that had previously formed part of
the duchy of Anhalt. In 1595 Prince Johann Georg had imposed Cal-
vinism on the principality and forbidden all other forms of public worship, a ban which lasted for almost a century until it was relaxed in
1693 by Prince Emanuel Lebrecht. He had married a Lutheran, Gisela
Agnes von Rath, and yielded to her pleas to permit again the celebration of Orthodox rites. Soon a Lutheran school was opened, and a
new Lutheran church, the Agnuskirche, was dedicated on 7 May 1699.
After the prince's premature death in 1704 Gisela Agnes founded also a
seminary for young titled ladies. Leopold, her eldest child and heir to
the title, was only ten when his father died, but already he was showing signs of unusual musical talent. Cöthen supported no permanent
*Kapelle*, but by 1707 the young prince had become sufficiently skilled
as a bass viol player to persuade his mother to employ three musicians
at court with whom he could join in chamber music. During the years
1708–10 he studied at the Ritterakademie in Berlin and then completed his musical education by touring the Low Countries, England,
France, and Italy. When he returned to Cöthen in April 1713 he was
a skilled player of the violin, bass viol, and harpsichord, and a good
bass singer.

Back in Cöthen, Leopold set about building up a *Kapelle* (or *collegium*

*musicum*, as he himself called it) in imitation of those he had encountered during his years of study and travel. In Berlin the new king of
Prussia, Friedrich Wilhelm I, had disbanded the court orchestra, and
Leopold was able to secure seven of the musicians who had lost their
jobs, including Augustin Reinhard Stricker, whom he appointed *Kapellmeister* on a three-year contract. Stricker's wife also joined the establishment as a singer; their combined salary was 276 thalers per annum. In
1716, by which time he had reached his majority and succeeded his
mother as ruler, Leopold increased the number of his musicians to eighteen. As well as *Kapellmeister* Stricker and his wife, there were now
three violinists, two flautists, two trumpeters, one player each of bass
viol, cello, oboe, bassoon, timpani, and organ, and three 'ripienists' (less
capable musicians who did not play solo parts). Among these it is appropriate to mention the viol player Christian Ferdinand Abel, whose
more famous son Carl Friedrich later collaborated with Bach's youngest
son Johann Christian in a celebrated series of London concerts.

The princely residence at Cöthen stood more or less in the centre
of the town, but isolated from it by a moat surrounded by spacious gardens (see Plate 11). Bach and his family seem not to have lived
in the castle, but their dwelling place in Cöthen has never been
established. A long tradition places it in the Wallstrasse, where a bust of
the composer by Heinrich Pohlmann was erected to commemorate his
bicentenary in 1885. More recently it has been suggested that Bach
lived first in the Stiftstrasse and moved to the Holzmarkt in 1721;[1]
No. 44 Schalaunische Strasse has also been suggested, at least as a temporary residence.[2] The seventh and last child born to Maria Barbara
was baptized on 17 November 1718 in the castle chapel, but this
should not be taken to indicate that the Bachs were living there. The
chapel was presumably chosen because Bach's employer and his
brother and sister had consented to act as godparents. Leopold Augustus (the child took the names of his exalted godfathers) did not survive
the first year of infancy; he was buried on 28 September 1719 in the
graveyard of the Agnuskirche, the church at which the Bachs worshipped in Cöthen.

---

[1] Walter Emery in S. Sadie (ed.), *The New Grove Dictionary of Music and Musicians*, i, 792.
[2] M. Petzoldt, *Bachstätten aufsuchen* (Leipzig, 1992), p. 68.

Bach took up his new appointment in time to celebrate Prince Leopold's twenty-third birthday on 10 December 1717.[3] A few days later he was in Leipzig testing and reporting on the organ that Johann Scheibe had built for the university church (the Paulinerkirche) the previous year. This was, as far as is known, his first visit to Leipzig, and the first of several visits he was to make to various places during his time at Cöthen. Between about 9 May and 15 June 1718 he and five other members of the *collegium musicum* attended Prince Leopold at the fashionable spa of Carlsbad (now Karlovy Vary) in Bohemia. Early the following year Bach paid what was perhaps a second visit to Berlin in connection with the purchase of a new harpsichord, and it was probably on this occasion that he came into contact with Margrave Christian Ludwig of Brandenburg, to whom two years later he dedicated the Brandenburg Concertos. The harpsichord itself was a large two-manual instrument and it was probably on this that the solo cembalo part in the Fifth Brandenburg Concerto was played for the first time. It is mentioned in an inventory of 1784 as the work of Michael Mietke, instrument maker at the Berlin court from 1697 until his death in 1719.

In May 1719 Bach's exact contemporary, George Frideric Handel, left London for the Continent to engage singers for the new Royal Academy's first opera season, planned for the following year. After visiting the electoral court at Düsseldorf, he stayed for a time at his birthplace, Halle, where his mother and other relatives were still living. When Bach heard that one of the most universally admired musicians of the time was staying only about 20 miles from Cöthen, he immediately set out by stagecoach to visit him, but arrived in Halle to find that Handel had left that very day. Ten years later, while Bach was unwell in Leipzig, Handel again visited Halle. Unable this time to make the journey himself, Bach sent his son Friedemann with a message inviting Handel to visit him, but Handel was unable to do so. According to the writer from whom this information derives (perhaps C. P. E. Bach), it grieved Bach not to have become personally acquainted with 'this truly great man of whom he thought so highly'.[4]

In May 1720 Bach again accompanied Prince Leopold to Carlsbad,

[3] He was born on 28 November (old style) 1694.
[4] *Allgemeine deutsche Bibliothek*, 27 February 1788.

leaving Maria Barbara to look after their four children in Cöthen. After what was no doubt a welcome and refreshing change of surroundings, he was totally unprepared, on his return in July, for the sorrowful news that his wife had fallen ill and died—indeed, had already been buried on the 7th of that month. The cause of her sudden death is not recorded—it would be idle to speculate on whether it might have been associated with a seventh pregnancy—but it is not difficult to imagine its distressing effect on Bach. He had learnt, like so many of his contemporaries, to live closely with death and perhaps to accept the loss of those near to him; but life at Cöthen, which until then had been the happiest he had known, must now have become distasteful to him. This, at any rate, can be inferred from his journey to Hamburg towards the end of the year to register his candidature there for the post of organist at the Jakobikirche, left vacant by the death in September of Heinrich Friese. Erdmann Neumeister, the cantata librettist, had been head pastor there since 1715, and there were other reasons as well for Bach's interest in the post. Hamburg, as he well knew from earlier visits, was favoured with some of the finest organs and most gifted organists in Germany. The Jakobikirche organ had been built by the famous Arp Schnitger in 1689–93, with four manuals and sixty speaking stops; Schnitger had also built fine instruments for Hamburg's Nikolaikirche and Johanniskirche. Bach evidently spent some time playing all these organs, to the delight and astonishment of those who heard him, and it was probably during this visit that he performed for over two hours in the Catharinenkirche to an audience that included the organist of that church, J. A. Reincken, by then a very old man. His half-hour extemporization on the chorale *An Wasserflüssen Babylon* was praised by Reincken with the words 'I thought such art was dead, but I see it still lives in you'—a compliment the more gracious since Reincken's own lengthy fantasia on the same melody was one of his most celebrated compositions.

Only four of the eight candidates for the Jakobikirche post presented themselves for the *Probe* on 28 November. Bach was not among them, having had to return to Cöthen five days before, perhaps to prepare for the celebrations in connection with Prince Leopold's birthday. However, before the post was offered to anyone else an attempt was made to persuade Bach to accept it, and it was not until his letter of refusal had been received that Johann Joachim Heitmann (about whom little else is known) was elected. Bach's refusal may be attributed to his unwillingness to acquiesce in the simony that apparently accompanied such appointments in Hamburg. (Heitmann contributed 4,000 marks to the church funds after his election.) A few years later Johann Mattheson referred to the appointment, without naming names, in the following scornful terms:

> I recall, as many others will too, that some years ago a certain great musician [Bach], whose merits have since earned him an important cantorate [at Leipzig], competed for the post of organist in a town of no small size [Hamburg] and exhibited his mastery on several of the finest organs, arousing universal admiration. But there was also present, among other incompetent journeymen, the son of a wealthy tradesman [Heitmann] who could prelude better with thalers than with his fingers, and it was he (as might easily be guessed) who was given the post, although most people were furious about it. It was Christmastide, and the eloquent chief preacher [Neumeister], who had not consented to the simony, took as his text the Gospel story of the angels' music at the birth of Christ . . . and ended his sermon with a remarkable pronouncement something like this: He was quite certain that if one of the angels at Bethlehem had come down from heaven and played divinely to become organist at St J [Jakobikirche], but had no money, he might just as well fly away again.[5]

March 1721 saw the completion and dedication of the six Brandenburg Concertos, which are among the most buoyant and inspiriting of all Bach's works. But the year as a whole cannot have been easy for him without the support of the one with whom he had shared thirteen years of happy marriage, and its early months were further darkened by the death on 22 February of his elder brother Johann Christoph at Ohrdruf. By a tragic coincidence his brother Jacob in Sweden had lost his wife only a few months before Maria Barbara died. In October 1721 Jacob found a new wife in Ingeborg Magdalena Swahn (née Norell), and only a few weeks later, on 3 December, Bach also remarried.

His new bride was Anna Magdalena, youngest daughter of Johann

---

[5] *Der musicalische Patriot* (Hamburg, 1728), 316.

Caspar Wülcken, court trumpeter at Weissenfels and before that at nearby Zeitz, where Anna Magdalena was born on 22 September 1701. Although Bach may have become acquainted with her eldest sister Anna Katharina when he visited Weissenfels in 1713, there is nothing to link his name with Anna Magdalena's before 25 September 1721, when they both acted as godparents to the son of Prince Leopold's butler, Christian Hahn. But they must have known each other well by then, for Anna Magdalena is described in the baptismal register as 'a court singer here'. Bach's second marriage was as fortunate as his first had been. Anna Magdalena was a gifted singer, well trained in music by her father and her maternal uncle, Johann Siegmund Liebe, town and court organist at Zeitz. Her salary at Cöthen brought an increase of fifty per cent to the family income, and after the move to Leipzig in 1723 she continued to be of professional service to her husband as a neat and accurate copyist of his music. Above all, she became stepmother to Maria Barbara's four surviving children, and added a further thirteen to the family during the course of a marriage which lasted until Bach's death. His affection for her can be sensed in the contents of two *Clavierbüchlein* (Little keyboard books) which he compiled for her during the first four years of their life together. Along with the *Clavier-Büchlein* begun earlier for his eldest son Friedemann, these collections open a window on the family music-making of the Bachs, in which instruction went hand-in-hand with enjoyment. Some of the pieces they contain later found a place in works more explicitly didactic: the fifteen Inventions and Sinfonias, the *Clavier-Übung* part I, and *Das Wohltemperirte Clavier* (The Well-tempered Clavier).

At the time of Bach's first marriage in 1707 financial assistance had come from a share in the estate of his uncle Tobias Lämmerhirt. By a strange coincidence, Tobias's widow, Martha Catharina, died at Erfurt in September 1721, less than three months before Bach's marriage to Anna Magdalena. The will was read on 26 September and once again Bach was a beneficiary, but settlement of the legacy was this time delayed by legal wrangles and it was not until over a year later, in December 1722, that he received the full amount due to him. This must have been about 500 thalers—well over a year's salary.

About a week after Bach and Anna Magdalena were married another wedding took place at Bernburg, some 12 miles north-west of Cöthen, which was to affect their future in a very different way. On 11 December 1721 Prince Leopold married his twenty-year-old cousin Friederica Henrietta of Anhalt-Bernburg; there followed five weeks of festivity at Cöthen, to which Bach contributed a congratulatory cantata, now lost, and no doubt other music as well. To the newly wedded Bachs the festivities must have seemed like a celebration of their own happiness, but they were soon to see their new princess in a quite different light. It turned out that Friederica shared none of her husband's delight in music, and indeed seems to have been indifferent to all forms of culture: an 'amusa' was how Bach later described her to his friend Georg Erdmann.[6] Her presence at Cöthen soon became so disruptive of the friendly relations that Bach had until then enjoyed with his prince that he began to find his position at court exceedingly difficult. It is unlikely that this was an overriding consideration in Bach's decision to leave Cöthen, but it was certainly a factor in it.

On 5 June 1722, about six months after Prince Leopold's marriage, Johann Kuhnau, Kantor of the Thomasschule in Leipzig, died at the age of sixty-two. He had been active at Leipzig for nearly forty years (the last twenty of them as Kantor) and had striven to uphold the status of church music there in the face of increasing secularization in the musical life of the city. The appointment of his successor was placed in the hands of an *Enge Rat*, a committee consisting of three burgomasters and nine other council members. Of the three burgomasters, who played a leading part in their deliberations, Adrian Steger and Abraham Christoph Platz were in favour of appointing someone who would make a good Kantor for the Thomasschule, able and willing to teach academic subjects (especially Latin), whereas the third, Gottfried Lange, was more concerned that Leipzig should have a gifted musician and composer as its *Director musices*. The post was one of considerable esteem, and it is not surprising that when the *Enge Rat* met on 14 July the list of applicants to be considered included some well-known names. The six candidates were: Johann Friedrich Fasch, *Kapellmeister* at Zerbst and a former pupil of Kuhnau; Georg Lenck, Kantor at Laucha, near Naumburg and later at Weissenfels; Christian Friedrich Rolle, Kantor

[6] See Bach's letter, quoted in full on pp. 119–21.

at Magdeburg, who had collaborated with Bach and Kuhnau in testing the Liebfrauenkirche organ at Halle in 1716; Georg Balthasar Schott, organist at the Neukirche in Leipzig and director of the *collegium musicum* founded by Telemann in 1702; Johann Martin Steindorff, Kantor at Zwickau; and Georg Philipp Telemann, since July 1721 Kantor at Hamburg.

Telemann was by far the strongest candidate for the post. He had already spent four years in the city (1701–5) as university student, opera director, founder of the *collegium musicum*, and organist of the Neukirche; as early as 1703 the council had invited him to succeed Kuhnau, who was at the time very ill. There can have been little surprise in Leipzig when he was elected Thomaskantor on 11 August 1722 and formally appointed to the post two days later. Possibly there was little surprise, either, when the Hamburg authorities refused to release Telemann. Instead they increased his salary and dropped the objections they had previously raised to his involvement in public concerts and opera. So, on 23 November, the committee met again to consider the remaining candidates and two others whose names had been added to the list: Georg Friedrich Kauffmann, organist and director of church music at Merseburg; and Andreas Christoph Duve, Kantor at Brunswick. Test cantatas by Kauffmann, Duve, and Schott were heard on the first Sunday in Advent (29 November), but the contest was still open, and by 21 December two more candidates had presented themselves: Johann Christoph Graupner, *Kapellmeister* at Darmstadt and a former pupil at the Thomasschule in Leipzig; and J. S. Bach. Graupner was clearly the favourite among the five candidates who remained when he performed his two test cantatas on 17 January 1723, and he was immediately offered the post. But, like Telemann, he was forced to withdraw when he failed to secure his release from Darmstadt, where he was compensated by a handsome increase in salary and the promise of a pension for his dependants in the event of his death. Possibly foreseeing that this might happen, the council at Leipzig had meanwhile conducted examinations of the other candidates (Bach performed Cantatas 22 and 23 in the Thomaskirche on 7 February), and when Graupner's refusal was received in April they resolved to invite Bach to accept the post.

There are good reasons to doubt the suggestion, frequently made, that Bach's agreement with the Leipzig council was entered into reluctantly by both parties. Five days before the meeting at which Graupner's refusal was announced, an event occurred that might have persuaded Bach also to reconsider his application. On 4 April 1723, less than three months after her twenty-first birthday, the 'amusa', Princess Friederica Henrietta, died at Cöthen. If this failed to persuade Bach to remain as Prince Leopold's *Kapellmeister* it can only be because by then he genuinely desired the Leipzig cantorate. His continued presence in Leipzig after performing his *Probe* supports this, as also (in a different way) does the amazing productivity of the next five or six years. As to the council's supposed reluctance to employ him, this rests chiefly on a misunderstanding of what was said by one of their number at the meeting of 9 April 1723. Councillor Platz is usually quoted as having said on that occasion: 'Since we cannot get the best man, we shall have to be satisfied with a mediocre one',[7] the inference being that the 'best man' was Telemann and the 'mediocre one' Bach. There were in 1723 very good reasons why the council might have held such views, but in fact Platz said something quite different, as the minutes of the meeting show. After the members had been informed that none of the three remaining candidates (Bach, Kauffmann, and Schott) was willing to teach nonmusical subjects, they were reminded that when Telemann had been under consideration it was suggested that these duties might be undertaken by someone other than the Kantor. It was at this point that Councillor Platz intervened: 'This suggestion he [Platz] has good reason to find inexpedient. Since the best [*die beste*, pl.] cannot now be engaged one must accept the mediocre. Many good things had recently been said about someone at Pirna . . .'[8] Clearly, when Platz spoke of 'the best' he was thinking not only of Telemann and Graupner but also of Bach, Kauffmann, and Schott, all of whom were disqualified, in his view, because of their unwillingness to teach Latin. That being so, one must accept someone less able, and presumably Platz had reason to think that the man at Pirna (no doubt the Kantor there, Christian Heckel) would be willing to undertake all the duties traditionally connected

---

[7] Translation from Karl Geiringer, *The Bach Family*, 163.

[8] Ratsprotokoll, 9 April 1723 (Stadtarchiv, Leipzig, Tit.VIII.60a, f. 197v–198r); in *Bach-Dokumente*, ii, No. 127. The minutes break off at this point.

with the post. But when it came to the final election on 22 April the committee voted unanimously for Bach, who had already secured his release from Prince Leopold and undertaken to pay a deputy to teach Latin if the need arose.

On 5 May Bach signed an undertaking which set out, in fourteen clauses, the duties and observances required of him as Kantor, and ten days later he entered officially upon his new duties. On 22 May two carriages and four wagons brought his family and their belongings from Cöthen to their renovated quarters in the Thomasschule. Cantata 75, the first of the sacred masterpieces that Bach was to write for Leipzig's two principal churches, was heard in the Nikolaikirche on 30 May, and two days later the new Kantor was formally introduced to the staff and pupils of the Thomasschule. The induction ceremony proved to be an occasion for some disagreement between the council and the consistory as to whose representative should present the new Kantor to the school, but Bach can hardly have seen this as a portent of the troubles in store for him in Leipzig.

# CHAPTER 6

# Orchestral, Instrumental, and Keyboard Music

THE DISTINCTION MADE TODAY BETWEEN ORCHESTRAL AND chamber music is not one that would have been generally observed by Bach and his contemporaries. They would have classified as chamber music (*musica da camera*) anything not intended for the church (*da chiesa*) or the theatre (*da teatro*). Genres such as sonata, concerto, and suite therefore cut across the modern division between orchestral and chamber music: a trio sonata might be performed with several players to each part, while a concerto could be for a group of soloists (as in Bach's sixth Brandenburg Concerto) or even for a single player (as in his *Italian Concerto* for harpsichord). The public face of Bach as an orchestral composer can be seen in the four orchestral suites (especially Nos. 3 and 4) and in some of the secular cantatas of the 1730s; but many of what we would now classify as orchestral pieces (for example, the concertos) were intended for the same kind of intimate musicmaking as the chamber works.

## Concertos

The concerto was the most ambitious and widely cultivated form of *musica da camera* during the late Baroque period. Bach devoted himself to it at three important periods in his life, and in three quite different ways. At Weimar he came into close contact with the concerto style of the Venetians by arranging works by Vivaldi and other composers for the clavier or organ. Even before engaging in this activity, he must have been familiar with the latest developments in concerto composition coming from Italy. In 1709 the violinist J. G. Pisendel, then employed in the court orchestra at Ansbach, visited Bach at Weimar, bringing with him a concerto by Albinoni (and no doubt other works of that type) which he was to perform with the *collegium musicum* in Leipzig. A copy in Bach's hand of a continuo part for the second concerto in Albinoni's *Sinfonie e concerti* Op. 2 (1700) suggests that he may have been familiar with the genre even earlier than this, and the importance to Bach of concertos by Giuseppe Torelli (d. 1709) has been demonstrated by Jean-Claude Zehnder.[1]

The importance of Bach's arrangements of other composer's concertos to his own stylistic development cannot be overstressed, but the arrangements also had an immediate practical purpose. Most, if not all, were probably made in 1713–14 for the instruction and enjoyment of the young prince Johann Ernst. The evidence for this is circumstantial, but convincing. J. G. Walther, the prince's teacher, also made keyboard arrangements of concertos, but never, as far as is known, of the same ones that Bach arranged.[2] Moreover, Bach's arrangements included four concertos by Johann Ernst himself, and he is unlikely to have chosen these merely to acquaint himself with the modern concerto style. As to the date of these arrangements, it was in July 1713 that the prince returned from Holland, where he had studied for two years at the university of Utrecht. Earlier in 1713 he had stayed for a time in Amsterdam, and he may have heard there the blind organist of the Nieuwe Kerk, Jan Jacob de Graaf, who delighted in playing the latest Italian concertos on the organ. Almost certainly he would have brought back to Weimar a collection of such works, either in manuscript or from the presses of the famous Estienne Roger of Amsterdam, and it is likely that Bach made his arrangements from these copies. It may also be presumed that they were made before the prince left Weimar in July 1714, in a vain attempt to cure the illness that was to kill him the following year at Frankfurt, when he was only nineteen.

[1] J.-C. Zehnder, 'Giuseppe Torelli und Johann Sebastian Bach: zu Bachs Weimarer Konzertform', *Bach-Jahrbuch*, lxxvii (1991), 33–95. On Albinoni, see G. G. Butler, 'J. S. Bach's Reception of Tomaso Albinoni's Mature Concertos', *Bach Studies 2*, 20–46.

[2] Only fourteen of Walther's numerous arrangements survive. They are printed in *Denkmäler deutscher Tonkunst*, xxvi and xxvii, ed. M. Seiffert.

It is noticeable that Bach's concerto arrangements concentrate more than Walther's extant examples on the modern Venetian masters. There are in all twenty of them, sixteen for harpsichord (BWV972–87) and four for organ (BWV592–4, 596).[3] Nine are by Vivaldi and one each by the Venetians Alessandro and Benedetto Marcello; German composers are represented by Telemann and Johann Ernst himself, and the composers of four works remain unidentified. All but four are in the Venetian three-movement form that Bach was later to adopt for his own concertos. He seems never to have made any alterations to the actual substance of the originals, but his detailed revisions are numerous and repay close study. They consist broadly of filling out the continuo harmony in the left hand (often with arpeggio figuration), adding middle parts when the texture invites it, ornamenting the melody in slow movements, and sometimes altering and enriching the harmonies. His approach is exemplified in the harpsichord arrangement of the slow movement from Vivaldi's Violin Concerto in G minor RV316 (BWV975)[4] (Ex. 6.1). Bach's aim, however, was not to transcribe the original as if it had been conceived from the start for harpsichord or organ. The figuration is often foreign to his usual keyboard style, or else it is

**Ex. 6.1**

[3] Not included in this total are BWV595 (another version of the first movement of BWV984) and BWV597 (probably not a concerto and not by J. S. Bach).

[4] Vivaldi's original version of the concerto is lost, but its first two movements were printed in his Op. 4 No. 6 (RV316a).

adopted as keyboard figuration through the experience of these transcriptions.

The chronology of Bach's own concertos is far from clear. Neither the three violin concertos (BWV1041–3) nor the six Brandenburg Concertos (BWV1046–55) are mentioned in the Obituary, and they were evidently unknown also to J. N. Forkel in 1802. They have usually been assigned to the Cöthen period (1717–23), along with other solo concertos known only from keyboard arrangements made in the 1730s for Bach's *collegium musicum* in Leipzig (see pp. 191–3); but some movements of the Brandenburg Concertos are almost certainly earlier than this, and a later, Leipzig origin for at least two (and perhaps all three) of the violin concertos has recently been proposed.[5] Autograph parts dating from about 1730 exists for the solo Violin Concerto in A minor and for the Double Concerto in D minor. These may have been copied, of course, to replace missing parts, and attempts to bolster a composition date of *c.*1730 with stylistic analysis have not so far proved convincing. Evidence in support of a Leipzig origin for the A minor concerto may, however, be provided by a passage in the first movement (bars 165–9; see Ex. 6.2) which evidently points to limitations in the technical skill of the rank-and-file violinists that would have been more likely to occur in Bach's largely amateur *collegium musicum* than in his wholly professional orchestra at Cöthen. He was evidently unwilling to trust his orchestral violinists with the upward scale to a top *e'''* at bars 165–6; in the corresponding passage earlier in the movement (bars 78–81, a fourth lower) the violins remain in unison with the soloist throughout.

**Ex. 6.2**

BWV1041/i, bars 165–9

[5] See especially C. Wolff, 'Bach's Leipzig Chamber Music', *Bach: Essays on his Life and Music*, 223–38.

All Bach's violin concertos are in the three-movement Vivaldi form, but the invention is remarkably fresh, even for Bach, and each work shows a new approach to standard structures, especially in the outer movements. A comparison between the Weimar arrangements and the later works shows clearly how Bach adapted the ritornello structure of the first movement to his own use, enriching its textures with thematic, accompanimental, and contrapuntal detail seldom to be found in Vivaldi's more straightforward (although far from schematic) ritornello movements. In the typical Vivaldi movement an opening tutti (or part thereof) returns in related keys, and finally in the tonic. Between each return (or ritornello) a solo episode introduces new virtuoso material and effects a change of key in preparation for the next ritornello. The structure may be likened to an arcade, with the ritornellos representing the pillars and the episodes the arches. The first movement of Vivaldi's Bb major concerto (RV381), which Bach arranged for solo harpsichord in G (BWV980), furnishes a fairly typical example (lower-case letters indicate minor keys):[6]

| Bar nos. | No. of bars | Function | Keys |
|----------|-------------|----------|------|
| 1–19 | 19 | Ritornello 1 | Bb |
| 19–38 | 20 | Episode 1 | Bb—F |
| 38–43 | 6 | Ritornello 2 | F |
| 43–50 | 8 | Episode 2 | F—d |
| 50–59 | 10 | Ritornello 3 | d—Bb |
| 59–77 | 18 | Episode 3 | Bb |
| 77–87 | 11 | Ritornello 4 | Bb |

The solo violin doubles the orchestral violins in the ritornellos, and in the episodes the accompaniment is mainly a single line (unison violins or cello continuo) or a simple transparent texture. The distinction between ritornello and episode is very clearly made (although it is slightly oversimplified in the above analysis, which does not show references to ritornello material at bars 19–22 and 68–70).

Bach's ritornello structures, like Vivaldi's, rest on the opposition of

[6] Bach's arrangement is not (as often said) of Vivaldi's Op. 4 No. 1 (RV383a), which has different episode material in the first movement, and quite different second and third movements.

soloist and tutti, and there is rarely any real difficulty in determining where a ritornello ends and an episode begins (the converse is often less easily recognized). The first movement of the A minor Violin Concerto, for example, may be shown as follows:

| Bar nos. | No. of bars | Function | Keys |
|----------|-------------|----------|------|
| 1–24 | 24 | Ritornello 1 | a—e |
| 25–51 | 27 | Episode 1 | a—C |
| 52–84 | 33 | Ritornello 2 | C—e |
| 85–142 | 58 | Episode 2 | e—a |
| 143–71 | 29 | Ritornello 3 | a |

The significant difference between this and the Vivaldi movement analysed above is not that Bach's can be shown to have fewer main sections, or that his modulating ritornellos make for a more dynamic structure (modulating ritornellos are by no means unknown in Vivaldi's concertos, or particularly common in Bach's other works). Where the ritornello structure of Bach's A minor concerto represents an advance over that of Vivaldi and other contemporaries lies principally in the following points:

1. A firmer cohesion is achieved by frequently interrupting the ritornellos (after the first) with solo passages, and by introducing brief returns of ritornello material into the episodes. The long second episode, in particular, is punctuated by structurally important orchestral references to the opening at bars 102–5 (D minor) and 123–6 (A minor); it might almost be considered a development section.
2. There is a freer interchange of thematic material between soloist and orchestra.
3. A strong element of recapitulation exists within the episodes as well as the ritornellos (compare, for example, bars 44–51 with 135–42).
4. There is a richer orchestral texture in the episodes. Only for about a dozen bars does Bach reduce his accompaniment to a single line.

It is not, however, only in such particulars as these that the violin concertos show Bach to be an innovator. He is ready, too, to introduce into the ritornello pattern features normally associated with other forms. The first movement of the E major Violin Concerto, for example,

follows exactly the design and key scheme of the da capo aria stereo-
type, while in the Double Concerto the opening ritornello is a fugal
exposition. The last movements are scarcely less diversified: the A minor
imbues a ritornello structure with the driving energy of a gigue; the E
major has a rondo of dance-like symmetry; and the D minor derives
its restless character from the superimposition of a 2/4 rhythm in the
orchestra onto the basic 3/4 pulse, already weakened by the soloists'
close canon at the unison (a favourite device in the concertos for gen-
erating tension) (Ex. 6.3). The slow movements of all three concertos
are of unusual melodic beauty. In each of the solo concertos the violin
cantilena is underpinned by a quasi-ostinato bass figure; in the Double
Concerto the soloists interweave their beguiling melodic lines, almost
in the manner of an operatic love-duet, above a gently lulling
accompaniment.

This variety of structure and expression is even more marked in the
Brandenburg Concertos, where it extends to the instrumentation as

**Ex. 6.3**

well. Although not conceived as a group, these six extraordinary works seem to have been brought together to demonstrate different ways of writing 'concertos for several instruments', as the autograph title-page calls them. The first concerto, in F major, is scored for two horns, three oboes, bassoon, violin,[7] strings, and continuo—a most unusual ensemble, it might seem, but one that Vivaldi used (with two oboes instead of three) in no fewer than four concertos (RV568, 569, 571, and 574). What *is* unusual—perhaps unique—is the work's structure. At first glance it might appear that Bach has merely added a French-style minuet to the usual three movements; but in fact the work's genesis is more complicated than that. An earlier version (BWV1046a) without the *violino piccolo* has only the first two movements and the minuet (this last lacking the string polonaise that in the later version forms the second of its three trios). This is called a 'sinfonia', a suitable designation for a work that shows little of the solo—tutti contrast typical of the concerto, but one that Bach, in his ensemble music, would have used only for an introduction to a longer work. It has been suggested that the sinfonia originally belonged to Cantata 208, written for the birthday of Duke Christian of Weissenfels, probably in 1713; the re-scoring with *violino piccolo* was presumably done when the present third movement was added and the polonaise inserted into the Minuet. The new Allegro, with its important part for *violino piccolo*, makes the work much more of a concerto, but even so the style and structure of the added movement point to Bach's secular vocal music rather than to his other orchestral works. He did, in fact, use it again, in D major and with some slight expansion at bars 58–9 and 78–9, as the opening chorus of the secular cantata *Vereinigte Zwietracht der wechselnden Saiten* (BWV207), written for the installation of Gottlieb Kortte as Professor of Jurisprudence at Leipzig University in 1726. The music sounds more at home there, with trumpets (and drums) replacing the horns, and the *violino piccolo* part filled out and allotted to the voices (SATB). To adapt a concerto movement in this way as a da capo chorus, with negligible alterations

[7]More precisely, *violino piccolo* (small violin). This instrument was usually tuned a fourth higher than the normal violin, but here (as in Cantatas 96 and 140) Bach uses one tuned a minor third higher.

to the actual substance, presupposes an almost unbelievable degree of skill; Alfred Dürr has called it 'one of Bach's most remarkable achievements.'[8] In fact, it is not unreasonable to suppose that both the concerto movement and the cantata chorus originated in some still earlier vocal composition, now lost. This might help to explain the tuning of Bach's *violino piccolo* and also the unusual nature of the solo part, which, with its frequent multiple stops, is quite unlike the composer's other writing for *violino piccolo*, and different, too, from the solo violin parts in the other concertos. Michael Marissen, on the other hand, relates Bach's instrumentation in this concerto (and the others) to the social and musical hierarchy at Cöthen, and argues that the status of the *Konzertmeister*, as first violinist, is here deflated by having him play on a small violin and giving him little in the way of a real solo part to play on it.[9]

If the first concerto was designed to flatter the margrave's taste for things French (Bach's dedication was also in elegant French), the other five are much more Italianate in structure, if not always in their solo–tutti relationships. The second concerto, in F major like the first, has a solo group consisting of trumpet, recorder, oboe, and violin. In performances on modern instruments the brilliant high-pitched writing for the F trumpet tends to dominate the music in the outer movements, and it must always have been one of the most exciting features of the concerto. But to criticize Bach for bringing together such a heterogeneous collection of instruments in a concerto is to misunderstand his whole approach to instrumentation—an approach in which a coherent balance and blend, such as late eighteenth- or nineteenth-century composers aimed for, was by no means of paramount importance. Bach could have chosen these instruments deliberately, knowing that their lack of 'blend' would serve the ruggedness of the music (one is reminded of his unorthodox organ registrations), or he could have written for them simply because they were there. In either case, performances of Brandenburg No. 2 on original instruments and in rooms of an appropriate size have shown the trumpet writing to be not nearly as dominating, nor the recorder part as inaudible, as we are sometimes led

[8] *Die Kantaten von Johann Sebastian Bach*, 681.
[9] M. Marissen, *The Social and Religious Designs of J. S. Bach's Brandenburg Concertos.*

to believe. During the slow movement the trumpeter looks on while the other soloists elaborate the initial violin phrase, or at times a simple 'sigh' motif, over a continuo bass whose quaver movement is halted only at cadences.

The third concerto, in G major, is a very different work, scored for strings only in nine parts (plus continuo bass). They join together to form a tutti or divide into concertino groups (of violins, violas, and cellos) or individual solo instruments. The first movement is clearly modelled on the tonal structure of a da capo aria: A1, bars 1–46; B, 46–77 (ending in B minor); A2, 78–136. But the final section (A2) is not an exact repetition of the first; it leads the music into hitherto unexplored tonal regions, brings fresh developments, and accompanies the main ritornello theme with a counter-melody on the first violins which, at the opening of the movement, had been hidden in the middle of the texture (Ex. 6.4).

**Ex. 6.4**

BWV1048/i, bars 78–80

The last movement is also unusual: except for the dances that conclude the first Brandenburg Concerto and belong more to the suite tradition, it is the only concerto movement by Bach to use a binary dance form, with each section marked for repeat. The proportions are also unusual, the second section being three times as long as the first. It is, however, the imperfect (Phrygian) cadence separating these two movements that constitutes a unique structural feature of the concerto, and one that has aroused endless discussion. These isolated chords would normally be found at the end of a slow movement in E minor, serving as a link to the final Allegro (as in the fourth Brandenburg Concerto, for example). But in this case there is no slow movement. There can be no question of it having been lost from the presentation copy, since the two Adagio chords come in the middle of a page; nor does it seem likely that Bach would have 'short-changed' the margrave by omitting a movement. What the Cöthen orchestra played at that point may never be known. In modern performances a short improvisatory cadenza by the first violinist is perhaps the most acceptable of the various solutions that have been tried. Another is simply to omit the cadence altogether.

The fourth and fifth concertos, in G and D major respectively, are the most conventional in their organization of solo and tutti sections. For various reasons they are thought to have been composed later than the others, and certainly the fact that their violone (bass) parts were written for an instrument without the low C string suggests that they were intended for a different group of players.[10] In the fourth concerto the violin outshines the other two soloists (recorders), just as the trumpet does in the second concerto, while in the fifth the harpsichord is promoted from its traditional role as continuo instrument to that of principal soloist. Violin and flute share the limelight, but it is the harpsichord that is given a long and elaborate cadenza in the first movement; Bach probably played it himself on the new instrument brought from Berlin in 1719. This work has attracted the attention of historians as the earliest known example of a keyboard concerto with orchestra, but a greater influence on the development of the genre was exerted by the concertos that Bach arranged for one or more harpsichords during his Leipzig years (see pp. 191–3).

The sixth Brandenburg Concerto, in B♭ major, is generally thought to be the earliest of the set, but there is nothing in the style of the music to support the very early date (before 1710) that several scholars have assigned to it. The instrumentation (two violas, two bass viols, cello, violone, and harpsichord continuo) may seem archaic, but it was well tailored to the Cöthen forces—perhaps to a small group of players such as Prince Leopold took with him on his Carlsbad journeys. The bass viol parts are undemanding and may have been written for Leopold himself to play with C. F. Abel. Together with the violone (and, of course, the harpsichord) they form an accompanying group of older instruments, while the modern violas and cello make up the solo group

---

[10] On the Brandenburgs' bass parts, see L. Dreyfus, *Bach's Continuo Group*, 142–51.

and join with the others for the ritornellos. In the central Adagio (which is unusual in beginning in E♭ major and ending in G minor)[11] the viols are silent, the three solo instruments being accompanied only by the continuo, with the violone shadowing the cello. The ritornello structure of the two outer movements is exceptionally clear (again arguing for a fairly late date of composition). To assist in this the ritornellos themselves are given distinct characteristics: in the first movement close canon at the unison, which is relaxed only at chord changes; in the last some attractively lilting syncopations which support the opinion that this concerto might easily be the most popular of the six were it not for the difficulty of finding the players to perform it.

Without taking too Romantic a view of the relationship between a composer's life and his work, it is possible to see the Brandenburg Concertos, with their major-key exuberance, their tunefulness, their rhythmic vitality, and their effortless counterpoint, as a true reflection of Bach's situation at Cöthen: a composer at the height of his powers writing for a patron 'who both loved and understood music'.[12] The qualities that place them in a special category within Bach's oeuvre have also earned them devotees even among those for whom his other music has few attractions.

## Orchestral Suites

It is impossible to arrive at a chronology for Bach's four orchestral suites (BWV1066–9). The principal source material, some of it in Bach's hand and some copied under his supervision, dates from the Leipzig years, but it is not impossible that at least some of the works themselves were composed during the Cöthen years; they were clearly not designed as a set, and their composition could have spanned a considerable period. Nor is there any proof that the second suite, with its scintillating *Badinerie*, was written for the celebrated French flautist Pierre-Gabriel Buffardin, known for his agility in rapid music. French style does, however, pervade all four suites, and it is noticeable that the allemande (or

[11] Cf. the slow movement of the Organ Sonata BWV526, which begins in E♭ major and ends in C minor, with a link to the dominant. Cf. also the Adagio of Corelli's Violin Sonata Op. 5 No. 5, which has the same tonal structure as the Bach concerto movement. 'Modulating' slow movements are present also in some of Handel's sonatas.

[12] See the letter to Erdmann, pp. 119–21.

German dance), which appears in nearly all the keyboard and string suites (even the so-called French suites for harpsichord), is here absent. In fact, the orchestral suites (or 'Ouvertures') belong to a quite different tradition, in which the emphasis was less on the regular dances of the classical German keyboard suite than on the *Galanterien* of the French: gavotte, minuet, bourrée, and light movements not in a specific dance rhythm (e.g. the *Badinerie* of Bach's second suite and the *Réjouissance* of the fourth). There is no reason, however, to relate these works to Bach's early experiences of French music such as that he might have heard played by the Celle court orchestra. German court composers wrote 'overture-suites' of this kind by the dozen to satisfy the frenchified tastes of their employers. Contemporaries such as Fasch, Kuhnau, and Graupner produced them in great numbers, and the 135 surviving orchestral suites of Telemann represent only a fraction of those he is known to have written. It was these composers, not Lully and his successors in France, who provided the model for Bach's incomparably greater examples of a popular entertainment genre.

Each of Bach's four suites begins with an overture in the form |: A1 :| |: B—A2 :| (the second repeat is sometimes omitted in present-day performances). The music is so obviously in the French overture mould that the sources do not provide tempo indications. But while the design is French, the style represents a *réunion des goûts*. The majestic first section (A1, recalled at the end, though never exactly) features the dotted rhythms and rapid scalic upbeats (*tirades*) of the French style; the central quick section (B) unites fugue and ritornello in lively Italianate concerto movements. The soloists are in the first suite the woodwind instruments (two oboes and bassoon), in the second a flute, and in the third a violin; in the overture of the fourth suite the various sections of the orchestra detach themselves from the tutti, rather as they do in the first movement of the first Brandenburg Concerto.

All the other movements, except for the Rondeau in the second suite, are in the usual binary dance form. The melodic charm of the dances in Nos. 2 and 3 (which include the aforementioned *Badinerie* and the incongruously nicknamed 'Air on the G string') has earned those suites a greater popularity than the others, but the C major suite (No. 1) is in many ways the most interesting of the four. It contains the only example Bach wrote of a forlana, a lively dance, possibly of

**Ex. 6.5**

north Italian or Slavonic origin, taken over into the French court tradition. No fewer than four of the other dances (Gavotte, Menuet,
Bourrée, and Passepied) are to be played *alternativement*, that is as a pair
of similar dances (numbered I and II) with the first repeated after the
second, exactly as in the Classical minuet and trio. Two of the second
dances do in fact use a three-part texture: Bourrée II is played by the
three woodwind instruments, and Passepied II repeats the theme of
Passepied I in the upper strings with a new counter-melody for the
oboes (Ex. 6.5a). Even more striking, and perhaps of particular significance to Bach's first audiences, is Gavotte II, in which unison violins
and violas repeat what sounds like a military call (Ex. 6.5b). It is in fact
identical with the trumpet call that punctuates the opening chorus of
Cantata 70, and very similar versions are to be found in a number of
other works (BWV20/viii, 119/vii, 127/iv, 130/iii, 143/v, 172/iii, 214/
iii, 214/vii, and 1046/i). Possibly it is related to the French military
signal *A cheval*, though Klaus Hofmann has suggested that Bach may
have used it as a symbol for worldly or divine authority.[13]

A fifth orchestral suite, in G minor, attributed to 'Sigr. Bach' in a
set of parts copied by one of Bach's last pupils, Christian Friedrich
Penzel (1737–1801), was included in *BG* and entered (as BWV1070) in

[13] K. Hofmann, ' "Grosser Herr, o starker König": ein Fantarenthema bei Johann Sebastian
Bach', *Bach-Jahrbuch*, lxxxi (1995), 31–46. See also M. Boyd, 'Bach, Telemann und das Fanfarenthema', ibid., lxxxii (1996), 147–50, and K. Hofmann, 'Nochmals Bachs Fanfarenthema',
ibid., lxxxiii (1997), 177–9.

the first edition of Schmieder's catalogue. Although still occasionally performed and recorded as a genuine work by J. S. Bach, it is now considered spurious; Bach's son Wilhelm Friedemann has been suggested as its likely composer.

## Instrumental Works

Bach's mature music is remarkable for its order and symmetry, both in the structure of individual works and in the shape of the oeuvre as a whole. This is something that first becomes apparent during the Cöthen years, and one of its manifestations is the collecting together of pieces in groups of six: the Brandenburg Concertos, the French and English Suites, the violin sonatas, the sonatas and partitas for unaccompanied violin, and the cello suites. In some cases this may have been done with a view to eventual publication (it was customary to print instrumental pieces in dozens or half-dozens), but it also illustrates what seems to have been a guiding impulse in Bach's creative life—the desire to bring a particular genre to completion and then to turn from it to other things. Rarely did he go over the same ground more than once, except when (as in the cantata cycles) it was part of his original plan to do so.

The two main instrumental genres that Bach cultivated at Cöthen were the suite and the sonata. The suite (Bach also used the terms 'partita' and 'partia') had by then assumed its classical layout of allemande, courante, sarabande, and gigue, with other dances perhaps interpolated between the last two. This is the layout that Bach adopts, though not slavishly, in his Cöthen suites. The form is at its most classical in the six suites for unaccompanied cello (BWV1007–12), where his concern for symmetry is apparent also in the additional dances: the first two suites include a pair of minuets, Nos. 3 and 4 a pair of bourrées, and Nos. 5 and 6 a pair of gavottes, in each case to be played *alternativement*. In addition, each suite begins with a prelude.

This uniformity might suggest that the suites were planned as a set from the start, perhaps for one of the Cöthen cellists, C. F. Abel or Christian Bernhard Linike. But there are good reasons for thinking that the last two may have originated independently of the others. In the first place, they are noticeably more difficult to play, with a higher proportion of multiple stops and (in No. 6, at least) more virtuoso passagework. They are also somewhat longer, No. 5 beginning with an extended prelude and fugue. More than this, No. 6 is actually for a different instrument, one with an extra string tuned to *e'* (a fifth higher than the normal top string),[14] while No. 5 employs scordatura, the highest string being tuned down from *a* to *g*. Scordatura was often used in violin music by Bach's German predecessors (the sonatas of Biber provide some familiar examples), but why Bach employed here a practice that he never used elsewhere is something of a puzzle. It cannot have been to facilitate fingering, which is often more awkward than with normal tuning, and it seems unlikely that it was done to give the music a darker colouring, as has often been suggested. Possibly the answer is in some way connected with the fact that the suite exists also in a version in G minor for lute (BWV995), an instrument tuned in fourths; if this came first, it might also explain why the cello version sometimes seems to need completion by another strand (Ex. 6.6). However, the autograph of BWV995 dates from 1727–31, several years after Anna Magdalena's fair copy of the cello suites. While this does not rule out the existence of an earlier version for lute, it seems just as likely that in the fifth cello suite Bach was reviving a tuning that had been standard in the early history of the instrument and that was occasionally revived in the late seventeenth century as a scordatura—for example, by Luigi Taglietti (*Suonate da camera*, Op. 1, 1697) and Jacob Klein the younger (6 Duetti, Op. 2).

The six suites are today in the repertory of every cellist who can master their technical challenges, whether as recital pieces or music to refresh the spirit. In a similar way the six sonatas and partitas (BWV1001–6), which demand even more of the performer, occupy an unchallenged position in the literature of solo violin music. It is likely that Bach wrote them for a particularly gifted player—Pisendel and Volumier of Dresden, and Joseph Spiess, leader of the Cöthen band, have all been suggested—but they also reflect his own mastery of violin technique. Very little in the way of a solo violin tradition lies behind these works. J. P.

[14] Spitta (ii, 100) states that this suite was composed for the *viola pomposa* (see Plate 13), an instrument said by Franz Benda to have been invented by Bach. Benda described it as somewhat larger than a viola, tuned like a cello with an extra *e'* string, and fitted with a supporting strap so that it could be held 'in front of the chest' and 'on the arm'. Bach's *viole pompose* were made by Johann Christian Hoffmann of Leipzig, which suggests that if Bach did invent the instrument it was after he wrote the cello suites.

**Ex. 6.6**

von Westhoff, a violinist at the Weimar court when Bach was first appointed there in 1703, published a set of six partitas for unaccompanied violin in 1696, and Biber, J. J. Walther, and Pisendel also wrote a few similar works.[15] Bach would certainly have known all, or most, of these, but his set of sonatas and partitas far surpasses them in both technique and musical interest.

Despite advances made in violin playing during the last two-and-a-half centuries, Bach's unaccompanied violin music is in one respect even more taxing for the modern performer than it was for an eighteenth-century one. This is because the development of the concave Tourte bow at the end of the eighteenth century, together with the introduction of higher and more curved bridges, made the bowing of multiple stops more hazardous for the player (and in some performances more painful for the listener). A return to 'authentic' instruments has shown

---

[15] It is perhaps no mere coincidence that all these composers were active at Dresden. In a Dresden MS once belonging to Pisendel, Bach's sonatas and partitas existed alongside solo violin works by Italian composers. The MS was destroyed in World War II.

how natural and appealing such passages can sound. Multiple stops are particularly prominent in the sonatas. These follow the *da chiesa* pattern of four movements (slow–fast–slow–fast), in the first and third of which the player has to provide harmonic support to a declamatory or cantabile line. The second movement is always a fugue, where the texture is often in three or even four parts. Only in the binary-form Allegro or Presto with which each sonata ends is there no multiple stopping, except occasionally at cadences.

This lighter, single-line texture is prevalent in the partitas, although by no means to the exclusion of the other. The overall design here is much looser than in the cello suites. The first partita ends not with the usual gigue, but with a bourrée (or 'borea'; Bach uses Italian spellings throughout the first two partitas); each movement is followed by a variation (or 'double'). To the four classical dances in the second partita (D minor) is added the famous Chaconne, often performed separately and frequently transcribed for piano or other instruments. Its sixty-four variations constitute a compendium of eighteenth-century violin technique, even if they may be felt to labour the four-bar chord progression on which they are based. The third partita (E major), in contrast to the other two, is entirely French in style, beginning with a Prelude which has become a favourite among violinists, and was evidently a favourite with Bach himself; he used it again, transcribed for organ and orchestra, in Cantatas 120a (?1729) and 29 (1731). In this partita the only dance of the classical suite to remain is the gigue, the others being replaced by the more specifically French Loure, Gavotte (en rondeau), Menuet I and II (played *alternativement*), and Bourrée. Whether or not this indicates a different recipient (Volumier perhaps?) is a matter for speculation.

In accompanied sonatas for violin, flute, or bass viol Bach preferred a fully composed harpsichord part to the continuo accompaniment that was then the norm. His sonatas for these instruments are therefore mostly in the nature of trio sonatas, with one of the 'solo' parts given to the right hand of the keyboard player. An important manuscript source of the six violin sonatas (BWV1014–19), in the hand of Bach's pupil and son-in-law Altnickol, actually has the title *Sechs Trios für Clavier und die Violine*. The kind of texture typical of these sonatas is one in which two imitative upper parts are supported by a bass which fulfils a continuo role (the left hand of the harpsichord could be doubled by a bass viol if desired) but also threads itself from time to time into the contrapuntal fabric of the upper parts. This is essentially the texture of the three-part Sinfonias (or Inventions) for clavier, and it is used in fifteen of the twenty-five movements in the violin sonatas, in both slow and quick tempos. But Bach's approach in other movements is extremely original and varied. In the expressive Largo of the F minor sonata (No. 5) the 'three-part Sinfonia' texture is given entirely to the keyboard; the violin part is mostly independent of it. Sometimes (especially in the slow third movements) the bass has a purely accompanimental role, and in some movements this goes for the right hand as well, anticipating a kind of sonata texture more characteristic of Haydn, Mozart, and even Schubert (Ex. 6.7).

**Ex. 6.7**

Striking for their textural variety, the violin sonatas are no less fascinating as studies in form. Nos. 1–5 all use the four-movement *da chiesa* pattern, but individual movements embrace a wide variety of ritornello, binary, da capo, and through-composed structures, often combined with fugal or concerto elements. The third movement of No. 2 is an effortless and graceful canon between the two upper parts over a bass mostly in staccato semiquavers; that of No. 3 is a modulating chaconne. The only sonata not in four movements is No. 6, in G major, whose various versions suggest a compilation from heterogeneous origins to make up the customary number for the set. There are three versions, the final and definitive one (published in *BG* and *NBA*)

having five movements, of which the first two and the last would make a coherent concerto structure. Additional to this are a binary Allegro (E minor) for harpsichord alone and a second slow movement in B minor—fine movements, both, but curiosities in the context of the whole set.

The other accompanied sonatas attributed to Bach include a number of spurious or doubtful works, one of which is a G minor sonata for violin or flute (BWV1020) now thought to be by his son Carl Philipp Emanuel. Of the three sonatas for bass viol and harpsichord (BWV1027–9) the first, in G major, exists also in a two flute and continuo version, generally considered now to be earlier (BWV1039); its transformation from trio to solo sonata is indicative of Bach's whole approach to the writing of accompanied sonatas. The second sonata, in D major, is perhaps of less musical interest than the other two, but it is more likely (though not certain) to be an original work for bass viol. On the other hand, the three-movement structure of the third (G minor), with both outer movements in ritornello form, suggests a possible origin in an earlier double concerto.

The flute sonatas pose even greater problems of attribution and chronology. Only four of the six solo sonatas printed in *BG* are generally accepted now as authentic, two with a fully composed harpsichord part (BWV1030 and 1032) and two with basso continuo (BWV1034–5). They are usually listed as products of the Cöthen period, but their chronology is in fact most uncertain. The A major sonata (BWV1032) exists in an incomplete autograph dating from about 1736. It resembles a concerto in form, with a slow movement in the unusual key of A minor, and it has been suggested that it was originally a flute concerto with the outer movements in C major.[16] Of the two sonatas with basso continuo, the E minor (BWV1034) perhaps dates from the early Leipzig years and the E major (BWV1035) is known only from a nineteenth-century copy bearing a note that suggests it was composed in 1741 for Michael Gabriel Fredersdorf, an amateur flautist and valet in the service of Frederick the Great at Potsdam. Even the B minor sonata (BWV1030), which exists in an earlier (though possibly still post-Cöthen) version in G minor,

[16] It may be relevant that the autograph shares pages with the C minor concerto for two harpsichords (BWV1062).

may not have reached its final form until the mid-1730s, the date of the earliest known copy.[17]

This last is undoubtedly the masterpiece among Bach's flute music. Its first movement is a long and very beautiful Andante which uses a spacious ritornello design as the framework for intertwining solo lines whose chromatic contours are heavy with the kind of expression to be found in much of the Passion music. Robert Marshall has drawn attention to the resemblance between the opening and the first chorus of Cantata 117, but no less striking is its similarity to the Vivace from a flute sonata (also in B minor) by Telemann, published in 1732 as No. 1 in his *Continuation des Sonates méthodiques* (Ex. 6.8). None of the other movements matches this Andante in design and expressiveness, but together they make an admirable complement to it. Bach here reverses the usual order of the middle movements, placing the binary Largo in D major second and following it with an attractive fugal Presto which calls for some nimble fingering from flautist and harpsichordist alike. This leads straight to a gigue-like finale notable for its playful syncopations.

**Ex. 6.8**

The other authenticated flute pieces are a trio sonata in G major for two flutes and continuo (BWV1039, an earlier version of the bass viol sonata BWV1027) and a partita for unaccompanied flute (BWV1013), probably the earliest of Bach's surviving flute pieces and not entirely idiomatic to the instrument, despite some attractive movements.

---

[17] The authenticity and chronology of Bach's flute music have been fully discussed by Robert L. Marshall in the *Journal of the American Musicological Society*, xxxii (1979), 463–98; see also Hans Eppstein's reply in the *Bach-Jahrbuch*, lxvii (1981), 77–90.

## Keyboard Works

While Bach's chamber music at Cöthen was written mainly for members of Prince Leopold's *collegium musicum*, the keyboard music of the period originated in the composer's family circle or in his activities as a teacher. The two cannot really be separated: his wife and children were among his pupils, and his other pupils often lived as members of the family. His eldest son, Wilhelm Friedemann, was nine in November 1719, and the following January Bach began compiling for him an anthology of pieces to instruct him in good keyboard style and the elements of composition. The *Clavier-Büchlein vor Wilhelm Friedemann Bach* proceeds from an explanation of the clefs to an *Explication* of the most important ornaments and an *Applicatio* (BWV994) which gives practice in playing some of them and also shows the elements of fingering. The pieces that Bach (or sometimes Friedemann himself) continued to add to the manuscript up to 1725–6 include early versions of the two-part Inventions and three-part Sinfonias and of some of the preludes later included in the *Well-tempered Clavier*.

In 1722 Bach started on a similar compilation for his new wife Anna Magdalena,[18] the most important contents of which are the first five French Suites, some of them incomplete; he later added a sixth to complete the set (BWV812–17), probably during his early years in Leipzig. The title was not Bach's own, but was adopted later to distinguish these works from the English Suites and the Partitas. Except for the Gigue of No. 1, with its dotted rhythms and short, rapid scale figures, and for some of the *Galanterien* (e.g. the Loure of No. 5), there is nothing distinctively French about them. Each one follows the classical German layout, without even the prelude usual in the keyboard suites of D'Anglebert and other French composers. As might be anticipated from the nature of their origins, the French Suites are of modest proportions and among the easiest to play of all Bach's keyboard works. While there is no lack of contrapuntal interest in some movements, particularly the gigues, the accent is more than usually on right-hand tunefulness, and this has endeared them to young pianists and their teachers, while recitalists have tended to neglect them for the more substantial and impressive English Suites.

[18] The term 'notebook' often used for this and for a second *Clavierbüchlein* for Anna Magdalena (1725) is a mistranslation of the German *Notenbuch*, meaning simply 'music-book'.

The English Suites (BWV806–11) are even less English in style than the French Suites are French. They owe their title, according to Forkel, to having been composed for an 'Englishman of rank', and although there is no evidence to support this, it could well be true. Being bigger and more difficult works than the French Suites, they might be expected also to be later ones, but this seems not to be the case. According to recent research, the first one in the collection may have been written as early as 1715 at Weimar, but the structural uniformity of the set as a whole is more typical of the Cöthen years and suggests that the suites were planned from the start as a group. Each one uses the classical layout preceded by a prelude and with an extra dance-pair, played *alternativement*, before the gigue. In Nos. 1 and 2 the additional dance is a bourrée, in Nos. 3 and 6 a gavotte, in No. 4 a minuet, and in No. 5 a passepied. While the dances are hardly less attractive than those in the French Suites, it is the preludes that are particularly outstanding. The shortest is No. 1 in A major, a kind of three-part invention similar in style to the E major Sinfonia (BWV792). This is of special interest because its opening is recalled in some of the dances that follow, resulting in a cyclic unity less common in Bach's suites than in those of some other composers (Ex. 6.9). The other five preludes are all more imposing, combining fugal and ritornello elements in movements as extended as some of those in the concertos. Like the *Italian Concerto*, they require a two-manual instrument to make their best effect, but they never sound like concerto arrangements.

Companion works to the French and English Suites are the six Partitas, published in Leipzig in 1726–31 under the general title of *Clavier-Übung*, but possibly including material dating from the Cöthen years. These are discussed together with other parts of the *Clavier-Übung*, in Chapter 10 (see pp. 193–7).

The didactic purpose behind some of the suites is still more explicit in the other keyboard works that Bach wrote at Cöthen: the Inventions, the Sinfonias, and the *Well-tempered Clavier*. The fifteen two-part Inventions (BWV772–86, originally called *Preambulum*) and the fifteen three-part Sinfonias (BWV787–801, originally *Fantasie*) were included in the *Clavier-Büchlein* of Wilhelm Friedemann, who may even have had a hand in writing some of them. As mentioned earlier (see p. 48), Bach

**Ex. 6.9**

BWV806

may have borrowed the title 'invention' from F. A. Bonporti's ten *In-venzioni* Op. 10, published in 1712; it is now frequently applied to both the two- and the three-part works. Both sets explore the tonalities normally available to keyboard players at the time, with up to four sharps (E major, but not C♯ minor) and four flats (F minor, but not A♭ major). Polished and re-ordered in an ascending sequence of keys, starting with C major and ending with B minor, the two sets were brought together in 1723 with a catch-all title which itself could serve as a model of how to develop an idea: 'A clear method not only (1) of learning to play cleanly in two parts, but also with further practice (2) to proceed correctly and well to three obbligato parts, and also to acquire at the same time not only good *inventiones* but also the ability to develop them well, and above all to cultivate a cantabile style of playing and to gain from the beginning a strong foretaste of composition'.

By 'inventiones' Bach meant 'musical ideas', 'themes', 'motifs', and the Inventions mostly work out an initial germinal idea on a simple tonal framework shaped by a few strong cadences. The compositional process seen here on a small scale is one that was basic to Bach's creative thinking, resulting eventually in such works as the *Musical Offering* and the *Art of Fugue*.[19] It involves not so much the technique of *Fortspinnung* (the quasi-automatic continuation of a short figure over changing harmonies), of which also Bach was a master, as integral contrapuntal development, and the ability to see the possibilities for such development in any *inventio*. The first Invention shows this process at its most rigorous, the initial figure ($x$) or its inversion being present in every half-bar except those approaching the cadence points at bars 7 (G major), 15 (A minor), and 22 (C major) (Ex. 6.10). Not all the Inventions are as tightly organized as this. In some there is still room for poetic fancy, for example in the dreamy E major Invention, classical in its poise and pre-Classical in its recapitulation of the first section at the end of the second. This is the only Invention in binary form.

**Ex. 6.10**

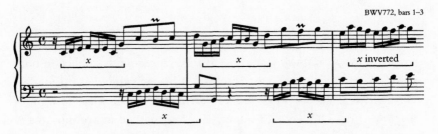

BWV772, bars 1–3

---

[19] On the concept of invention as a fundamental element of Bach's compositional method, and as a critical tool in analysing his music, see especially L. Dreyfus, *Bach and the Patterns of Invention*.

Binary forms are completely absent from the three-part Sinfonias, where the contrapuntal working-out of the initial idea often results in something very much like a fugue. In fact, the only structural difference between some of the Sinfonias and the three-part fugues in the *Well-tempered Clavier* of 1722 (BWV846–69) is that in the former 'subject' and 'counter-subject' are heard together from the start. In their fugal textures and their systematic deployment of the available major and minor keys, the Sinfonias can be seen as a preparation for the *Well-tempered Clavier*, the first book of what we now know as the '48'. The grouping of pieces in as many different keys as practicable was by then well established, and several composers had begun to extend the boundaries of tonal space in works involving keyboard instruments. Pachelbel's clavier suites of 1683 use seventeen different keys in an ascending sequence like that of the *Well-tempered Clavier*, except that minor keys are placed before the corresponding major ones; F minor and all keys with signatures of more than four sharps or flats are omitted. B major is among the sixteen different keys employed in each of the five cycles of sonatas for violin and continuo by J. C. Pepusch, dating from the early 1700s. Mattheson's *Exemplarische Organisten-Probe* (1719) goes even further by including examples in all twenty-four major and minor keys. One of the most important precursors of the *Well-tempered Clavier* was the *Ariadne musica* of Johann Caspar Ferdinand Fischer, a set of very brief preludes and fugues in twenty different keys (including the Phrygian mode) published at Schlakenwerth in 1702.[20] Thematic resemblances between fugues in the same key by Fischer and Bach have been exaggerated, but the E major fugue from Book II of the '48' does suggest that Bach knew Fischer's collection. It also demonstrates, even in its opening bars, the superiority of his invention and craftsmanship (Ex. 6.11).

The term 'well-tempered' in Bach's title need not necessarily be taken as indicating our modern temperament in which all twelve semitones in the octave are equal. Bach's contemporaries were reluctant to abandon what his pupil Johann Philipp Kirnberger once referred to as 'the variegation of the keys', and several irregular 'well-tempered' tunings were

---

[20] The date given by J. G. Walther in his *Musicalisches Lexicon* (Leipzig, 1732). The earliest extant edition dates from 1713.

**Ex. 6.11**

J. C. F. Fischer

Bach, BWV878, bars 1–5

proposed, including a particularly influential one by the organist and
theorist Andreas Werckmeister. Bach was certainly influenced by Werckmeister's ideas (not only about temperaments), but his preferred tuning
(if it was not in fact equal temperament) may well have been nearer to
one proposed by the Italian composer and theorist Francesco Antonio
Vallotti.[21] Such a system would allow all twenty-four keys to be used,
while making some more 'equal' in temperament than others and so
preserving a perceptible 'variegation'. The logical succession of preludes
and fugues in upward semitone steps through all the major and minor
keys gives the *Well-tempered Clavier* a planned and orderly appearance,
but in many respects it is more of an anthology. We are accustomed

[21] See John Barnes, 'Bach's Keyboard Temperament', *Early Music*, vii (1979), 236–49.

nowadays to hearing it performed as a complete cycle or from a complete recording, but in Bach's time there would have been no occasion
to play the whole volume. Eleven of the preludes had appeared
earlier (without fugues) in Wilhelm Friedemann's *Clavier-Büchlein*, and
evidence suggests that some items were transposed before being allotted
their place in the *Well-tempered Clavier*. Some preludes (e.g. those in E♭
minor and B♭ minor) seem to belong inseparably to the fugues they
precede, and others are united by thematic cross-reference,[22] but most
could be interchanged (after suitable transposition) without violating
Bach's intentions.

The *Well-tempered Clavier* is remarkable more for its variety than for
its unity. This is most obvious, of course, in the preludes, since they
have no fixed structure. Some of them elaborate a chord progression
in the manner of a toccata or an improvisation, the best known being
No. 1 in C major. Bach's contemporaries would have recognized the
figuration as imitating the *style brisé* of the French lutenists, a style much
used by the clavecinistes of the period for improvisatory preludes. Only
a Romantic composer such as Gounod would feel the piece to be
incomplete.[23] Other preludes (Nos. 8 and 10) spin out a highly orna-
mented arioso line in the manner of a concerto slow movement. Others
again might have found a place among the two-part Inventions (Nos.
13, 14, and 20) or the three-part Sinfonias nos. 18 and 19) on which
Bach was working at about the same time. One (No. 7) is a double
fugue so thoroughly and extensively worked out as to overshadow
completely the fugue that follows it.

The fugues vary in texture from two parts (No. 10, reducing to what
is in effect a single line in two passages of bold octaves!) to five (the
ricercare types, Nos. 4 and 22); the majority are in three or four parts.
Among these there is again the utmost variety of styles. No. 17 is a
gavotte; others are dance-like without suggesting particular types. Some

---

[22] See the B major (openings of prelude and fugue) and the B minor (prelude, bars 23–4;
fugue, bars 18–19). Some writers have found other parallels, but such motivic relationships
are of little importance in the *Well-tempered Clavier* as a whole.

[23] That it is now impossible for many people to hear Bach's prelude without also recalling
the sentimental melody that Gounod added to it is a tribute to the success of the Frenchman's
misguided aim. Fortunately he was less successful with a second *Ave Maria*, based on the C
minor prelude for lute (BWV999).

seek out the possibilities of fugal resource: No. 1 is a stretto fugue, Nos. 6 and 20 make a feature of inversion, No. 8 of augmentation. Some have short diatonic subjects (Nos. 9, 17, 19), others lengthy chromatic ones (Nos. 10, 14, 24). If the opening prelude was intended to show how sweet the triads of C major could sound on a well-tempered keyboard, the final fugue might have been designed to demonstrate the adaptability of the same tuning to a plangent, totally chromatic subject (Ex. 6.12).

**Ex. 6.12**

BWV869, bars 1–4

It is, of course, such fugues as this that test a particular tuning more effectively than a sequence of separate pieces in different keys, since what counts is the ability to encompass the most extreme flat and sharp keys in the same piece. Two other works that set out to do this are the *Kleines harmonisches Labyrinth* (BWV 591), a work of doubtful authorship now generally attributed to the Dresden composer J. D. Heinichen, and the well-authenticated Chromatic Fantasia and Fugue in D minor (BWV 903). The final section of the fantasia spans keys as remote as B flat minor and C sharp minor in a few phrases of 'recitative' supported by chromatic and enharmonic harmonies. The middle section of the fugue similarly goes beyond the keys one might expect to find there, containing entries of the chromatic (although not, this time, totally chromatic) subject in B minor (bars 76–83) and E minor (bars 90–7). A 'good' temperament is not the only cause the music promotes. Chromatic and enharmonic *tours de force* in which a composer might display his daring, as well as his learning, were not uncommon in vocal as well as in keyboard works of the period; the famous exchange of cantatas between Gasparini and Alessandro Scarlatti in 1712 provides just one example. The boldness of Bach's harmony in the Chromatic Fantasia and Fugue has encouraged performances and arrangements that emphasize the bravura element, but much of the music is inward-looking.

By 1742 Bach had completed a second set of twenty-four preludes and fugues in all the major and minor keys (see pp. 210–11). Although obviously designed as a companion volume to the first set, Book II served also to inaugurate the contrapuntal works of Bach's final period as Thomaskantor in Leipzig. It is to the early years of that cantorate that we now turn.

CHAPTER 7

# Leipzig

(1723–30)

L EIPZIG WAS SECOND ONLY TO DRESDEN AS THE MOST IMPOR-
tant city in Saxony. It had for centuries been a centre of learning
and commerce before Bach and his family took up residence there in
1723. Its university, founded in 1409, was regarded as one of the most
important and progressive in Germany, and the city's pre-eminence in
publishing and as a centre for the book trade was widely acknowledged.
Ever since the twelfth century its regular trade fairs had attracted numerous visitors, as they still do today. Leipzig's principal churches, the
Thomaskirche and the Nikolaikirche, and the schools attached to them,
ensured its prominence in the development of church music, and until
1720 the city had also supported an opera house, for which Telemann
had composed at least five operas (over twenty, according to his autobiography). Friction between the opera and the church, which had to
compete for the services of the university students, had caused difficulties for Bach's predecessor, Johann Kuhnau. Support from the students was crucial to the success and happiness of any music director at
Leipzig, as Bach was soon to discover.

It is important to an understanding of Bach's duties and status in
Leipzig to know that his appointment as Kantor was at the St Thomas
School (Thomasschule) and not, as English-language writers have frequently stated, at the Thomaskirche. The two were, of course, closely
connected. The school building, in which Bach and his family had their
lodgings, stood next to the church, forming with it two sides of the

Thomaskirchhof (see Plate 12). The school was demolished in 1902, but other monuments remain to remind the visitor of Bach's association with the church and its immediate vicinity. Not far from the place in the Thomaskirchhof where in Bach's time a stone water-trough stood is Carl Seffner's statue of the composer, erected in 1908, and nearby stands the Bach monument unveiled by Mendelssohn in 1843. Opposite the church at No. 16 Thomaskirchhof stood the house of Georg Heinrich Bose, with whose family the Bachs were on friendly terms; the building now houses a permanent exhibition illustrating Bach's connections with Leipzig as well as the Leipzig Bach-Archiv, an important centre for Bach research. Then there is the Thomaskirche itself, its west front and interior much altered since Bach's time; in its chancel now lie what are thought to be the composer's mortal remains, transferred there after World War II from the bombed Johanniskirche.

Bach, however, was not specifically connected with the Thomaskirche in any professional capacity. His family worshipped there, his last twelve children were baptized at its ancient font, and very likely he himself preferred the Thomaskirche, with its spacious west gallery, for performances of his large-scale choral works. But as Kantor his duties were at the Thomasschule, and as *director musices* they extended equally to the larger and senior Nikolaikirche. This was the official town church until 1755; it was there that the superintendent, Salomon Deyling, preached, and it was there that the annual service was held to mark the election of a new town council. It was in the Nikolaikirche, too, that some of Bach's greatest choral works were heard for the first time, including the *St John Passion*, the *Christmas Oratorio*, and about half of the cantatas.

The Leipzig cantorate was one of the most prestigious in Germany. The writer and publisher Georg Rhau (1488–1548) and the composer, theorist, and mathematician Sethus Calvisius (1556–1615) had been among early holders of the post. Johann Hermann Schein (1586–1630) was Kantor from 1616 until his death, and the succession had then come down to Bach through an illustrious line: Tobias Michael (Kantor 1631–57), Sebastian Knüpfer (1657–76), Johann Schelle (1677–1701), and Johann Kuhnau (1701–22). In the hierarchy of the Thomasschule the Kantor ranked third, after the Rektor (headmaster) and Konrektor and immediately above the Tertius. His duties, as laid down in the *Ordnung* published in 1723, were to teach music and other subjects to the foundationers (boarders) of the *coetus superior* (upper school) and to give individual practical tuition where this was called for. He had to direct the *chorus primus* at the two main churches on alternate Sundays, to oversee the work of the organists and other musicians there, and to be responsible for the performance material (scores and parts) and the musical instruments. He was paid extra for attendance at weddings, and other *Accidentien* included payment for funerals and a share in what was collected at the school *Kurrenden*. Every fourth week he had to take his turn with the other senior masters (including the Rektor) in acting as inspector. During his week of duty he would have to ensure that the school was roused at 5 A.M. (6 A.M. in winter), say prayers fifteen minutes later and again in the evening, supervise meals in the refectory, and generally take responsibility for school discipline.

Many of these duties must have seemed irksome to Bach after six years of court life at Cöthen, and he soon persuaded the Tertius, Carl Friedrich Pezold, to take over his non-musical teaching for a payment of 50 thalers a year—an arrangement that the council had approved in advance of Bach's appointment but that they were nevertheless to hold against him later on, especially as Pezold seems to have discharged his obligations very badly. The 50 thalers Bach paid Pezold represented a large proportion of his regular salary as Kantor. Most of his income, which might amount in all to some 700 thalers, came from other sources, the irregularity of which was a cause of annoyance to him. It was not long before he was delegating to prefects some of his other duties at the Thomasschule, including the midday singing classes and even the direction of wedding music. Clearly he preferred to regard himself as *director musices* rather than as Kantor.

As *director musices* Bach's duties were to provide music for civic occasions and to supervise the church music of the city as a whole. They also included responsibility for festal services at the Paulinerkirche, the university church. In 1710 the university had instituted a regular Sunday service of its own, known as the *neu Gottesdienst* (new service), and appointed its own music director. But Kuhnau, as official *director musices*, had insisted on his right to direct the *alt Gottesdienst* (old service), for which he was paid 12 gulden per annum, and to safeguard his connections with the university he had even undertaken to direct the new services as well, without extra payment. After Kuhnau's death Johann Gottlieb Görner, organist of the Nikolaikirche (and before that of the Paulinerkirche), was invited to take over at the university until a new *director musices* was appointed, but after Graupner's withdrawal he applied for and was granted permanent directorship of both old and new services. The scene was set for the first of Bach's many brushes with officialdom at Leipzig.

In September 1723 Bach petitioned the university council for restitution of his right to the old service and the salary that went with it. The university tried at first to reject his claim out of hand, but eventually agreed to restore to him the old service and, after further persistence on Bach's part, half the salary (6 gulden). Not satisfied with this, Bach took his case to King August II in Dresden, asking that the university be made to grant him control of both the old and the new services, together with the full stipend and *Accidentien* accruing from them. After receiving a report from the university and Bach's lengthy reply to it, August ruled in January 1726 that Bach should be granted the old service and its full salary, but that the new service, which he saw as having no connection with the other, should be disposed of as the university thought fit. Whether or not this very reasonable judgement satisfied Bach we do not know, but he seems to have lost interest even in the old service after this; Görner remained as director of the Paulinerkirche and Bach associated himself with the university only on special occasions.

One such occasion was in December 1726, when Gottlieb Kortte was installed as Professor of Jurisprudence and Bach wrote the congratulatory cantata *Vereinigte Zwietracht der wechselnden Saiten* (BWV207). Bach was again preferred to Görner when he conducted the students in another cantata (now lost), *Entfernet euch, ihr heitern Sterne* (BWV Anh9), to celebrate the king's birthday. It was performed before the monarch on 12 May 1727 in front of the merchant Apel's house in the market-place, where the Saxon royal family always stayed on visits to Leipzig.[1] When, however, it came to a ceremony in the Paulinerkirche to commemorate the electress Christiane Eberhardine, who died in

[1] Built in the first decade of the eighteenth century, the house was almost completely destroyed in World War II. It was rebuilt in 1965–7.

September 1727, Görner was determined to claim his rights as the university's music director. The ceremony had been proposed by a student, Hans Carl von Kirchbach, who commissioned the poet, philosopher, and university teacher Johann Christoph Gottsched to write a *Trauer Ode* and Bach to set it to music. Görner, with support from some of the university professors, threatened to deny Bach permission to take part in the ceremony, but the university council decided that since he had already written most of the music and been paid for it the performance should go ahead, but under Görner's direction. Kirchbach, however, refused to dishonour the contract he had made with Bach and offered Görner a fee of 12 thalers in compensation. Görner accepted on condition that Bach signed a document that would have pledged him not to enter into future negotiations with university personnel without official permission. He might as well have asked for the moon. Bach flatly refused to sign, and the performance of the *Trauer Ode* went ahead as planned on 17 October, Bach directing the music from the harpsichord and Kirchbach delivering his funeral oration between the first and second parts.

In disputes like this Bach might well have felt himself at some disadvantage through not having had a university education. Certainly he was aware that in changing the livery of a *Kapellmeister* for the robes of a Kantor (even of the Thomaskantor) he had dropped a rung in the social and professional ladder.[2] He was therefore careful to retain the title of *Kapellmeister von Haus aus* at Cöthen,[3] and during his early years at Leipzig he maintained friendly contacts with his former employer. He continued to write music for Cöthen, despite a heavy schedule of work at home, and made guest appearances there with Anna Magdalena. In 1726 his newly published Partita No. 1 for clavier was dedicated to Prince Leopold's infant son Emanuel Ludwig, born to the prince's second wife on 12 September. Prince Leopold died shortly before his 34th birthday on 19 November 1728, and in the following March Bach and his wife, this time with their eldest son Wilhelm Friedemann, travelled to Cöthen for the interment and funeral ceremony, at which the

---

[2] See the letter to Erdmann, pp. 119–21.

[3] A courtesy title, placing the recipient under no obligation except that of composing music for the court from time to time.

(lost) cantata *Klagt, Kinder, klagt es aller Welt* (BWV244*a*) was performed; they received the considerable sum of 230 thalers for their services.

After Prince Leopold's death Bach lost no time in securing for himself another court title. For many years he had enjoyed the patronage of Duke Christian of Weissenfels, and in February 1729 he spent several days there during the celebrations for the duke's birthday. With him was his pupil Carl Gotthelf Gerlach, who later that year became organist at the Neukirche in Leipzig. The visit achieved its purpose, and the title of *Kapellmeister (von Haus aus)* to the Court of Saxe-Weissenfels was one that Bach enjoyed from this time until the death of Duke Christian in 1736.

These visits to Cöthen and Weissenfels were by no means the only ones that Bach made during these years. He continued to be in demand as an inspector of new and renovated organs, and as a recitalist. In November 1723 he was at Störmthal, a village near Leipzig, to inaugurate an organ by Zacharias Hildebrandt and to perform a new cantata, *Höchsterwünschtes Freudenfest* (BWV194); just over six months later, on 25 June 1724, he travelled the 40 miles to Gera to inspect new organs in the Johanniskirche and the Salvatorkirche, receiving a fee of 30 thalers and expenses which included 7 thalers 8 groschen for wine.[4] Dresden was also a powerful magnet during these years, and indeed for the rest of his life; recitals on the Silbermann organ in the Sophienkirche are documented for 19–20 September 1725, but there must have been many other visits of which no records exist.

Such excursions were but short breathing-spaces for the industrious Kantor, whose main efforts were concentrated on composing, rehearsing, and performing music for the two main Leipzig churches. Bach's creativity in these few years was phenomenal. C. S. Terry (177–8) marvelled at his having composed 'at least 265 cantatas . . . in little more than twenty years, at the rate, on the average, of one cantata every month'. We now know that all but a few of these were written during Bach's first five or six years as Thomaskantor, at the rate of about one a *week*, and in addition there were the Passions and the Magnificat, as well as sundry motets and other pieces. Somehow Bach managed to

---

[4] Presumably he delayed his departure until after the first performance that morning, at Leipzig, of the superb cantata *Ach Herr, mich armen Sünder* (BWV135).

accomplish all this while coping with a demanding school routine and a household throbbing with pupils and a growing family. Five children had accompanied the parents from Cöthen to Leipzig in 1723; by 1728 Anna Magdalena had borne another five. Only two of these survived beyond the age of five: Gottfried Heinrich (1724–63), a talented keyboard player but mentally impaired, and Elisabeth Juliana Friederica (1726–81), who was to marry one of Bach's most gifted pupils, J. C. Altnickol. With the arrival of Elisabeth there were altogether eleven Bachs occupying the Kantor's dwelling in the Thomasschule,[5] and it was probably to accommodate them all that alterations were carried out there between November 1726 and April 1727. At the same time a new iron stove, weighing two-and-a-quarter hundredweights, was installed.

Soon after entering into controversy with the university authorities over the old and new services, Bach came into conflict for the first time with the Leipzig town council. The occasion was the performance of the Passion music on Good Friday 1724. Concerted Passion music was not heard in the two main Leipzig churches until 1721, when Kuhnau's *St Mark Passion* was given in the Thomaskirche, but it had been established from the start that performances should alternate annually between the two main churches. In 1724 it was the turn of the Nikolaikirche, but that year Bach had librettos printed for a performance of his *St John Passion* in the Thomaskirche. When the superintendent of the Nikolaikirche, Dr Johann August Hölzel, complained to the council about this, Bach replied that to perform the Passion in the Nikolaikirche more room would have to be made in the choir loft and the harpsichord would have to be repaired. The council agreed that all this should be seen to at their expense, Bach promised to consult Superintendent Deyling on such matters in future, and the performance went ahead in the Nikolaikirche on 7 April.

Not all disputes were resolved as amicably as this. In 1728 there was some disagreement with the sub-deacon of the Nikolaikirche over who should choose the hymns at Vespers, but this was only a foretaste of the serious trouble that Bach found himself in with the council two years

---

[5] This total includes Friedelena Margaretha (1675–1729), eldest sister of Bach's first wife Maria Barbara, who had lived with the family since at least 1709.

later. At a meeting on 2 August 1730 complaints were raised about his absenting himself without permission and neglecting the daily singing class, as well as other shortcomings and misdemeanours. Worst of all, it seems, Bach refused to offer any explanation for his conduct. Instead he submitted to the Council a 'Short but much-needed outline for a well-regulated church music, together with some impromptu thoughts on the decline of the same'. This important and much-quoted Memorandum, dated 23 August 1730, contains revealing and in many ways astonishing information about the vocal and instrumental forces for which Bach wrote his greatest cantatas and Passions. Twelve singers, he says, are required for each of the churches where part music is sung (the Thomaskirche, Nikolaikirche, and Neukirche). In addition, at least eighteen instrumentalists are needed at the church where the cantata is to be performed, made up as follows:

| 2 (or 3) first violins | 2 second violas |
|---|---|
| 2 (or 3) second violins | 2 violoncellos |
| 2       first violas | 1 violone (double bass) |
| 2 (or 3) oboes | 3 trumpets |
| 1 (or 2) bassoons | 1 kettledrums |

If flutes are needed this will bring the minimum number of players to twenty. He goes on to say that the number of instrumentalists regularly available to him in 1730 is eight: four *Stadtpfeifer* (town musicians, proficient mainly on wind instruments), three *Kunstgeiger* (string players) and an apprentice. The remainder must be recruited from the university students, who no longer receive the remuneration they once did and are understandably reluctant to give their services free, and from the *alumni* of the Thomasschule itself, which necessarily depletes the choirs. The situation is made worse because standards of musical ability on admission to the school have been allowed to decline. Bach ends his Memorandum by listing and grading the fifty-four *alumni* (boarders) of the Thomasschule: seventeen are described as proficient, twenty as requiring further training before they can be used in concerted music, and the rest as incompetent (*untüchtige*).[6]

[6] Bach elsewhere mentions the number of *alumni* as fifty-five, which was the maximum admitted to the school at any one time. He could, of course, draw also on the *externi* (day

Bach had good reason to describe his superiors at Leipzig as 'odd, and little interested in music' (see the letter to Erdmann). But while it must seem incomprehensible to us now that the council should have failed to provide Bach with the modest resources he needed to perform his music—and amazing that he was able to go on creating such masterpieces as the *St Matthew Passion*, knowing that they might never receive adequate performance—it must be said that the blame for the decline in church music at Leipzig was not entirely the council's, or that of a weak and aging Rektor. Bach had reacted to an unsatisfactory situation by showing himself uncooperative and neglectful, or (as a councillor put it on this occasion) 'incorrigible'. His refusal to defend his attitude and his actions must have infuriated the Leipzig council as much as it had the Arnstadt consistory in 1706. The unanimous decision to deprive Bach of some of the *Accidentien* to which he was entitled might seem petty and spiteful, but it must have appeared entirely justified at the time.

Temperamentally unsuited to the career of a school Kantor, and unable, because of circumstances, to exercise the role of *director musices* as he would have liked, Bach felt increasingly frustrated in Leipzig. Two months after penning the Memorandum to the Leipzig council he expressed his feelings in a letter to his friend Georg Erdmann in Danzig. Erdmann, it will be remembered, had been a schoolfriend in Ohrdruf and Lüneburg. He had then gone on to university to study law, and in 1713 he went to Lithuania as adviser to the military tribunal under Prince Anikita Ivanovich Repnin. When Bach wrote to him in 1730 he had been employed for twelve years as Russia's diplomatic representative in Danzig and legal adviser to the Russian court. He had visited Bach at Weimar in about 1717, and the two men had exchanged letters in 1726, when Erdmann had furnished information about himself and requested Bach to do the same.[7] Bach's second letter is fashionably sprinkled with French and Latin words and

boys), including his own sons, for his choirs and orchestras. The implications of the Memorandum for the performance of Bach's Leipzig church music will be mentioned in a later chapter, p. 144.

[7] The discovery of Bach's earlier letter to Erdmann was reported by G. Pantielev in *Sovetskaya muzika* in 1983 (No. 74ff). For a German translation of Pantielev's article see *Beiträge zur Musikwissenschaft*, xxv (1983), 143–6 and *Bach-Jahrbuch*, lxxi (1985), 83–97.

couched in the respectful terms normally used even between close friends and relatives; it is one of the few intimate letters of the composer that remain, and by far the most interesting. It must therefore be quoted in full:

Most honoured Sir.

Your Honour will be good enough to excuse an old and faithful servant for taking the liberty of troubling you with this. It must be nearly four years now since Your Honour favoured me with a kind reply to the letter I sent you. Since you then, as I recall, graciously requested news of what had befallen me, I shall obediently furnish this herewith. You are well acquainted with my *fata* from my youth until the *mutation* that took me to Cöthen as *Kapellmeister*, where I had a gracious Prince who both loved and understood music, and with whom I had expected to end my days. But it had to happen that the said *Serenissimus* married a Bernburg princess, as a result of which it seemed that his musical *inclination* weakened somewhat, especially as the princess seemed to be an *amusa*.[8] So God ordered it that I should be called here as *director musices* and Kantor at the Thomasschule. Now, it seemed to me at first not at all the right thing to become a Kantor after being a *Kapellmeister*, and I postponed my *resolution* for three months; but this *station* was described to me as so *favorable* that finally (especially as my sons seemed to be inclined towards [university] studies) I risked myself in the name of the Most High and came to Leipzig, took my *Probe*, and accepted the *mutation*. And here, following God's will, I have remained until now. But since now (1) I find that this post is not as remunerative as it was described to me, (2) many of the *accidentia* of the *station* have been withdrawn, (3) the cost of living is very high here, and (4) the authorities are odd, and little interested in music, with the result that I must live with almost constant vexation, envy, and harassment, I shall be compelled, with help from the Most High, to seek my fortune elsewhere. If Your Honour should know of or could find a *convenable station* in your city for an old and faithful servant, may I humbly request you to put in a gracious *recommendation* for me; for my part, I shall not fail to give *satisfaction* and to justify your gracious support and *intercession*. My present station is worth about 700 thalers, and if the death-rate is higher than *ordinairement* then the *Accidentia* increase in

---

[8] That is, someone indifferent to the arts (muses).

5   Part of Bach's letter to Georg Erdmann in Danzig, 28 October 1730

proportion; but if the air is healthy they fall accordingly, as last year, when there was a reduction of over 100 thalers in the *Accidentien* I would normally receive for funerals. In Thuringia I can live better on 400 thalers than I can here on twice that amount, because of the excessive cost of living.

Now I must tell you a little about my domestic situation. I have married a second time, my late first wife having died at Cöthen. From my first marriage three sons and a daughter are still living, whom Your Honour will graciously remember meeting in Weimar. From my second marriage one son and two daughters are still living. My eldest son is a *studiosus juris* [law student], the other two are still at school, one in the first and the other in the second class, and my eldest daughter is as yet unmarried. The children of my second marriage are still young; the eldest is a boy, aged six. But they are all born musicians, and I assure you that I can form a vocal and instrumental ensemble from my family, especially as my present wife sings a very pleasing soprano, and my eldest daughter can also join in not too badly. I should almost overstep the bounds of courtesy were I to *incommode* Your Honour further, and therefore hasten to close with my most devoted and lifelong *respect*, remaining Your Honour's most obedient and devoted servant,

Leipzig, 28 October 1730                                    Joh: Sebast: Bach

It seems unlikely that Bach seriously hoped for a suitable position in Danzig, and yet he would hardly have written as he did without considering the possibility of one. Perhaps he was aware that the organist of St Catherine's Church there, Theophil Andreas Volckmar, had recently resigned his post, but although the church had a fine organ and had employed some notable musicians in the past, an appointment there could hardly have been regarded as an improvement on Leipzig. Possibly Bach had his eyes on the much more attractive and prestigious post of Kantor at St Mary's Church. This had been held since 1699 by Maximilian Freisslich, who died in 1731 at the age of 68. What reply Erdmann made to his friend's call for help we do not know; but Bach was to remain at Leipzig for the rest of his life.

# Music for the Leipzig Liturgy

ORE THAN HALF OF THE VOLUMES IN THE BACH-
gesellschaft edition of Bach's works are devoted to vocal music
for the church. If we bear in mind that most of this incomparable
repertory was written during Bach's first five or six years at Leipzig
we can begin to appreciate the phenomenal creative effort involved. It
is as if the composer had until then been saving himself for the creation
of a 'well-regulated church music' and now devoted all his energy
to it.

In the Obituary the church music is listed as follows:

1. Five annual cycles of church pieces [cantatas] for every Sunday and feast
   day
2. Several oratorios, Masses, Magnificat, separate settings of the Sanctus . . .
3. Five Passions, including one for double chorus
4. Some double-chorus motets

Bach seems to have set out at Leipzig to provide a five-year cycle of
cantatas and Passions for use in the two main churches. Perhaps his
intention was to repeat each work after a five-year interval, and the
fact that about two-fifths of them cannot now be traced does not mean
that they never existed. Other composers have fared even worse. G. H.
Stölzel, J. T. Römhild, and J. F. Fasch each composed twelve annual
cycles, or about 1,150 works. Only some 450 of Stölzel's cantatas survive, 235 of Römhild's and a mere 70 or so of Fasch's. Compared with

the cantata production of these composers, or with the 2,000 and more that Telemann wrote, Bach's five cycles seem very modest. But, as we shall see, his cantatas are far more substantial and varied than those of any other composer; their quality is, of course, another matter altogether.

## Cantatas

The secular cantata was of Italian origin, as its name suggests. Its development during the seventeenth century ran parallel with that of opera, but its cultivation in learned and aristocratic circles encouraged experiment and made it more of a genre for connoisseurs. By the beginning of the eighteenth century a more or less standard structure was established, thanks largely to the prolific Alessandro Scarlatti, in which two or three (sometimes more) da capo arias were separated by recitative. Cantata subjects were amatory and pastoral, less usually historical or humorous. An important sub-genre, the *cantata spirituale*, had a religious or moralistic theme, but it was not liturgical, and the poetic imagery of its vernacular text was strongly influenced by the secular type. A well-known example is Scarlatti's Christmas cantata, *O di Betlemme altera*.

The impact of the Italian cantata on German music was limited at first to those centres where Italian opera flourished and where Italian musicians were employed. Reinhard Keiser in Hamburg was a leading composer of solo cantatas to both Italian and German texts. Bach wrote only two Italian solo cantatas. *Amore traditore* (BWV203) is of doubtful authenticity and of interest mainly for the written-out keyboard accompaniment to the second of its two da capo arias, a feature also of cantatas by the Dresden composer J. D. Heinichen. *Non sa che sia dolore* (BWV209) has a stronger claim to authenticity on stylistic grounds. It was evidently conceived as a farewell cantata, and in fact its rather curious text includes passages from G. B. Guarini's madrigal 'Partita dolorosa' (1598), as well as others from Metastasio's librettos for *La Galatea* (1722) and *Semiramide riconosciuta* (1729). Allusions in it to the town of Ansbach have led some commentators to suggest as its recipient J. M. Gesner, whom we shall meet later as Rektor of the Thomasschule in Leipzig from 1730 to 1744, but who before that was Rektor of the gymnasium in Ansbach. Lorenz Mizler, another member of Bach's circle in Leipzig who will enter the narrative in a later chapter, has also been suggested, and Alberto Basso has found references in the text that seem to point to a young man departing on military service.[1] Whatever the occasion for the cantata's composition, it was one that gave rise to some very fine music, contained in the standard structure of two recitatives and two arias preceded, in this case, by a particularly attractive instrumental sinfonia for flute, strings, and continuo. There are also three solo cantatas with German words: two of them are wedding cantatas (BWV202 and 210) and the other, *Ich bin in mir vergnügt* (BWV204), reflects on how it is more pleasurable to be contented than to be rich. This last may have been written, as Alfred Dürr has suggested, for an intimate circle of family or friends.

Most of Bach's other secular cantatas are large-scale works written for the birthday, name-day, or accession of a royal or aristocratic patron, or for some academic ceremony. More of these are lost than survive, but some are wholly or partly recoverable from the printed librettos and the re-use Bach made of the music when he adapted it to new words in the form of sacred 'parodies' (see p. 178). Their celebratory character, and often their suitability for open-air performance, is reflected in the orchestration, particularly in the cantatas written in the 1730s for the Dresden court (see p. 167), with their trumpets and drums. Of the pre-Leipzig works only three survive complete in their original form. *Durchlauchtster Leopold* (BWV173a) is a birthday cantata composed for Prince Leopold at Cöthen and parodied in the church cantata *Erhöhtes Fleisch und Blut* (BWV173). Like the other secular cantatas for the Cöthen court (known mainly from parodies), its arias are strongly dance-influenced, and indeed may possibly have accompanied some form of dancing. This is particularly true of the two duets (the first of them explicitly marked 'Al tempo di menuetto'), in each of which the instrumental ritornellos occupy exactly the same number of bars as the vocal sections (seventy-two and forty-eight respectively). *Die Zeit, die Tag und Jahre macht* is another Cöthen work, for New Year 1719, and again its lyrical items are imbued with dance rhythms; in April 1724 it too served as the basis for a sacred cantata, *Ein Herz, das seinen Jesum*

[1] A. Basso, 'Non sa che sia dolore', in M. Boyd (ed.), *Oxford Composer Companions: J. S. Bach* (London, 1999), 318–19.

*weiss* (No. 134). The delightful hunting cantata *Was mir behagt* (BWV208) was composed for the birthday of Duke Christian of Weissenfels in 1713. In this work the duke's character is flattered in recitative, six arias, a duet, and two choruses (or rather ensembles, since they would have been sung by the four soloists). The arias include the well-known 'Schafe können sicher weiden' ('Sheep may safely graze'), whose first couplet has misled many into associating it with the Good Shepherd. As the rest of the strophe makes clear, the 'good shepherd' is in this case not Christ, but Christian:

> Schafe Können sicher weiden
> Wo ein guter Hirte wacht.
> Wo Regenten wohl regieren,
> Kann man Ruh und Friede spüren
> Und was Länder glücklich macht.

Sheep may safely graze where a good shepherd is watching. Where a ruler governs well one may look for peace, freedom, and a happy people.

While this aria seems never to have been transferred to a sacred work, both the bass aria 'Ein Fürst ist seines Landes Pan!' and the soprano aria 'Weil die wollenreichen Herden' were re-used in Cantata 68 (1725), the second of them being fitted out with a completely new vocal line from which it is now indissociable (Ex. 8.1).

The secular cantata made an important impact on Bach's church music (other examples will be mentioned later), but in the seventeenth century the main form of Lutheran church music—usually referred to simply as the *Stück* (piece) or the *Musik*—developed independently of it. Gospel settings, psalm settings, and works based on chorales gradually assumed particular importance because the textual division into verses (whether scriptural or poetic) encouraged the mixing of musical styles that was to become a hallmark of the genuine cantata. Towards the end of the century *ad hoc* poetic texts became more frequent, and with the combining in one work of various textual elements the move towards a genre that might be distinguished as 'cantata' received added impetus. Particularly important were works that combined arias and biblical texts in what has been called the 'concerto–aria' cantata. This normally began and ended with a setting of a biblical text for the combined forces,

## Ex. 8.1

(BWV208: As long as fleecy flocks [graze] on this treasured pasture
BWV68: My faithful heart, be joyful, sing and be merry, your Jesus is here)

between which verses of a hymn or other text were set for soloists or small ensembles. Works of this kind (not yet called 'cantatas') were composed by Buxtehude, Pachelbel, and many others, including Bach's predecessors at Leipzig, Knüpfer, Schelle, and Kuhnau. Bach's own Mühlhausen cantatas, mentioned in a previous chapter, also stem from this tradition (see pp. 32–4)

With further textual mixing (for example, the introduction of a final chorale into the 'concerto–aria' type) and a clearer division into separate movements, the genre began to approach the 'modern' type of church cantata associated with Bach at Weimar and Leipzig. The decisive step of mixing the Italian operatic constituents of recitative and da capo aria with the forms of traditional German church music has usually been seen as having been taken in two cycles of cantata texts by the theologian and poet Erdmann Neumeister published in 1711 and 1714. We now know, however, that this 'modern' type of church cantata had been anticipated some years earlier at the Meiningen court of Duke Ernst Ludwig, who may himself have been the author of texts of this type set by his *Kapellmeister* Georg Caspar Schürmann.[2] Neumeister's printed sets were nevertheless influential, and his example was soon followed by other poets, notably Salomo Franck and Georg Christian Lehms, both of whom provided texts for Bach.

The term 'cantata' was included in the title of Neumeister's first published cycle (*Geistliche Cantaten statt einer Kirchenmusik*), and it is found occasionally in other collections, but it was not generally applied at the time to church compositions in Germany. Bach used it for only seven cantatas (Nos. 30, 54, 56, 82, 173, 195, and 197), most of them works for solo voice or parodies of secular compositions; the others he called simply 'Stück' or 'Concerto', or else he used no generic title at all. His debt to the pre-1700 type of cantata is evident above all in the importance he assigned to the chorale and in the way he combined it with other elements. In some late cantatas (Nos. 97, 100, 112, 117, 129, 177, and 192) he even set complete, unparaphrased chorales *per omnes versus*, reverting to a type of text that for his contemporaries had become obsolete. The diversity of form used by Bach in both individual movements and the cantata as a whole (resulting in part from collaboration with various different librettists) is also characteristic of the older type of cantata.

The effect on Bach of the reforms associated with Neumeister is first seen in the cantatas he wrote at Weimar from March 1714, when he was appointed *Konzertmeister*. Two of them (Nos. 18 and 61) do in fact use texts by Neumeister, and there are also two by Lehms (Nos. 54 and 199), but the majority (probably about twenty among the extant works) are to words by the Weimar court poet, Salomo Franck. The mystical, even pietistic, sentiments of Franck's verse—much of it expressing a yearning for death as a sweet release from earthly suffering—are enhanced by the intimacy of Bach's settings, even if this was to a large extent imposed by conditions at Weimar. The cantatas dating from before mid-1715 vary a good deal in their scoring. Three of them (Nos. 54, 152, and 199) are for one or two solo voices only, and *Tritt auf die*

*Glaubensbahn* (No. 152) is scored for solo instruments as well (recorder, oboe, viola d'amore, bass viol, and continuo). Its chamber-music character is typical of the Weimar cantatas. The Whitsunday cantata *Erschallet, ihr Lieder* (No. 172), on the other hand, requires four soloists, chorus, trumpets, and drums, as well as oboe and a full complement of strings (with divided violas, another feature of the period). Clearly the duke's *Kapelle* could be reinforced for important festivals.

It is unfortunate that all but one of the cantatas presumably performed at Weimar during the first five months of 1715 have been lost,[3] for it is evident that by June, when *O heilges Geist- und Wasserbad* (No. 165) was heard, Bach and Franck had established a type of cantata that remained standard for the rest of the year and much of 1716. It took the form of two or, more commonly, three arias (the term here includes duets) separated by recitative and followed by a plainly harmonized chorale. All the cantatas of this type use four soloists (soprano, alto, tenor, and bass), and it may be presumed that they also sang the chorale. The instrumentation is correspondingly small-scale: strings (now with only one viola part) and an obbligato wind instrument, usually an oboe. Another feature is the inclusion of a bassoon, which usually reinforces the bass but in *Mein Gott, wie lang, ach lange* (No. 155) is given an important solo part.

*Mein Gott, wie lang, ach lange* is not one of Bach's finest cantatas, though both Spitta and Schweitzer admired it. It was composed for the second Sunday after Epiphany (19 January) 1716. Franck's text, which refers obliquely to the gospel for the day (Christ's miracle at the marriage at Cana, as told in John 2:1–11), is constructed as a kind of spiritual drama, like many other cantatas. In the opening recitative (D minor), accompanied by strings and continuo, the solo soprano sings of the cares to be endured without the support of the Lord. The first eleven-and-a-half bars proceed above a tonic pedal, suggestive of anxiety according to Schweitzer, from which the voice finally liberates itself for some characteristic word-painting on 'Freudenwein' (wine of joy) and 'sinkt' (sinks) (Ex. 8.2). The duet that follows (A minor) is for alto and tenor,

---

[3] One of them (BWV80a) was adapted between 1727 and 1731 as *Ein feste Burg ist unser Gott* (No. 80); another may have been an early version of *Alles nur nach Gottes Willen* (No. 72), the text of which is from Franck's *Evangelisches Andachts-Opffer* (1715).

**Ex. 8.2**

(I lack the wine of joy; all assurance fails me)

with an agile obbligato bassoon part: 'You must have faith, you must hope, you must trust in God'. The bass singer in the next recitative represents the voice of God, who will bring 'wine of comfort and joy for bitter tears', and the soprano, restored in spirit, sings of Jesus's goodness in a cheerful through-composed aria (F major). The cantata ends with a straightforward four-part harmonization in F major of the chorale melody *Es ist das Heil uns kommen her*, sung to the twelfth strophe of Paul Speratus's hymn (1524).

This cantata was presumably followed by others at the rate of about one a month throughout 1716, but none is known for certain until December, when a sudden acceleration of activity resulted in cantatas for the second, third, and fourth Sundays in Advent.[4] As we have seen, this may be attributed to the death of Samuel Drese on 1 December 1716, and the apparent halt in cantata production after 1716 can be explained by Bach's disappointment at not succeeding him as *Kapellmeister*.

With Bach's appointment as Thomaskantor in Leipzig there began his most important and productive period as a church composer. He now had to perform a cantata each Sunday and feast day except during the penitential season of Lent and on the last three Sundays in Advent, when there was no concerted music in church. The number of cantatas needed for an annual cycle was about sixty, and so if Bach assembled five cycles, as stated in the Obituary, there must have been altogether some 300 in his cupboard in the Thomasschule. The number of lost works is difficult to estimate, since the 198 published in *BG* and listed by Schmieder include some spurious ones, as well as others for weddings, funerals, and other occasions not included in the church's year. Also, the Obituary's five annual cycles quite possibly included cantatas by other composers copied and used by Bach. That a considerable number (perhaps as many as 100) have been lost is, however, without question.

Cantatas were normally performed at the principal service, or *Hauptgottesdienst*. This was the Lutheran equivalent of the Catholic Mass; Anglicans might think of it as a combination of Matins and Holy Communion, including a sermon and (except at certain festivals) the Litany. At Leipzig the service began at 7 a.m. and usually lasted until about 11 a.m. The music included organ voluntaries and preludes, Latin motets (selected for the most part from Erhard Bodenschatz's *Florilegium Portense*), hymns, and plainchant, as well as the chief musical item, the *Stück* (cantata), accompanied by organ and instruments. The cantata was

---

[4] BWV70a 186a, and 147a, known only in their Leipzig recensions.

usually related in subject matter to the gospel reading, which it followed either immediately or after the intoning of the Latin Credo. The sermon, which came shortly after, began at about 8 a.m. and lasted an hour, so the cantata, usually about twenty to twenty-five minutes in length, must have started some time between 7.30 and 7.40 a.m.—not the best time of day, one might think, for young choristers and instrumentalists to get to grips with some of the most demanding new music in the whole of western Europe! On cold mornings the boys were allowed to leave the choir loft after the cantata, but they were to remain when there was a second part, or a second cantata, to be sung later in the service. Cantatas for the winter months are on the whole shorter than those for the other seasons.

The cantata was sung by the first choir of the Thomasschule at the two main churches on alternate Sundays. On the first day of the three major festivals (Christmas, Easter, and Whitsun) it was sung at the Nikolaikirche in the morning and repeated at the Thomaskirche in the afternoon; the following day this procedure was reversed, and on the third day only the Nikolaikirche heard the cantata. Bach inaugurated his first annual cycle (or *Jahrgang*, to use the convenient German term) at the Nikolaikirche on the first Sunday after Trinity (30 May) 1723 with *Die Elenden sollen essen* (BWV75); the cycle then extends to Trinity Sunday 1724. With so many new duties to attend to, especially during the weeks preceding Christmas and Easter, Bach naturally drew on the cantatas he had written at Weimar, and on a number of occasions he also adapted new texts to old music, mainly from secular cantatas. But the majority (at least thirty-seven) of the 1723–4 cantatas were new, and they show the composer experimenting with various structures and evidently with various librettists, although the texts are in nearly every case anonymous. The first two cantatas (Nos. 75 and 76) are both large-scale works in two parts, with the following structure:

I Chorus—R—A—R—A—R—Chorale
II Sinfonia—R—A—R—A—R—Chorale
(R = recitative; A = aria)

Their structural similarity is even closer than this outline suggests. The opening choruses, to a psalm text, both take the form of a prelude and fugue; and in both cantatas the chorale in Part I is spaced out with orchestral interludes and repeated (to a different strophe) at the end of Part II. No other Bach cantatas use precisely this structure, but the choral 'frame' (an elaborate chorus at the beginning and a plain chorale at the end) is typical of the Leipzig cantatas as a whole. Symmetry in the organization of the internal movements is also something that continued to interest Bach.

Bach obviously intended his first cantatas to impress the clergy, officials, and congregations at the two main Leipzig churches, and he seems to have succeeded to judge from a contemporary newspaper report that No. 75 had been heard 'mit guten applausu'. But a choir and orchestra deprived for two years of the services of a Kantor, and unused to the particular demands of Bach's music, cannot have found them easy, and the other new cantatas in the first *Jahrgang* are on a more modest scale. Alfred Dürr has drawn attention to the following groundplans which recur with particular frequency:

1. Chorus (biblical text)—R—A—R—A—Chorale (Nos. 25, 46, 69a, 77, 89*, 104, 105, 109, 136, 179)
2. Chorus (biblical text)—R—Chorale—R—A—R—Chorale (Nos. 40, 48, 64, 65, 67, 153)
3. Chorus (biblical text)—A—Chorale—R—A—Chorale (Nos. 37, 44, 86*, 144, 166*)[5]

Several cantatas in the first *Jahrgang* consist only of recitative and arias with a final chorale, like the 1715 Weimar cantatas, a number of which were revived at this time. With Christmas music (including the Magnificat) and the *St John Passion* to prepare, Bach clearly did not wish to overtax his choir.

Bach's second *Jahrgang*, in contrast to the first, was evidently planned from the start as a unified cycle of chorale cantatas. The setting of a chorale text strophe by strophe (*per omnes versus*) had been one of the main German 'cantata' types in the second half of the seventeenth century, but by 1700 it had been superseded by others using mixed texts, such as those of Bach's first cycle. For 1724–5 Bach and his unknown

---

[5] A. Dürr, *Die Kantaten von Johann Sebastian Bach*, 41–2. In the cantatas marked with an asterisk (*) the opening Biblical text is set as a bass solo and not as a chorus. The third groundplan is found again in three cantatas of the second *Jahrgang* (Nos. 6, 42, and 85) and in No. 79 (31 October 1725).

librettist devised an entirely new type of chorale cantata, in which the first and last strophes (exceptionally others, too) were set unaltered, the rest being paraphrased in poetic form for recitatives and arias.[6] The hymn tune itself forms the basis for a large-scale chorale fantasia to open the cantata, usually with thematically independent orchestral ritornellos, and the last strophe is given a plain chordal setting with the instruments doubling the voices. The internal movements are usually independent of the chorale melody, except in those cases where the librettist has retained portions of the original text.

One of the finest chorale cantatas is No. 93 *Wer nur den lieben Gott lässt walten,* for the fifth Sunday after Trinity (9 July) 1724, based on the hymn by Georg Neumark first published in 1642 (Ex. 8.3a). The cantata opens with a magnificent chorale fantasia in which each line of the hymn is preceded by a contrapuntal elaboration of the same, first by (?solo) soprano and alto (lines 1 and 2), then by tenor and bass (lines 3 and 4) and finally by all four voices (lines 5 and 6). Meanwhile the orchestra develops its own material within a ritornello framework. The cantata's central movements, arranged symmetrically as R—A—duet—R—A, all refer in one way or another to the chorale tune. Some of its transformations are shown in Ex. 8.3b–f.

The cantata ends with the usual straightforward four-part harmonization of the chorale melody. It might seem to modern ears that a more satisfying musical architecture would have been achieved by beginning the work in this way and placing the large-scale chorale fantasia at the end. But this is to apply a criterion of the concert-hall to a piece designed for the liturgy. When Schelle was Thomaskantor at Leipzig the custom was to precede the sermon with a chorale cantata and to follow it with the same chorale sung by the congregation. There is no evidence to support congregational singing of the final chorales in Bach's cantatas (in fact the alterations Bach often makes to the melody argue against it, but of a *feeling* of communal participation in the chorale would have been enough to secure the sense of completeness that a modern concert performance might seem to miss.

The series of chorale cantatas came to a premature end after 25 March 1725 (Feast of the Annunciation), when one of the loveliest of them

---

[6] An exception is No. 107, which reverts to the old *per omnes versus* type.

all, *Wie schön leuchtet der Morgenstern* (BWV1) was performed. Why Bach abandoned the cycle at this point is something of a mystery. It has been suggested that he simply wanted a change after writing the same type of cantata for nine months, but this seems unlikely. Another possibility is that for some reason he lost the services of his librettist, and it is worth noting that in all the later chorale cantatas he revived the old *per omnes versus* type. Perhaps there were changes in choir personnel that had something to do with it. Of the twelve cantatas spanning the period between Easter and Trinity Sunday 1725, no fewer than five use an SATB chorus only for the final chorale. The last nine of these are all to texts by the Leipzig poet Christiane Mariane von Ziegler, whose

**Ex. 8.3**

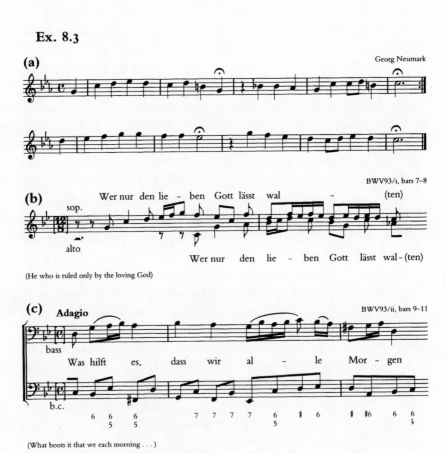

(He who is ruled only by the loving God)

(What boots it that we each morning . . . )

**(d)**

tenor — BWV93/iii, bars 17–20

Man hal - te nur___ ein___ we - nig stil - le

(One is still for a little)

**(e)**

sop. — BWV93/iv, bars 1–2

Er kennt die recht - en Freu – den - stun - den

(He knows when it is right to be joyful)

**(f)**

tenor — BWV93/v, bars 1–2

Denk' nicht in dei - ner Drang - sals Hit - ze

b.c.

♭7     5     6
                    4
                    2

(Think not in the heat of tribulation)

emphasis on the faith and feelings of the individual may have commended her verses to Bach at this time.

Cantata 176, *Es ist ein trotzig und verzagt Ding*, brought Bach full circle to Trinity Sunday, but this time he did not immediately start on a new *Jahrgang*. For the next six months he seems to have either revived old cantatas or used those of other composers. The only new ones from this period are Nos. 168, 137, and 164, for the ninth, twelfth, and thirteenth Sundays after Trinity respectively, and No. 79, for the Reformation festival (31 October); No. 137 is a chorale cantata *per omnes versus*, possibly written to fill a gap in the previous *Jahrgang*. Bach's intention may have been to readjust his cantata cycles to coincide with the church's year, beginning with the first Sunday in Advent. It is unfortunate, therefore, that we have no record of what was done on that Sunday in 1725, but it may be significant that the cantata for Christmas

Day, *Unser Mund sei voll Lachens* (BWV110), begins with a French overture (adapted from the Orchestral Suite No. 4). Only five other extant cantatas begin in this way, and at least four are associated in some way with an inauguration:[7] No. 61 was for the first Sunday in Advent 1714, No. 119 for the inauguration of the town council at Leipzig in 1723, No. 194 for the dedication of a new organ at Störmthal in November 1723, and No. 20 to open Bach's second cantata cycle in 1724. No. 110 may therefore mark the beginning of the third *Jahrgang*, or possibly Bach felt an overture to be appropriate for the feast celebrating the beginning of Christ's life on earth.

From Christmas 1725 to Advent 1726 the sequence of new cantatas is virtually unbroken (the lacunae occur mostly around Whitsun), but they form a strangely heterogeneous cycle. Some of them include orchestral movements composed at Cöthen, some are for one or two solo voices, and several performed between 28 July and 3 November feature a virtuoso solo part for the organ. By no means all of them are by Bach. Between the Feast of the Purification (2 February) and the thirteenth Sunday after Trinity (15 September) he used on at least eighteen occasions cantatas by his distant cousin Johann Ludwig Bach, (1677–1731), *Kapellmeister* at Meiningen. One of these, *Denn du wirst meine Seele*, for Easter Sunday, was included in *BG* as an original work by J. S. Bach (BWV15). The librettos of J. L. Bach's cantatas have a distinctive two-part design, Part I beginning with an Old Testament (OT) passage and Part II with a New Testament (NT) passage. The organization of the rest of the cantata may vary slightly, but the standard design is:

I: OT—R—A          II: NT—A—R—Chorus—Chorale

(R = recitative; A = aria or duet)

The same design is found in seven out of the nine or ten new cantatas that J. S. Bach composed for the normal Leipzig services during the same period: Nos. 17, 39, 43, 45, 88, 102, and 187. Walter Blankenburg (*Bach-Jahrbuch*, lxiii [1977], 7–25) suggested that the texts may have been by the pastor Christoph Helm of Rudolstadt, but it now seems more probable that they were the work of Duke Ernst Ludwig of Saxe-Meiningen, as mentioned earlier (see p. 127).

---

[7] It is not known for what occasion No. 97 was composed.

Dürr and others see the third cantata cycle as extending to Septua-
gesima (9 February) 1727. The question of a fourth *Jahrgang* to texts by
Picander is one that has engendered much controversy among Bach
scholars. The arguments on both sides hinge on the inference to be
drawn from a passage in Picander's preface to the first edition (now lost)
of his *Cantaten auf die Sonn- und Fest-Tage durch das gantze Jahr* (Leipzig,
1728):

> I have decided to complete the present cantatas to the glory of God, urged
> thereto by good friends and by my own devotion. I have undertaken the
> task the more willingly since I may flatter myself that any lack of poetic
> charm may perhaps be made good by the beauty of [the music of] the
> incomparable Herr *Kapellmeister* Bach, and that these songs may be per-
> formed in the services of the main Leipzig churches.

Clearly, Picander wrote the texts especially for Bach, and probably in
collaboration with him; instead of following the church's year they begin with St. John's Day and end with the fourth Sunday after Trinity.
But only seven of Bach's settings (BWV145, 149, 156, 159, 171, 174, and
188) and fragments of another two (BWV197a and *Ich bin ein Pilgrim auf
der Welt*) remain. If, as on balance seems likely, Bach did compose the
others as well, their disappearance represents one of the most regrettable
losses in all music.

Of the fifth *Jahrgang* mentioned in the Obituary there remains now
not the slightest trace, unless, as Christoph Wolff has suggested (*Bach-
Jahrbuch*, lxviii (1982), 151–2), the 1723–4 cycle was a complete *Doppel-
jahrgang* of cantatas to be sung before and after the sermon. Many of
the post-1728 cantatas were composed to fill lacunae in the earlier sets.
They include several parody movements and a good deal of virtuoso
writing both for instruments and for solo voices. A splendid example
of the latter is the 'Allelujah' that ends Cantata 51, *Jauchzet Gott in allen
Landen*, probably the most brilliant solo Alleluia setting before the one
in Mozart's *Exsultate, jubilate* (K165/158a).

The variety of structure and scoring in Bach's cantatas is in contrast
to the uniformity generally apparent in the cantata cycles of his Lutheran contemporaries. Even their tonal structure is comparatively irregular. The usual practice in both sacred and secular cantatas was to

begin and end in the same key, but in about a quarter of Bach's Leipzig cantatas this does not happen. The presence of the same hymn tune in both opening and closing movements does ensure tonal unity in all the chorale cantatas, and Bach seems to have regarded the relative major or (more surprising, perhaps) the relative minor as a surrogate tonic for this purpose; but in many cases the initial and final tonalities are less closely related. It has been suggested that in some cantatas, such as No. 104 (beginning in G major and ending in A major), Bach used 'progressive tonality' as a means of text illumination, but in many others it can be shown to result from changes made during the course of the works' history. The tonal scheme of Cantata 136 (beginning in A major and ending in B minor) lends support to Dürr's theory that the work re-uses a lot of old material.

In totally new works the expressive connotations of particular keys played an important role. Cantatas for the major church festivals, splendid civic occasions, or (in their original forms) princely celebrations are mostly in C major or D major, the keys in which the trumpets of Bach's day were usually pitched. F major, the horns' key, was similarly favoured for cantatas with an outdoor 'setting', such as No. 1, *Wie schön leuchtet der Morgenstern* (How beautifully shines the morning star). For the expression of darker sentiments G minor is most often chosen, and B minor seems to have been associated in Bach's mind with passive suffering, as witness its use in the Passions and the B minor Mass.[8] Hardly less personal is the use of A major and E major for expressing tenderness and eroticism; a fine example is Cantata 49, *Ich geh und suche mit Verlangen*, one of several dialogues in the cantatas between Christ as bridegroom and the Soul as bride.

The most impressive sections of the church cantatas are the huge choral movements with which most of them begin. Chorale fantasias predominate, but other structures are also found. The significance of the French overture in this context has already been mentioned. More common are ritornello forms indebted to (and sometimes borrowing from) concerto models, and dance-like da capo movements

---

[8] W. Mellers: *Bach and the Dance of God*, 137, and *passim*. Stephen Daw, on the other hand, finds that 'for Bach B minor is a key of profound joy' (*Bach: the Choral Works*, 264).

frequently taken from secular works. Fugues, in either a strict *stile antico* with instruments doubling voices or in a modern style with independent orchestral support, are also quite common. The term 'permutation' has been used for a type of fugue with three regular counter-subjects which are passed from voice to voice in various keys and combinations. The practical advantage of this highly organized fugal texture was that the music was easily learnt and remembered. An early and very attractive example is in the opening chorus of *Himmelskönig, sei willkommen* (No. 182, 1714), which however is not a fugue but a da capo chorus whose first section is fugal. In chorale fantasias Bach found an equally valuable way of saving rehearsal time and guarding against accidents in performance by placing the chorale melody in long notes in the soprano line (sung by boy trebles), and perhaps doubling it with a wind instrument: horn, trumpet, or cornett. The great opening chorus of the *St Matthew Passion* provides a familiar example, but no less masterly are many of the chorale fantasias in the cantatas, such as *Wie schön leuchtet der Morgenstern* (No. 1), with its concerto-like ritornellos, and *Jesu, der du meine Seele* (No. 78), which is at once a chorale movement and a passacaglia.

Choruses such as these are rightly prized among Bach's greatest achievements, and yet the cantatas are not primarily choral works. Recitatives and arias far outnumber other types of movement, and choirs that include the cantatas in their repertories must accustom themselves to remaining silent for much of the time. The nature of Bach's recitative has frequently been misunderstood, and it is still misunderstood when a singer declaims it with a studied regard for the written note-values or looks for meaningful expression in conventional melodic formula. Bach's recitatives are rarely of more intrinsic merit than those of contemporary opera composers; their association with sacred texts has encouraged singers and commentators to seek in them a level of expressivity that properly belongs to the arias. His recitatives nevertheless have qualities that make them more memorable than those of most operas of the period, and Bach had one great advantage over the opera composer: with no stage action to advance, he could respond to all the possibilities in the text for lyrical expansion and for symbolic or pictorial word-painting. The results once or twice border on the grotesque, as in the much-quoted bass recitative in Cantata 152, where the words 'zum Fall' are accompanied by a leap downwards of a tenth to a low *D♯*, or in Cantata 78/v, where an even wider leap downwards is used to suggest the grave; but usually Bach's taste matches his imagination. Words expressing motion almost unfailingly attract the appropriate melisma; 'pain', 'grief', 'torment' etc. are usually expressed harmonically by a diminished seventh or some other chromatic chord, or melodically by the interval of a diminished fifth or fourth; and words like 'Freude' (joy) and its derivatives are matched by melismatic passages, sometimes in dotted rhythms and often of considerable length.

Such word-painting belongs to the stock-in-trade of all Baroque composers of vocal music. Bach applies it with more than ordinary inventiveness, but it is in the arias and duets that we find his true originality at work, modifying and advancing accepted structures in ways that set them completely apart from the arias of his contemporaries. Several arias, particularly in the pre-Leipzig cantatas and again in the second *Jahrgang*, are based on chorale melodies. If the chorale text is also used, the melody is normally given to the voice, with an independent, newly composed instrumental counterpoint. A familiar example is 'Zion hört die Wächter singen' in Cantata 140; another is 'Ach bleib' bei uns' in No. 6. Their trio texture and the shapeliness of their new counter melodies made these arias obvious candidates for organ arrangements when Bach was asked to provide some chorale preludes for the publisher J. G. Schübler in about 1748.

The da capo aria (A—B—A) makes an early appearance, but those in the pre-Weimar cantatas are brief, rudimentary in key-scheme and ritornello design, and (because of the nature of the texts) few in number. Under the influence of the Italianate Weimar court Bach's da capo arias increased in size and importance, with substantial ritornellos integrated into the vocal phrases. A good example is 'Kreuz und Krone sind verbunden' in Cantata 12 (1714), which may be said to have inaugurated a common type of minor-key aria whose plangent expressiveness owes much to the participation of a solo oboe. The long, sinuous oboe melody of the opening ritornello (Ex. 8.4.) is repeated in its entirety after the initial vocal phrase and again at the end of the aria's first section. This means that the bars quoted in Ex. 26 are heard altogether six times, unaltered and in the same key.

**Ex. 8.4**

BWV12/iv, bars 1–7

Bach continued to employ the conventional da capo structure (especially in secular cantatas, where it is used for choruses as well) but he soon became aware of its two main shortcomings: repetitiousness and a ponderous emphasis on the tonic key. One way to avoid these was to dispense altogether with the da capo and to repeat the second half of the strophe instead of the first. An example is the following tenor aria from Cantata 78:

> 1. Das Blut, so meine Schuld durchstreicht,
> 2. Macht mir das Herze wieder leicht       A
> 3. Und spricht mich frei.
>
> 4. Ruft mich der Höllen Heer zum Streite,
> 5. So stehet Jesus mir zur Seite,       B
> 6. Dass ich beherzt und sieghaft sei.

(The blood [of Christ], wiping away my guilt, makes my heart light again and sets me free. If the army of Hell should rise against me, with Jesus at my side I should be fearless and victorious.)

A conventional setting would reach a cadence in the tonic at the end of line 3 and then repeat lines 1–3 (A) after lines 4–6 (B). What Bach does, however, is to reach the relative major with line 3 and then to set the B section twice to make an extended binary design (A—B1—B2), leaving the instrumental ritornello (flute and continuo) to furnish the required element of recapitulation. The structure may be summarized thus (Rit = part only of ritornello):

| *Section:* | Ritornello—A—Rit—B1—Rit—B2—Ritornello |
|---|---|

| *Key:* | g . . . . .     g→ B♭ . . . B♭→ E♭→ c→ g . . . . . . |
|---|---|

The relevance of arias such as this to the ritornello structure of the Baroque concerto needs no stressing.

When this kind of structure is allied to a da capo text (A2 substituting for B2 in the above scheme) the result is what modern analytical studies of Bach's music frequently refer to as a 'free da capo' aria. The term is apt in those cases where A1 and A2 differ as much as B1 and B2 do in the example just analysed. But in many others it happens that the A2 section, far from being a 'free' da capo of A1, stands in the same relation to it as does the recapitulation to the exposition in Classical sonata form. In other words, A2 recapitulates the music of A1 with only such adjustments as are necessary to finish in the home key. Our analytical vocabulary is short of a term to distinguish this structure; 'modified da capo', although not entirely satisfactory, will be used here with this specific meaning.

This aria type did not originate with Bach—an embryonic form is to be found in Alessandro Scarlatti's early opera, *Gli equivoci nel sembiante* (1679), and in operas by Carlo Pallavicino (d. 1688)[9]—but Bach seems to have been the only one to cultivate it in the first half of the eighteenth century. Isolated examples can be found in the Weimar cantatas (e.g. BWV54/iii; 63/v; 182/iv, vi), but it was not until the Leipzig years that they began to appear almost as frequently as the conventional da capo aria. Cantata 22, written for the Leipzig *Probe* in 1723, contains a modified da capo aria, 'Mein Jesu, ziehe mich nach dir', dir,' in C minor with oboe obbligato which makes an interesting comparison with the one from Cantata 12 mentioned earlier; in this case only the first clause of A1 is recapitulated. The first aria in the New Year cantata *Gott, wie dein Name, so ist auch dein Ruhm* ( BWV171, ?1729) shows a more developed example of the structure (see the outline on p. 143).

In this, as in most other modified da capo arias, the 'recapitulation' begins in the tonic, but occasionally Bach introduces the da capo in the

[9] J. Smith, 'Carlo Pallavicino', *Proceedings of the Royal Musical Association*, xcvi (1969–70), 57–72.

| Section | Key | Text | Bars |
|---|---|---|---|
| A1 ('Exposition') | A major | [Ritornello, 2 violins, bc] | 1–15 |
| | A major | 1. Herr, so weit die Wolken gehen | 15–26 |
| | | 2. Gehet deines Namens Ruhm | |
| | | 1. | |
| | | 1. | |
| | | 2. | |
| | | 1. | |
| | | 2. | |
| | E major | [Ritornello, shortened] | 26–34 |
| B (Middle section) | E major | 3. Alles, was die Lippen rührt | 34–44 |
| | | 4. Alles, was noch Odem führt | |
| | | 5. Wird dich in der Macht erhöhen | |
| | | 3. | |
| | | 4. | |
| | | 5. | |
| | B minor | [Ritornello, part] | 44–46 |
| | | 3. | 46–56 |
| | | 4. | |
| | | 5. | |
| | | 3. | |
| | | 4. | |
| | | 5. | |
| | F♯ minor | [Ritornello, part] | 56–60 |
| A2 ('Recapitulation') | A major | 1. ⎤ | 60–71 |
| | | 2. ⎬ as in 'exposition' | |
| | | 1. ⎦ | |
| | | 1. ⎤ | |
| | | 2. ⎬ transposed to end in tonic | |
| | | 1. ⎥ | |
| | | 2. ⎦ | |
| | A major | [Ritornello, complete] | 71–85 |

subdominant, anticipating a procedure sometimes found in sonata movements by the young Schubert and his immediate Viennese predecessors. In such cases the music of the first section can be repeated exactly at the new pitch, the only changes being those necessary to keep the parts within the appropriate vocal or instrumental compass. Possibly the earliest example of a subdominant da capo in the cantatas occurs in the opening duet of *Du wahrer Gott und Davids Sohn* (BWV23, 1723). This may have been prompted by the desirability of exchanging the solo soprano and alto parts in the da capo, and similar considerations perhaps governed the choice of a subdominant da capo in the terzetto 'Ach, wenn wird die Zeit erscheinen' in Part V of the *Christmas Oratorio* (presumably a parody). But subdominant da capos are present also in perhaps half-a-dozen solo arias. The charge of laziness sometimes levelled (with little justification) against Schubert for his subdominant recapitulations cannot apply here, since the conventional alternative actually requires less effort. The relevance of the Bachian modified da capo aria to the emerging sonata form is something still requiring investigation.

The illustration of particular images in the text is necessarily tempered in the arias by purely musical considerations which do not apply to recitatives, but Bach usually contrives to work in an appropriate melisma when the words call for it. 'Freude' in particular never fails to evoke the natural response, sometimes at considerable length (Ex. 8.5).

The constitution of Bach's choir in Leipzig has been the subject of much controversy ever since Joshua Rifkin proposed that many—perhaps most—of the cantatas were performed there by a choir of only four singers, with one voice to each part.[10] Such a proposition seems to contradict Bach's own 1730 Memorandum to the town council, in which he set out his requirements for at least three (and preferably four) singers to each part (see p. 117). Rifkin, however, has argued that what Bach had in mind here was a pool of singers from which he could select the four normally required, as well as extra *ripieno* singers when a particular work called for them; in this way he would have been able to guard against the not infrequent absences through illness.

[10] J. Rifkin, 'Bach's Chorus: a Preliminary Report', *Musical Times*, cxxiii (1982), 747–54.

**Ex. 8.5**

BWV103/v, bars 47–52

O Freu — — — — —

— — — — — de!

(O joy!)

Rifkin's theory is backed up by evidence culled from a thorough study of the surviving performance material and other documents; it has so far proved impregnable to the many objections raised against it, and after much initial scepticism has attracted several followers among conductors and performers.

Bach's instrumentation in the cantatas is a study in itself, and can only be touched upon here.[11] Most of the Leipzig cantatas are scored for four-part chorus and usually three or four soloists, with an orchestra of strings, oboes, and continuo (organ), to which may be added trumpet (and drums if more than two trumpets are used), horn, flute, recorder, oboe d'amore, oboe da caccia, bassoon, *violoncello piccolo*, and bass viol. In addition, the cantus firmus of a chorale movement is often doubled by a cornett (a wooden, leather-covered instrument of great antiquity but limited technique) and in motet-like movements the lower voices, too, may be reinforced by trombones. Bach's instrumentarium is a rich mixture of the standard, the brand new and the near-obsolete, and no doubt the scoring of a particular cantata was determined largely by the players (and in some cases the instruments) available. One notices, for example, that the flute is rarely used until

[11] It has been the subject of thorough investigation in Ulrich Prinz's *Studien zum Instrumentarium Johann Sebastian Bachs mit besonderer Berücksichtigung der Kantaten* (Tübingen, 1979).

after the first *Jahrgang*, that parts for *violoncello piccolo* appear most frequently in April and May 1725, and that cantatas with obbligato organ are concentrated in the last months of 1726. Nevertheless it seems unlikely that the available forces at Leipzig would have changed as a rule from one week to the next, and yet if cantatas for successive Sundays and intervening feast days are placed side by side, it is surprising how infrequently adjacent works call for the same instruments.[12] Clearly Bach's choice of instruments was determined by other considerations as well, not the least of which was the nature of the text and its place in the church's calendar.

Bach's orchestral writing serves the symbolic and pictorial interpretation of the text in a number of ways, for example in the use of plucked strings. A pizzicato bass line is common enough in Bach's music, but he rarely asks the entire string section to play pizzicato except to illustrate some specific point in the text. In the bass recitative from Cantata 61, for example, pizzicato strings accompany the words from Revelation 3:20; 'Behold, I stand at the door and knock'. In other contexts pizzicato is used (sometimes with reiterated flute notes as well) to evoke the sound of funeral bells. A particularly beautiful example is the opening chorus of Cantata 8, *Liebster Gott, wenn werd ich sterben?* (Dearest Lord, when shall I die?); arias with similar bell-like effects are included in Cantatas 73 and 95. Perhaps the most elaborate passage of such tintinnabulation is the recitative 'Der Glocken bebendes Getön' (The tremulous ringing of the bells) in the *Trauer Ode* (BWV198), but no less striking is the entry of pizzicato strings at the words 'ach, ruft mich bald, ihr Sterbeglocken' (ah, call me soon, you funeral bells) in the aria 'Die Seele ruht' from Cantata 127 (Ex. 8.6a). What makes this passage so extraordinarily effective is that the upper strings are otherwise silent during the aria. Another telling piece of text illustration, this time involving the removal rather than the addition of string tone, occurs at the end of an accompanied recitative in Cantata 165. At 'wenn alle Kraft vergehet' (when all my strength departs) the sound of the upper

---

[12] Cantatas that can be grouped together in this way are Nos. 136 and 105 (July 1723); 10 and 89 (October 1723); 86, 37, and 44 (May 1724); 173 and 184 (May 1724); 116 and 62 (November–December 1724); 111 and 92 (January 1725); and 169 and 56 (October 1726). No distinction is made here between different varieties of oboe.

strings fades away, leaving only the bass, without continuo realization, to complete the cadence (Ex. 8.6b).

A special resource in the interpretation of the text—indeed, sometimes going beyond the bare meaning of the text—is the instrumental quotation of a chorale melody. This is a particular feature of the Weimar cantatas; for Leipzig revivals Bach often transferred the part to a voice with the appropriate chorale words. A dramatic example comes in the accompanied recitative in Part II of Cantata 70, which must, however, belong only to the Leipzig (1723) version, since Franck's Advent text, which Bach had set in 1716, contains no recitative. The interpolation presents a vision of the Last Judgement. At the phrase 'und der Posaunen Schall' (and the sound of the trumpet)[13] the trumpet enters with the chorale melody *Es ist gewisslich an der Zeit*, a kind of *Dies irae* popular during the Thirty Years' War. The effect is awe-inspiring, even to a modern audience for whom such associations do not exist; to Bach's congregation it must have been overwhelming.

Our knowledge and appreciation of the Bach cantatas have benefited enormously from the advantages of recording, especially in the format of long-playing and compact discs, and a number of complete cycles

**Ex. 8.6**

[13] Literally 'trombone'; the word 'Posaune' in this context has led several German composers, including Mozart, to represent the sound of the last trump by a trombone.

(Ah, call me soon, you funeral bells, I do not fear dying)

(. . . and restores me when all my strength departs)

are now available to the record collector. If, despite this, the cantatas have remained among the least performed of Bach's major works in the concert hall and in radio broadcasts, the reasons are not far to seek. Their lengths, their sometimes unusual instrumentation, and the frequent strangeness to modern audiences of their sentiments and language all help to make them difficult works to fit into a concert programme. It is perhaps to our advantage that we need to seek them out more determinedly than we do, for example, the Magnificat, the B minor Mass, or the Orchestral Suites. Bach can have had few expectations that the cantatas would long outlive him, and not every one is a masterpiece.

But the best things in them are unsurpassed in any of his other works, and the thrill of discovery can make them more highly prized than if their treasures were constantly paraded before us.

## Motets and Magnificat

In the Lutheran liturgy the motet was far less important than the cantata. Latin motets were sung at Vespers on Sunday afternoons and at the beginning of the main morning service, the *Hauptgottesdienst*; they might also be sung during communion. The Leipzig repertory was culled from Erhard Bodenschatz's *Florilegium Portense*, an anthology compiled in 1603–21 of mostly eight-part pieces by German, Italian, and Flemish composers of the sixteenth and early seventeenth centuries. Since the music was relatively simple and only a small proportion of the 270 motets in the anthology were used, they were easily learnt and remembered. Certainly the small importance that Bach attached to the motet is reflected in his 1730 Memorandum to the Leipzig council, in which he divided his available singers into three groups: those capable of taking part in figural music (i.e. cantatas), the motet singers, and those able to do no more than lead a chorale. A cursory examination of Bach's own motets is enough to show that we are dealing here not with works intended for normal use in the Leipzig churches, but with motets written for special occasions and requiring the best available singers. There are seven of them altogether, including *Lobet den Herrn* (BWV230), the authenticity of which has been vigorously contested. They seem to have been written mainly for funerals or memorial services.

As a genre the motet is distinguished from the cantata textually by its exclusion of 'madrigalian' verse,[14] and musically by the absence of solo numbers (recitative, arias, duets etc.) and independent instrumental parts. (An exception is *O Jesu Christ, mein Lebens Licht* [BWV118], which uses wind instruments; it was printed in *BG* among the cantatas.) Four of the motets are for double chorus, following a central German tradition to which other members of the Bach family also contributed. *Der Geist hilft unser Schwachheit auf* (BWV226) was written for the funeral on 20 October 1729 of the Rektor of the Thomasschule, J. H. Ernesti.

[14] *Komm, Jesu, komm!* uses two strophes of a funeral hymn by Paul Thymich (1697).

*Komm, Jesu, komm!* (BWV229) and *Fürchte dich nicht* (BWV228) were also probably written for funeral or memorial services, but cannot definitely be associated with particular occasions. All three works demonstrate an amazing command of a difficult medium, not least in the masterly combination of chorale and fugue in *Fürchte dich nicht*. Another feature is the almost total absence of the kind of sombre expression one might expect in funeral music. Indeed, so confident and cheerful are they that the possibility of the fourth eight-part motet, *Singet dem Herrn* (BWV225), also being a funeral piece should not be ruled out. Many writers, however, have considered it to be a New Year work, and Konrad Ameln, who edited it for *NBA*, suggested it may have been written for the birthday of Friedrich August I on 12 May 1727. For whatever occasion Bach intended it, he made it one of the sunniest pieces of counterpoint ever written, even by him. It was this motet that so impressed Mozart when he heard it in Leipzig in 1789.

More solemn in expression, and again probably a funeral piece, is the five-part *Jesu, meine Freude* (BWV227), the best-known of all Bach's motets. The six strophes of Johann Franck's hymn are separated by verses from Romans 8, forming a kind of ritornello structure of particularly striking symmetry:

| | | | |
|---|---|---|---|
| 1. Chorale, strophe 1 | E minor | à4 (SATB) |
| 2. Romans 8:1 | E minor | à5 (SSATB) |
| 3. Chorale, strophe 2 | E minor | à5 (SSATB) |
| 4. Romans 8:2 | E minor | à3 (SSA) |
| 5. Chorale, strophe 3 | E minor | à5 (SSATB) |
| 6. Romans 8:9 | G major | à5 (SSATB) |
| 7. Chorale, strophe 4 | E minor | à4 (SATB) |
| 8. Romans 8:10 | C major | à3 (ATB) |
| 9. Chorale, strophe 5 | A minor | à4 (SSAT) |
| 10. Romans 8:11 | E minor | à5 (SSATB) |
| 11. Chorale, strophe 6 | E minor | à4 (SATB) |

The motet is framed by two identical plain harmonizations of the chorale melody, while the other odd-numbered movements treat the same melody more freely: Nos. 3 and 7 with richer textures, No. 9 as a chorale prelude, and No. 5 as a free and extended paraphrase. No. 6 forms a fugal centrepiece. Nos. 4 and 8 are for the three highest and the three lowest voices respectively, their symmetry enhanced by thematic cross-reference (Ex. 8.7). The relationship between Nos. 2 and 10 is even closer, No. 10 being a parody (in a sixteenth-century as much as an eighteenth-century sense) of No. 2. (On Bach's use of parody techniques, see pp. 178–9.)

**Ex. 8.7**

(Since the law of the Spirit that gives life . . . )

(But if Christ is in you . . . )

The Magnificat was sung at Vespers, usually to plainchant and in Luther's German version (*Meine Seele erhebet den Herrn*). At the principal feasts, however, it was customary to perform a more elaborate setting in Latin. The first version of Bach's Magnificat (BWV234a), composed for Christmas Day 1723, was written in E♭ (although whether or not it actually sounded in that key is another matter) and scored for five-part chorus and soloists with an orchestra of recorders, oboes, trumpets, drums, strings, and continuo. The text is divided into twelve short sections, making for a pleasing variety of concise solo and choral movements, and allowing Bach scope for musical illustration of particular

words and phrases. The sudden entry of the chorus at 'Omnes gener-
ationes' and the recapitulation of the opening music at 'Sicut erat in
principio' (As it was in the beginning) are two examples of this; they
both follow a long tradition in Baroque settings, as does the special
treatment of 'dispersit' and 'deposuit'. In its original version the Magnificat includes four items of particular relevance to Christmas: three
choruses ('Vom Himmel hoch', 'Freut euch und jubiliert', and 'Gloria
in excelsis Deo') and a duet for soprano and bass ('Virga Jesse floruit').
The last is incomplete, but the music is recoverable from the parody
version in Cantata 110 (1725).

In 1728–31 Bach revised the Magnificat, and it is this new version (BWV243) that is most often performed today. The Christmas
interpolations were omitted (making the work suitable for any festival),
flutes were substituted for the recorders, and the whole work was transposed down a semitone. The changes in pitch and instrumentation
made necessary numerous other alterations in detail as well. Modern
critical opinion tends to prefer the original 1723 version, but it is not
easy to see why. D major seems a much more suitable key for this
music, especially for the joyous, extrovert choruses; not only was it the
normal key for trumpet parts in Bach's time, it is also a brighter key
for the string instruments, whether modern or 'authentic'. Also, the
Christmas interpolations are by no means representative of Bach at his
best, and their inclusion impairs the unity and continuity of the piece
without adding anything of real value to it.

## Passions

The reciting of the Passion story during Holy Week goes back to pre-
Reformation times, when the Gospel accounts of Christ's crucifixion
were sung in Latin, at first to plainchant and later, from the fifteenth
century, to a mixture of plainchant and polyphony. By the mid-
sixteenth century this type of responsorial (or 'dramatic') Passion had
been introduced into Lutheran Germany, a particularly influential example being the *St John Passion* (1561) of Antonio Scandello, an Italian
composer working at Dresden. The tradition persisted well into the
seventeenth century in the Passions of Heinrich Schütz, but by then a
new type of 'oratorio Passion' had taken root which introduced instruments into the performance and broke up the Gospel narrative with

hymns and free verses of a reflective kind. An early and important example is the *St John Passion* (1641) of the Hamburg Kantor Thomas Selle. It was this type of Passion that found its consummation in the incomparable settings of J. S. Bach.

If the Obituary is correct on this point, Bach composed five Passions, but only two of them, the *St John* and the *St Matthew*, have survived complete. One of the other three was the *St Mark Passion* (BWV247), performed in 1731. Only the libretto exists, but the music was made up largely of parodies, and some of it can be reconstructed from Cantatas 54 and 198. As to the other two Passions, these have been the subject of endless speculation. It would be consistent with what we know of Bach's comprehensive approach to particular genres for him to have written a setting of Luke's version also, but the *St Luke Passion* (BWV246) included in *BG* is quite unlike the music he was writing in 1730 (when it was probably performed), or for that matter at any other time. It seems incredible now that Spitta (ii, 526) not only accepted it as a genuine work of the early Weimar years but even thought it superior in some ways to the *St John Passion*.

A search for the two missing Passions might begin with an examination of those performed at Leipzig under Bach's direction up to 1739:

| Date | Church | Composer | Work |
|------|--------|----------|------|
| 7 April 1724 | Nikolaikirche | Bach | St John Passion |
| 30 March 1725 | Thomaskirche | Bach | St John Passion (2nd version) |
| 19 April 1726 | Nikolaikirche | ?F. N. Brauns | St Mark Passion |
| 11 April 1727 | Thomaskirche | ?Bach | ?St Matthew Passion |
| 26 March 1728 | Nikolaikirche | ? | ? |
| 15 April 1729 | Thomaskirche | Bach | St Matthew Passion |
| 7 April 1730 | Nikolaikirche | ? | ?St Luke Passion |
| 23 March 1731 | Thomaskirche | Bach | St Mark Passion |
| 11 April 1732 | Nikolaikirche | ?Bach | ?St John Passion (3rd version) |
| 3 April 1733 | (No Passion; mourning period for Friedrich August I) | | |
| 23 April 1734 | Thomaskirche | ? | ? |
| 8 April 1735 | Nikolaikirche | ? | ? |
| 30 March 1736 | Thomaskirche | Bach | St Matthew Passion |

| 19 April 1737 | Nikolaikirche | ? | ? |
| 4 April 1738 | Thomaskirche | ? | ? |
| 27 March 1739 | (No Passion; projected performance cancelled) | | |

Bach certainly went on performing Passions after 1739, including on at least one occasion (possibly 23 March 1742) his own *St Matthew* and on 4 April 1749 his *St John*; the other performances are not documented. His interest in the annual Good Friday performance seems to have waned during the 1730s, and to judge from his other church music it seems extremely unlikely that any Bach Passion performed after 1731 would have been a new work. That leaves 1728 as the only available year for a new Passion at Leipzig, but we know that Bach was reluctant to perform his large-scale works in the Nikolaikirche (see p. 116). If there is a lost original Passion, therefore, it probably dates from the Weimar years; but it is also possible that the five mentioned in the Obituary included the spurious *St Luke Passion* and perhaps a single-choir version of the *St Matthew* which was among the music left by C. P. E. Bach. In either case, the possibility is remote that a work of the stature of Bach's surviving Passions has been lost.

Of the two original Passions that survive complete, the *St John* (BWV245) was heard in the Nikolaikirche in 1724 and repeated in the Thomaskirche the following year. For the 1725 performance Bach made a number of changes, inserting a bass aria with chorale, 'Himmel reisse, Welt erbebe', into the scene before the high priest, replacing two tenor arias with new ones, substituting an elaborate setting of *Christe, du Lamm Gottes* for the final chorale, and supplying a new opening chorus, 'O Mensch, bewein' dein' Sünde gross', which was later transferred (a semitone higher) to the end of Part I of the *St Matthew Passion*; this 'new' material possibly includes portions of a Passion composed at Weimar and perhaps performed in Gotha in 1717 (see p. 43). For the third version, which survives incomplete, Bach removed the items he had substituted in the second and made other changes as well; the final version, for Good Friday 1749, reverts to something close to the original one of 1724. The *St Matthew Passion* (BWV244), until recently thought to date from 1729, was in all probability sung in 1727; it was revived in 1736 (it was then that the chorus 'O Mensch, bewein' dein' Sünde gross' was transferred from the *St John* to replace the simple chorale that had previously ended Part I) and again in the 1740s with further minor revisions.

In both Passions the story of Christ's arrest, trial, crucifixion, and entombment is unfolded on four interlocking levels: the narrative (or dramatic), the lyrical, the devotional, and the monumental. To the first level belong the recitatives of the Evangelist, Jesus, and the minor characters (including Peter and Pilate) and the short crowd (*turba*) choruses—in other words, the setting of the Gospel text. Bach's main concern here is for a vivid portrayal of the dramatic events; incidents such as the disciples' questioning of Jesus, 'Herr, bin ich's?' (Lord, is it I?), or the great shout of 'Barrabas!' that greets Pilate's question, 'Whether of the twain will ye that I release unto you?' (both in the *St Matthew*) are made dramatically effective with the simplest means. Where there is a point to be argued Bach employs counterpoint for the *turba* choruses, rather stiffly at times in the *St John Passion*, but with a tight control of the dramatic tension in the *St Matthew* (for example, when the Jews call for Christ's crucifixion). A feature of many *turba* choruses, particularly in the *St John Passion*, is the line of semiquaver scales and arpeggios for the first violins (and usually flutes as well), increasing the sense of urgency in the music. No less alive to dramatic and expressive possibilities is Bach's setting of the solo recitatives, and passages such as Peter's denial in the *St John Passion* (No. 12c)[15] or the final despairing cry of Jesus on the Cross ('Eli, Eli, lama asabthani?') in the *St Matthew* (No. 61a) are as memorable as anything in the arias and the large choral movements. (The sense of abandonment in the second of these two passages is heightened by the removal of the 'halo' of string sound that has until then sanctified the words of Christ.) Bach, however, would not have understood the modern practice of using the most distinguished and highly paid soloists for the roles of Jesus and the Evangelist; his best singers would have sung the arias, and might actually have sung the recitatives as well, as Joshua Rifkin has argued (see note 10 on page 144).

The arias introduce the lyrical or contemplative element into the Passion, representing a highly personal, even pietistic response to the events of the Gospel story. Their structures parallel those of the cantata

[15] The numbering here and elsewhere is that of the *NBA*.

arias already described, but they tend on the whole to be shorter; in the more expansive *St Matthew Passion*, however, they are mostly preceded by an expressive accompanied recitative or arioso. The instrumentation naturally excludes trumpets, which would have been thought out of place in celebrating the Passion, but it is nevertheless remarkably varied; only two arias in the *St Matthew Passion*, and none at all in the *St John*, have the same instrumental accompaniment. The inclusion of obsolescent string instruments (lute, viola d'amore, bass viol) is a particular feature of the *St John*, possibly reflecting the Weimar origins of some of the music. The bass viol, which has an important solo in the alto aria 'Es ist vollbracht' ('It is finished'), was closely associated with Lutheran sentiments about the sweetness of death; Bach used it also in funeral cantatas (Nos. 106 and 198). The two arias with bass viol in the *St Matthew Passion* contrast the melodic style of the Germans (No. 35) with the chords and wide leaps characteristic of French viol writing (No. 57). They belong to different 'choruses' in the work, and were presumably written for different players.

On a communal, or devotional, level there are the chorales—well-known hymn tunes in new harmonizations which, even in the eighteenth century, were recognized as models of their kind. Whether or not the Leipzig congregations actually joined with the choir in singing the chorales is of secondary importance; through them they became involved directly and corporately in the Passion as a liturgical observance. The choice and placing of the chorales was to a considerable extent determined by tradition, and it is therefore not at all surprising that the first chorale in each of the extant Passions should be the same: *Herzliebster Jesu, was hast du verbrochen* (the first strophe in the *St Matthew*, the seventh in the *St John*). What is more surprising is that the two works have only one other chorale melody in common (Heinrich Isaac's *O Welt ich muss dich lassen*), and Bach seems to have gone out of his way to associate each setting with a particular chorale. Melchior Vulpius's *Jesu, Kreuz, Leiden und Pein* appears three times in the *St John* (four times in the 1725 recension) and Hans Leo Hassler's *Herzlich tut mich verlangen* five times in the *St Matthew*. (The latter is now popularly known as the 'Passion chorale', although it was not exclusively associated with Passiontide; Bach used it again in the *Christmas Oratorio*.) Both Passions also include troped chorales, in which the lines of a hymn are separated to alternate (and sometimes to combine) with passages of an aria or arioso (*St John*, Nos. 24 and 32; *St Matthew*, Nos. 19, 20, and 60). These are among the most skilfully composed numbers in the Passions, and obviously exist on two expressive levels, the subjective and the communal, simultaneously.

The monumental aspect of the two Passions is conveyed by the massive choruses that frame them. The opening chorus in each case sets the scale for the whole work. 'Herr, unser Herrscher', which opens the *St John*, is a vast da capo movement whose middle section, far from introducing contrast, develops the material of the first. Even more imposing in its proportions and overwhelming in its effect is the opening chorus of the *St Matthew Passion*, a chorale fantasia on a scale unprecedented in the history of Passion music. The melody of *O Lamm Gottes* (the German Agnus Dei), sung by a separate treble choir, shapes the movement, but the antiphonal setting of Picander's words seems to proceed quite freely, as if coming from different groups within a 'surging crowd moving onwards with hymns of lamentation' (Spitta, ii, 564). The contrast between the tonality of the chorale (G major) and that of the movement as a whole (E minor) may go unnoticed by the listener, but it contributes subtly to the tension that exists between the two literary and musical constituents. Both Passions end with the traditional chorus of burial and farewell, which in the *St John* is followed by a final chorale. In each case the key is C minor and the metre and tempo those of a sarabande; they also have in common descending arpeggios in the accompaniment, symbolizing (with a general but not strictly a biblical appropriateness) the burial of Christ (Ex. 8.8). The *St Matthew* chorus is a da capo movement, fully written out; the *St John* chorus has a da capo of the first section, but it is in fact a rondo (A—B1—A—B2—A). In addition to these two framing choruses, and in keeping with the scale of the work as a whole, the *St Matthew Passion* includes also a magnificent chorale fantasia on the hymn *O Mensch, bewein' dein' Sünde gross* which, as mentioned earlier, brings the first part of the work to a close. Bach had set this chorale most expressively in the *Orgel-Büchlein* (see p. 53); the treatment it receives in the Passion is completely different, but like the organ piece it was composed at Weimar and was originally in the key of E♭.

While unfolding on these four different levels, the Passions also bring

## Ex. 8.8

([The grave that is promised] and no more distress encloses, opens Heaven to me)

(We sit down in tears)

into conjunction two distinct timescales: that of the biblical events and that of the present (whether Bach's or our own). The action is historical, but the reactions are contemporary, and it is this interaction of past and present that lends the Passions their powerful irony and layers of reference. Two examples may be mentioned from the *St Matthew Passion*, which is in this respect the richer work. In No. 27*a* of the *St Matthew Passion* the second chorus responds to the lament of the soprano and alto soloists ('My Jesus now is taken') with cries of 'Leave him, hold, bind him not!' The interjections are abrupt, homophonic, and *turba*-like, but they are not uttered by the crowd or the disciples in the Gospel narrative; in a short while the same singers will be calling for Jesus to be crucified. In No. 63*b*, 'Truly this was the Son of God', the irony is reversed. This time what we have *is* a *turba* chorus, but it should represent only a centurion and 'they that were with him' at the foot of the Cross. Bach would normally have had it sung by only one section of his choir, as happens in most of the other *turba* choruses except when eight-part antiphonal writing is involved. By employing his entire forces for this four-part passage and setting the text somewhat in chorale style, Bach turns the centurion's words into a universal affirmation of faith, and at the same time bridges the 2,000 years separating Christ's time from ours.

Which of Bach's two great Passions is the greater is something that has often been debated. Spitta was critical of many things in the *St John*, particularly the libretto, with its adaptations from the popular Passion oratorio of Barthold Heinrich Brockes set by Keiser, Telemann, Handel, Mattheson, and others; and he was critical, too, of the many musical repetitions among the shorter choruses. Spitta's evaluation coloured those of many subsequent writers, but although the work has benefited from recent reappraisals and now receives perhaps as many performances as the *St Matthew Passion*, there are few who would dispute the superiority of the later setting. It is often described as more contemplative than the *St John*, where events succeed each other more swiftly, and where the impact of the drama is more immediate and more painful. This is true, and yet the dramatic incidents in the *St Matthew* are extraordinarily vivid, and it was this work that the distinguished theatre director Edward Gordon Craig intended to adapt for the stage. Hubert

Parry wrote of the *St Matthew Passion* as 'the richest and noblest example of devotional music in existence', but it is not given only to believers to be moved by it. Bach's supreme achievement is also a work of profound humanity, and one of the most monumental dramatic masterpieces before Wagner's *Ring*.

CHAPTER 9

# *Leipzig*

## (1730–41)

THE YEAR 1729–30 WAS A CRUCIAL ONE FOR BACH AT LEIPZIG, culminating, as we have seen, in an appeal for help to Georg Erdmann in Danzig. There had been protracted disputes with the civic and university authorities, disappointment at the level of resources available for church music, and low morale among staff and pupils at the Thomasschule. No doubt all this contributed to Bach's unrest and caused him to neglect some of the duties expected of a Kantor. But the fundamental cause of his discontent probably lay deeper than this. How far he thought of himself as essentially a church composer is difficult to say. It had certainly been an early ambition to achieve a 'well-regulated church music', and yet the number of years Bach actually devoted to composing church music amounts to less than a quarter of his creative life. As an orthodox Lutheran he well understood music's role as a handmaid to theology, but as a composer he must have felt a wider allegiance to his art. A 'well-regulated church music' was only one of the aims he set himself, and once that aim had been fulfilled he needed a new one to spur his creativity. At the age of forty-five he might well have felt that he had achieved all he had set out to do at Leipzig, or at least as much of it as the difficult circumstances permitted; but new possibilities must have seemed frustratingly limited.

Even before the letter to Erdmann, Bach had entered a new sphere of activity by accepting control in spring 1729 of the *collegium musicum* that Telemann had founded in 1702. This was one of two such societies in Leipzig at the time; the other had been founded in 1708 by J. F. Fasch and was directed during the years 1723–56 by J. G. Görner, music director at the university church and organist of the Thomaskirche. Since 1720 the 'Telemann' society had been directed by Georg Balthasar Schott, organist of the Neukirche. When Schott left Leipzig in 1729 to become Kantor at Gotha, control of the *collegium musicum* should, by tradition, have passed to his successor at the Neukirche, Carl Gotthelf Gerlach, but Gerlach apparently ceded the position to his former teacher, Bach. The society was supported by university students and some professional musicians, and no doubt there was also a degree of family involvement, at least on the part of Bach's elder sons. Meetings were held during the winter months on Friday evenings at Gottfried Zimmermann's coffee house in the Catherinenstrasse, and in summer on Wednesday afternoons at his garden just outside the city. In addition to these ordinary meetings, to which the public was admitted, the *collegium musicum* was often called upon to provide music for royal or academic occasions, and for these Bach composed several cantatas and similar works. A typical *al fresco* scoring is for four voices and a 'full' orchestra of three trumpets, timpani, woodwind, strings, and continuo. The standard form is one of nine to fifteen sections, two choral movements framing a succession of recitatives (often orchestrally accompanied) and arias (mostly da capo).

There is unfortunately no record of the music played at the *collegium*'s 'ordinary' concerts, but it was presumably for these that Bach arranged his many harpsichord concertos, and no doubt the orchestral suites and a good deal of the chamber music found a place in the programmes. Vocal music was included, too, and Zimmermann's establishment was probably the place where two of Bach's most amusing cantatas were first heard. *Der Streit zwischen Phoebus und Pan* (BWV201) probably dates from 1729. It is a satire on the new trends in music, based on Ovid's *Metamorphoses* (11, 153ff.). Phoebus and Pan compete in singing and Midas is given a pair of donkey's ears for mistaking Pan's shallow, modern-style aria for true art. The polemical intention is unmistakable, even if Spitta's identification of Midas with J. A. Scheibe, who later criticized Bach's music, is without any sure foundation. The *Coffee Cantata* (BWV211, *c.* 1734–5) presents a little drama in which Liesgen, addicted to coffee despite her father's disapproval, agrees to give up the brew if she can marry—but (in an addition to Picander's libretto, no doubt designed to appeal to Zimmermann and his clients) she adds that her husband must allow her to indulge her weakness. Both works unite popular and *galant* elements, and may be understood as a lighthearted but none the less fascinating comment on the stylistic crisis that Bach went through in the 1730s. They are the nearest he came to writing an opera, but despite the quality of the music (perhaps even because of it) they do not suggest that he would have found much success as an opera composer.

Except for a period of two years (1737–9), when Gerlach took over temporarily, Bach remained in charge of the *collegium musicum* at least until 1741 (the year that Zimmermann died) and possibly until 1744. During that time there were many changes at the Thomasschule. Johann Heinrich Ernesti, who had been Rektor (headmaster) since 1684, died on 16 October 1729. He was an old man—over 70 when Bach was appointed to the school—and a respected scholar, but for years he had been resistant to change and under him the school had been allowed to deteriorate. Standards of conduct, discipline, and instruction had declined, and the physical condition of the buildings left much to be desired. Dormitories were overcrowded and insanitary, with boys sometimes having to share a bed, and as many as three different classes at a time were held in one schoolroom—all this despite a fall of about fifty per cent in the number of foundationers (i.e. boarders) during Ernesti's rectorship. Bach had had no personal quarrel with Ernesti, and indeed seems to have been on good terms with him; the Rektor's wife and daughter had on separate occasions stood godmother to two of Bach's children, and for Ernesti's funeral on 20 October 1729 Bach wrote the motet *Der Geist hilft unser Schwachheit auf* (BWV226). Nevertheless, it must have pleased Bach when Johann Matthias Gesner was appointed to succeed Ernesti as Rektor on 8 June 1730. Gesner had known Bach at Weimar and shared his views on the importance of music in both the school curriculum and the church service. He was, moreover, a sincere admirer of Bach's musicianship, and in a famous footnote to his edition of Quintilian's *Institutio oratoria*, published at Göttingen in 1738, he left a lively and agreeable sketch of the composer as organist and conductor (in rehearsal, one presumes):

You would think but slightly, my dear Fabius [Quintilianus], of all these [the accomplishments of the citharists], if, returning from the underworld, you could see Bach (to mention him particularly, since he was not long ago my colleague at the Leipzig Thomas-Schule), either playing our clavier (*polychordum*), which is many citharas in one, with all the fingers of both hands, or running over the keys of the instrument of instruments (*organon organorum*), whose innumerable pipes are brought to life by bellows, with both hands and, at the utmost speed, with his feet, producing by himself the most various and at the same time mutually agreeable combinations of sounds in orderly procession. If you could see him, I say, doing what many of your citharists and six hundred of your tibia players together could not do, not only, like a citharist, singing with one voice and playing his own parts, but watching over everything and bringing back to the rhythm and the beat, out of thirty or even forty musicians (*symphoniaci*), the one with a nod, another by tapping with his foot, the third with a warning finger, giving the right note to one from the top of his voice, to another from the bottom, and to a third from the middle of it—all alone, in the midst of the greatest din made by all the participants, and, although he is executing the most difficult parts himself, noticing at once whenever and wherever a mistake occurs, holding everyone together, taking precautions everywhere, and repairing any unsteadiness, full of rhythm in every part of his body— this one man taking in all these harmonies with his keen ear and emitting with his voice alone the tone of all the voices. Favorer as I am of antiquity, the accomplishments of our Bach, and of any others who may be like him, appear to me to effect what not many Orpheuses, nor twenty Arions, could achieve.[1]

Gesner came too late to smother the flames of dispute between Bach and the council, which had obviously been smouldering for some time. But he soon set about instituting much-needed reforms at the Tho-masschule, beginning in April 1731 with the reconstruction and extension of the building itself (see Plate 12). The cramped conditions under which masters and boys had struggled until then were relieved by the addition of two stories, an extensive rebuilding which took a year to complete. During this time the occupants had to be rehoused, and Bach

[1] Original in Latin; translation from *NBR*, 328–9.

and his family lived temporarily with Dr Christoph Donndorf in the Hainstrasse. Later, on 23 June 1732, Donndorf acted as godfather to Bach's sixteenth child, Johann Christoph Friedrich, who was subsequently employed at the court of Bückeburg and died there in 1795. The rebuilt Thomasschule was ready for occupation by the end of April 1732 and officially reopened on 5 June, Bach supplying for the occasion a new cantata, *Froher Tag, verlangte Stunden*, to words by J. H. Winckler, another master at the school. The music is lost.

The new building, which remained virtually unaltered until it was demolished in 1903, also offered better accommodation for the Kantor's family, which continued to increase in size, even though several children did not survive infancy. Of the seven born between 1730 and 1742, two died within a few days and one after about eighteen months. The other four were Johann Christoph Friedrich, the 'Bückeburg Bach' already mentioned, Johann Christian (later to find fame as a composer in London), and two daughters: Johanna Carolina and Regina Susanna. Regina Susanna was Bach's twentieth and last child, and the only one to carry the family name into the nineteenth century; she died in 1809. Of the elder children, Carl Philipp Emanuel remained at Leipzig until 1734, when he went to the University of Frankfurt an der Oder, still as a law student; from 1738 he served as harpsichordist to Prince Frederick, later Frederick the Great, in Berlin. Wilhelm Friedemann, the eldest son, completed his university studies in 1733 and then succeeded Christian Pezold as organist at the Sophienkirche, Dresden. Of Bach's third surviving son, Johann Gottfried Bernhard, there will be occasion to say more later in this chapter.

Friedemann's Dresden appointment was helped by an enthusiastic recommendation from the vice-*Kapellmeister* there, Pantaleon Hebenstreit, but the reputation his father enjoyed in the Saxon capital undoubtedly played its part, too. Bach went out of his way during the early 1730s to establish closer ties with Dresden, both through his *collegium musicum* performances and through visits to the city, and quite possibly he hoped for some permanent post there. In September 1731 he gave organ recitals in the Sophienkirche and at court, and during the same visit he probably attended, along with Friedemann, the première of Hasse's first Dresden opera, *Cleofide*, on the 13th. His friendship with Hasse, one of the most universally admired composers of the time, probably dates from this visit or perhaps from the previous year. According to Forkel, Bach took Friedemann to the Dresden opera several times 'to hear the pretty songs'—a phrase which has too readily been taken to indicate a deprecatory attitude to opera on Bach's part.

On 1 February 1733 the Elector of Saxony, Friedrich August I (King August II of Poland), died, and there followed five months of official mourning. It was during this time that Friedemann secured his appointment at the Sophienkirche, and Bach, relieved of the obligation to prepare and direct cantatas and a Passion at Leipzig during the mourning period, used part of the time to compose the Kyrie and Gloria that form the B minor *Missa*. (The rest of what we now know as the B minor Mass was compiled during the last years of Bach's life.) He took the parts of the *Missa* with him to Dresden in July and presented them to the new elector, Friedrich August II (King August III), together with a petition, dated 27 July 1733, in which he expressed the hope that His Royal Highness would look with clemency on 'this insignificant example of the skill that I have acquired in *Musique*' and might take him under his 'most mighty protection'. With surprising candour Bach set out his reasons for seeking a court title:

I have had for some years and until now the *Directorium* of the music in the two main churches in Leipzig, but I have had to endure various unmerited affronts and at the same time a reduction in the *Accidentien* connected with the office, which situation could, however, cease altogether if Your Royal Highness were to grant me your favour and confer upon me a title in your *Hoff-Capelle*, and let a decree to this effect be sent to the appropriate place.

The petition failed, perhaps because the elector was unwilling to associate himself with the minor court of Saxe-Weissenfels, where Bach still held the title of *Kapellmeister von Haus aus*. We have no record that the *Missa* was ever sung, but it seems unlikely that Bach would have taken a set of parts to Dresden unless a performance had been planned. Possibly it was heard in the Sophienkirche, with Friedemann at the magnificent Silbermann organ.

Despite the disappointment of not receiving a title, Bach continued to flatter the Dresden court with new works, as is clearly shown by the following list of pieces performed by his *collegium musicum* during the twelve months or so following the Dresden petition:

3 August 1733: *Frohes Volk, vergnügte Sachsen* (BWVAnh. I 12), for the name day of the elector (a reworking of the cantata written for the reopening of the Thomasschule);

5 September 1733: *Hercules auf dem Scheidewege* (BWV213), for the eleventh birthday of the elector's son, Prince Friedrich Christian;

8 December 1733: *Tönet, ihr Pauken! Erschallet, Trompeten!* (BWV214), for the birthday of Electress Maria Josepha;

19 February 1734: *Blast Lärmen, ihr Feinde!* (BWV205a), to celebrate the coronation of the elector as King of Poland (possibly performed two days earlier);

3 August 1734: unknown work, for the name day of the elector;

5 October 1734: *Preise dein Glücke, gesegnetes Sachsen* (BWV215), for the anniversary of the elector's accession to the Polish throne.

The last of these was a particularly festive occasion, with the elector himself present. At 9 p.m. 600 students formed a torchlight procession to the market place in Leipzig, where Bach's *collegium* performed the 'Abend-Music', *Preise dein Glücke*. The composer received 50 thalers, out of which he had to pay the musicians. One of these was the leader of the town *Stadtpfeifer* and Bach's principal trumpeter, Gottfried Reiche, aged sixty-seven, for whom the occasion proved too much. The next day he collapsed in the street and died, it was said as a result of the torch smoke and his exertions in the performance the previous evening.

While Bach's attention was directed towards Dresden and the change of monarchy there, he was not blind to changes at the Thomasschule which were to affect him no less. After the rebuilding of the school, Gesner began to institute some mild reforms in its organization. He upheld the importance of music in the curriculum, reminding his colleagues that 'our ancestors intended the school to be a seminary of music whereby the singing in all our churches might be provided',[2] and he secured for Bach the restoration of the *Accidentien* that the council

[2] *Gesetze der Schule zu S. Thomae* (Leipzig, 1733), p. 22; quoted and translated in Terry, 162.

had withheld from their 'incorrigible' Kantor. Under his headship Bach seems to have enjoyed a period of truce in his relations with the council. But before the effects of his reforms could be properly felt Gesner resigned his rectorship to become a professor at the university of Göttingen, where he made a distinguished career as a scholar. He was succeeded at the Thomasschule by Johann August Ernesti (1707–81), who had been Conrektor since the death of Carl Friedrich Pezold in 1731.

The new Rektor seems not to have been related to the previous Ernesti; he represented not only a new generation but also a completely different philosophy. At the age of only twenty-seven he had already earned a brilliant academic reputation, and it soon became clear that his aim was to transform the Thomasschule into a progressive academy embodying Enlightenment principles. Under the influence of the rationalism emanating from Locke and Newton in England, Descartes and Voltaire in France, and Leibniz and Christian Wolff nearer home, Ernesti challenged the basic assumptions of the old curriculum, and in particular the place of music as a handmaid to theology. Indeed, he seems to have been altogether opposed to school music, and the subject was not even mentioned in the new regulations he drew up for the Thomasschule in 1773. According to J. F. Köhler's *Historia scholarum Lipsiensium* (1776), if Ernesti came upon a boy practising a musical instrument, he would rebuke him by saying, 'Do *you* want to become a beer-fiddler as well?'

Until the effects of Ernesti's new ideas began to be felt in the Thomasschule, Bach seems to have got on well with the young Rektor. He composed a cantata, *Thomana sass annoch betrübt* (BWV Anh. I 19), for his installation on 21 November 1734, and Ernesti stood godfather to Bach's last two sons, Johann August Abraham and Johann Christian, in 1733 and 1735. Given their totally opposed views on music, however, a clash between Rektor and Kantor was in the long run inevitable. When it came it took the form of a violent struggle over the right to appoint and dismiss the school prefects, but behind it lay a deeper conflict of interests and convictions.

The trouble began when Bach's head prefect, Gottfried Theodor Krause, exceeded his powers and punished too severely some choirboys who had misbehaved while he was in charge of them at a wedding. One of the boys complained to the Rektor, who seized the opportunity

to undermine Bach's authority by ordering a public caning for the prefect. Rather than suffer what was a harsh punishment for a young man
of twenty-two about to enter university, Krause absconded, whereupon
Ernesti, without consulting Bach, appointed Johann Gottlob (or Gottlieb) Krause in his place. This Krause (not related to the other) had
only his seniority in the school to commend him for the position, being
incompetent in music and (as Ernesti himself admitted) of poor character. Ernesti nevertheless not only insisted on promoting Krause but
also threatened severely any scholar who might take Krause's place on
Bach's instruction. In letters to the council dated 12 and 13 August 1736
Bach objected to Ernesti's action, pointing out that the prerogative of
choosing the prefects had always belonged to the Kantor. On two successive Sundays there were disruptions in the two main churches as
Bach forcibly removed Krause from the choir loft and replaced him
with a university student, probably his former pupil Johann Ludwig
Krebs. Both disputants wrote further to the council, each defending his
actions and accusing the other of falsely stating his case. The council,
by failing to act swiftly and effectively, exacerbated what was already a
deplorable situation. It was not until 6 February 1737 that the 'Noble
and Most Wise Council of the Town of Leipzigk' formulated a statement on the matter, and even then they delayed issuing it for a further
two months, presumably to avoid having to make a decision about J. G.
Krause, who was due to leave school at Easter. As might be expected,
blame was apportioned more or less equally: Ernesti was admonished
for the way he had dealt with the initial affair of G. T Krause and for
summarily dismissing the prefect nominated in his place, and Bach for
neglecting his duty by not attending weddings in person and for en-
trusting the duties of prefect to someone from outside the school (i.e.
the university student). There were clear regulations governing the appointment of prefects (the council pointed out), and these were to be
strictly observed in filling the vacancy of head prefect after Easter.

The matter did not rest there. On 28 June 1736 Duke Christian of
Weissenfels had died, thus removing the only obstacle to Bach's appointment to a Dresden title. Bach renewed his petition in September,
and the title of *Hofcompositeur* was duly conferred on him on 19 November in a decree transmitted to him by his patron Count von Keyserlingk, who was probably influential in securing the title for Bach.

Bach now began to use his royal protection in the dispute with Ernesti, and it was as 'Compositeur von Königlicher Maj. in Pohlen Hoff-Capelle' that he signed a letter of 12 February 1737 placing his complaints before the consistory. As the council's April ruling failed to satisfy him, despite its recognition of Ernesti's mistakes, Bach again petitioned the consistory in August, this time arguing (with more than a touch of casuistry) that the school regulations of 1723 governing (*inter alia*) the appointment of prefects had never been officially ratified, that they were in various respects unfavourable to the Kantor, and that the old regulations should stand. The consistory passed on the contents of Bach's letter to the council, who once again dragged their feet, deciding six weeks later to 'do nothing for the present'. Bach then took full advantage of his Dresden appointment and petitioned the elector himself, again claiming the illegality of the 1723 regulations and requesting both restitution of his right to choose the prefects without hindrance and an apology from Ernesti. But if he hoped that the elector would reprimand the Rektor and the council, he must have been disappointed. Friedrich August merely ordered the consistory to take what measures they saw fit; the consistory again asked the council to report, and the council, as far as we know, did nothing. There the matter seems to have rested, unless, as Spitta suggested, the elector intervened personally when he came to Leipzig for the Easter fair in 1738 and was greeted by Bach's *collegium musicum* with an 'Abendmusik', *Wilkommen! Ihr herrschenden Götter* (BWVAnh. I 13), performed in front of the merchant Apel's house in the marketplace.

The 'battle of the prefects' has been described many times in the Bach literature.[3] It has been retold here at some length not so much to illustrate Bach's tenacity in defending his own position and the place of music in the community as to show his readiness to invoke the oldest laws and traditions in opposing 'enlightened' reforms with which he was out of sympathy. (A similar response to criticism of his own music was soon to result in the marvellous creations of his last years.) In other ways the whole affair reflects badly on both Rektor and Kantor. Bach had obviously been negligent in his observance of school regulations as they affected attendance at weddings and the appointment of prefects;

---

[3] Most of the documents relating to it are in *NBR* 172–96.

1   Portrait (not fully authenticated) of Bach, aged about thirty (c. 1715), attributed to
Johann Ernst Rentsch, the Elder.

2  View of Arnstadt, 1650. Engraving by Matthaeus Merian.

3  Bach's earliest surviving autograph (c. 1705): the organ chorale
*Wie schön leuchtet der Morgenstern* (BWV739).

4  The earliest printed music by Bach (1708): Cantata No. 71,
*Gott ist mein König* (opening of soprano part).

5  View of Mühlhausen, 1650. Engraving by Matthaeus Merian.

6    The Blasiuskirche, Mühlhausen. Engraved by J.F.G. Poppel, after Ludwig Rohbock.

7    The Wilhelmsburg castle at Weimar, showing the covered gallery. Based on
     old engraving in A. Doebber, *Das Schloss in Weimar*, 1911.

8   View of Halle, 1650. Engraving by Matthaeus Merian.

9   The ducal chapel (Himmelsburg) at Weimar, from a painting, c. 1660, by Christian Richter.

10 Prince Leopold von Anhalt-Cöthen, c. 1723. Painting by an unknown artist.

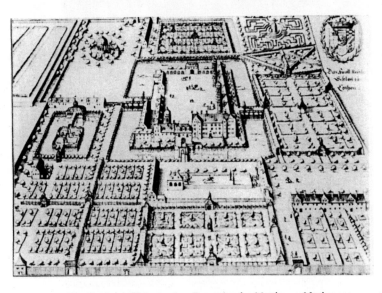

11 The Castle at Cöthen, 1650. Engraving by Matthaeus Merian.

12 Viola pomposa by Johann Christian Hoffmann, Leipzig, 1732.

13 The Thomaskirchof, Leipzig, with the rebuilt Thomasschule,
and, on the right, the Thomaskirche. Drawing by S. Hauptmann, 1868.

14 Johann Sebastian Bach, from a replica (1748)
by Elias Gottlob Haussmann of his 1746 portrait in oils.

15 The final page, in Bach's hand, of the unfinished fugue
from the Art of Fugue (BWV 1080).

Ernesti, for his part, had shown himself vindictive towards both Bach and the young people at his school. In addition, both men had under-mined the morale and discipline of the Thomasschule by airing their differences in public. The damage done was not easily mended.[4]

The Ernesti affair had no sooner died down than Bach was faced with trouble of a more personal nature. In June 1735 he had helped to secure for his son Johann Gottfried Bernhard the post of organist at the Marienkirche, Mühlhausen—the church where Eilmar had been pastor when Bach was organist at the Blasiuskirche in 1707–8. Gottfried Bern-hard seems not to have got on well with some of the Mühlhausen officals and, worse still, to have run into debt, so that in October–November 1736 his father inquired on his behalf about an organist's post at the Jakobikirche, Sangerhausen. In letters to the burgomaster, Johann Friedrich Klemm, Bach recalled his own appointment at San-gerhausen in 1702, and how Duke Johann Georg of Saxe-Weissenfels had intervened to secure the post for his own candidate (see p. 15–16) Divine Providence, he wrote, now made it possible for the Sangerhau-sen council to fulfil the promise they had made to him over thirty years ago by choosing his son as organist.[5] Gottfried Bernhard's application was successful, but Divine Providence soon withdrew its hand and by May 1738 the young man was in such serious financial difficulties that he had to flee the town and go into hiding, leaving behind debts and unpaid bills. Klemm wrote to Bach informing him of this, and Bach replied in terms that leave us in no doubt as to his distress:

> Your Honour will not take it amiss that absence has prevented my replying before now to your esteemed letter, but I returned from Dresden only two days ago. Your Honour, as a loving and caring parent yourself, can judge with what pain and sorrow I compose this reply. I have not set eyes on my unfortunately wayward son since last year, when I had the privilege of enjoying Your Honour's many kindnesses. You will recall that I not only paid his board then but also settled the Mühlhausen account (which prob-ably caused him to leave that town), and also left a few ducats behind to pay off some debts, thinking that he would now take up a different *genus*

[4] 'Since that time there has been little harmony between the Rektor and Kantor, although both posts have changed hands several times' (J. F. Köhler, *Notizen zur Schulgeschichte, c. 1776*).
[5] Bach actually wrote 'nearly thirty years ago'.

*vitae.* Now I learn, with the deepest dismay, that he has again contracted debts here and there, has not mended his ways in the slightest, but has absconded without giving me the least indication of where he is staying. What more can I say or do? Since no admonition, not even loving provision and *assistence*, will any longer suffice, I must bear my cross with patience and simply leave my undutiful son to God's mercy, not doubting that He will hear my sorrowful prayers and finally, according to His Holy Will, bring him to realize that conversion can come only from Divine Goodness. Since I have now opened my heart to Your Honour, I have every confidence that you will not impute to me the bad conduct of my son, but will recognize that a devoted father, whose children are dear to him, will do everything he can to help to promote their well-being. It was this that made me recommend my son, when you had the *vacance*, in the hope that the more civilized way of life at Sangerhausen and the eminent patrons there would in equal measure cause him to behave differently, on which account I once more offer my most dutiful thanks to Your Honour as author of his advancement. Nor do I doubt that Your Honour will try to persuade your Most Noble Council to postpone the threatened *mutation* until such time as his whereabouts can be ascertained (God being my omniscient witness that I have not seen him since last year), so that we may learn what he intends to do: to remain and alter his ways, or to seek his *fortun* somewhere else. I would not have your Most Noble Council inconvenienced, but I would request only such *patience* until he should turn up, or until it can be discovered where he is. Since also various *creditores* have been in touch with me, whose claims I cannot of course meet without my son's verbal or written admission of them (which is my legal entitlement), I beseech Your Honour to be so good as to make inquiries as to his whereabouts, and then you need only give me definite information so that a final effort may be made to see if, with God's help, his obduracy can be won over and he can be made to see his mistakes. Since he was fortunate enough to lodge with Your Honour until now, would you please let me know at the same time whether he took with him the little furniture he has, or what still remains of it. Awaiting an early reply, and wishing you a happier holiday than I shall have, I remain, with most humble respects to your wife, Your Honour's most devoted servant,

Leipzig, 24 May 1738                                          Joh. Seb. Bach

Gottfried Bernhard was in fact no further away than Jena, where he matriculated at the university on 28 January 1739 with the intention of studying law. But on 27 May that year an acute fever brought his plans, his short life, and his father's concern for him to an abrupt end.

When Gottfried Bernhard left Leipzig in 1735 there were four sons and daughters remaining in the Bach household, their ages ranging from three to twenty-six. The number was increased to five with the birth of Johann Christian in September, and to six two years later when Johanna Carolina was born. In October 1737 a nephew, Johann Elias from Schweinfurt, joined the family to assist Bach as secretary and to act as tutor to the younger children. Elias was born in 1705; his father was Bach's first cousin Johann Valentin Bach (1669–1720), a town musician at Schweinfurt. During the five years he spent at Leipzig Elias wrote many letters, and those that remain afford us most of the few glimpses we have of Bach's domestic life. Elias seems to have felt a special affection for Anna Magdalena, who was only three-and-a-half years his senior. In April 1738 he wrote to his mother in Schweinfurt, asking her to send some yellow carnations 'for our Frau Muhme, who is a great lover of gardening; I am sure it would make her very happy'. More carnations were ordered for her in August 1740, and in the same year he wrote to Johann Georg Hille, Kantor at the Georgikirche in Glaucha (near Halle), asking him if he would be prepared to sell a linnet whose singing, he said, would give Anna Magdalena particular pleasure. Elias's family evidently owned a vineyard in Schweinfurt, and more than once he requested gifts of wine for Bach. In August 1739 he wrote to Johann Wilhelm Koch, Kantor at Ronneburg, telling him of the 'extra fine' music they had enjoyed at home during a visit from Wilhelm Friedemann and his Dresden colleagues, the lutenists Silvius Leopold Weiss and Johann Kropfgans. It is from Elias, too, that we learn of Anna Magdalena's serious illness during July and August 1741, while Bach was visiting Carl Philipp Emanuel in Berlin. In a letter dated 9 August he even had to advise Bach to return immediately, as it was feared that Anna Magdalena might die; the following month she was still too weak to accept an invitation to visit Weissenfels.

Elias studied theology at the university while he was in Leipzig, and he left the city at the end of October 1742 to take up teaching at Zöschau, near Oschatz; the following year he returned to Schweinfurt as Kantor of the Johanniskirche. His letters from Leipzig give the impression of a busy, contented household. They say nothing about Bach's strained relations with Ernesti and the town council, nor about the distress caused by Gottfried Bernhard. They are silent, too, about another dispute that flared up during these eventful years—one which affected Bach deeply, since it involved his own music and therefore his deepest artistic convictions.

In May 1737 the theorist and composer Johann Adolf Scheibe published an anonymous criticism of Bach's music in the sixth issue of his periodical *Der critische Musikus*. Scheibe was the son of the organ builder Johann Scheibe (c. 1680–1748).[6] He had been a candidate for the post of organist at the Nikolaikirche in Leipzig in 1729, when Bach was one of the examiners, and it has been suggested that his criticism of Bach's music was motivated by his failure to secure the post. There is, however, no trace of vindictiveness in Scheibe's remarks, which reflect what many musicians of his generation must have felt about music that seemed out of touch with new trends.[7] He was expressing an Enlightenment view which prized simplicity, directness, and appealing melody as music's most desirable attributes. He acknowledged Bach's artistry as a performer and his technical mastery as a composer, but accused him of obscuring the beauty of his music with too much artifice, of writing for voices and instruments as though he were writing for his own clavier, of overlaying the melody with excessive written ornamentation, and of employing too much counterpoint. He ends thus: 'In short, he is to music what Herr [Daniel Cooper] von Lohenstein was to poetry. Turgidity has led them both away from the natural to the artificial and from the sublime to the obscure; one admires their onerous labour and exceptional care, which however count for nothing since they conflict with Nature.'

Bach did not himself reply to Scheibe's strictures, but he allowed himself to be caught up in the controversy that followed and probably had a hand in the reply drawn up by J. A. Birnbaum, a lecturer in

---

[6] Bach tested at least three of Scheibe's instruments: at the Paulinerkirche, Leipzig, in 1717; at the Johanniskirche, Leipzig, in 1744; and at the church in Zschortau in 1746.

[7] For a reappraisal of Scheibe's criticisms see G. J. Buelow: 'In Defence of J. A. Scheibe against J. S. Bach', *Proceedings of the Royal Musical Association*, ci (1974–5), 85–100.

rhetoric at Leipzig University; this was printed anonymously as a pamphlet: *Impartial Comments on a Dubious Passage in the Sixth Issue of 'Der critische Musikus'*. Birnbaum took exception to the term 'Musikant' by which Scheibe referred to Bach, and countered his attack on the music point by point. The controversy was carried on in further articles and pamphlets, and Bach's cause was taken up by Lorenz Mizler, founder of the Society of the Musical Sciences that Bach was later to join. As is usual in such polemics, neither side succeeded in convincing the other and the argument gradually petered out, though it was briefly taken up again by Christoph Gottlieb Schröter (another member of Mizler's society) in 1746. But the effect on the music Bach was to write during the last decade of his life was profound.

# CHAPTER 10

# *Parodies and Publications*

A FTER HIS FIRST FIVE OR SIX PRODIGIOUSLY CREATIVE YEARS at Leipzig, Bach seems virtually to have abdicated from composing music for the Lutheran church, and very nearly from composition altogether. Only ten of the extant cantatas after 1729 might be wholly original: Nos. 9, 14, 29, 51, 97, 100, 112, 140, 177, and 192. Possibly the latest of these is *Wär Gott nicht mit uns diese Zeit* (BWV14), for the fourth Sunday after Epiphany (30 January) 1735; this filled a gap in the second *Jahrgang* of chorale cantatas, there having been no fourth Sunday after Epiphany in 1725. Two wedding cantatas, Nos. 195 (*c.* 1742) and 197 (*c.* 1736–7), are at least partly revisions of earlier pieces. The *St Mark Passion* (1731) similarly used music from the *Trauer Ode* (BWV 198, 1727) and Cantata 54 (1714).

It would be wrong to suggest that Bach suddenly stopped writing church music simply because of his disputes with the Leipzig authorities, or because the vocal and instrumental forces at his disposal were inadequate. His disagreements had been with the university and the town council, not with the consistory, and they did not prevent his composing a new (or largely new) cantata (BWV 29) for the service to mark the council election on 27 August 1731. Still less is there any evidence to suggest that Bach's creative fire had burned itself out, as Rossini's and Sibelius's did, for example, at a similar stage in their lives. On the contrary, what is generally regarded as a *sine qua non* of musical inspiration—a gift for creating original and memorable melody—was never stronger than at this period of Bach's life. Works such as the cantata *Wachet auf, ruft uns die Stimme* (BWV140, 1731) and the Sinfonia ('Pastoral Symphony') in Part II of the *Christmas Oratorio* (1734) provide ample evidence of this.

One reason why Bach gave up writing cantatas and Passions for Leipzig after 1729 has already been suggested in the completion of his 'five-year plan' for a 'well-regulated church music' and the need to find new spheres of activity. Hence the involvement with the student *collegium musicum*, the letter to Erdmann, and the overtures to Dresden. But we are entitled to ask why his *collegium musicum* activities and his appointment as *Hofcompositeur* produced so little new music. Whatever the reasons (and it is, perhaps, the psychologist rather than the musicologist who will provide them), the fact remains that during these middle Leipzig years Bach's wholly original works amount to less than a dozen church cantatas, some keyboard music and a few serenata-type pieces, mainly in homage to the Dresden court. Even allowing for lost works, the quantity is not impressive; set beside the productivity of the years 1723–9 it is trifling.

Bach's main concern in the period after 1729 seems to have been to bring his music to some kind of final form. While he had never actually composed for posterity—the immediate commission, next Sunday's service, or an approaching church festival had provided sufficient reason to finish a piece—he now appears to have felt a desire to order and establish those works which he thought might survive him. Before 1726 only one or two cantatas had achieved publication, and even then not on his own initiative (see p. 33). In that year, however, he embarked on the systematic publication, at his own expense, of a series of keyboard pieces under the general title of *Clavier-Übung* (keyboard practice). He also revised and put into order a good deal of older music which did not find its way into print during his lifetime, but which may have been intended for eventual publication. Another manifestation of Bach's new awareness of posterity is his compilation, in 1735, of the *Ursprung der musikalisch-Bachischen Familie*, a genealogy of the musical members of the Bach family during the preceding two centuries. Brought up to date in 1774–5 by Carl Philipp Emanuel, this remains an important primary source of information on the Bach family history. Bach also looked after, made use of, and added to the *Alt-Bachisches*

*Archiv*, a manuscript collection of music by members of the Bach family probably compiled by his cousin Johann Ernst Bach at Eisenach.[1] Even the parodies of the 1730s may have been done with an eye to posterity, as an attempt to give permanence (in the form of oratorios and Masses) to music which he might not otherwise have expected to outlive its immediate purpose.

## Oratorios and Masses

When applied to Renaissance music the misleading but well-established term 'parody' is used for works (usually Masses) that incorporate material—not just melodic lines, but whole sections of polyphony—from earlier works (usually motets or madrigals). Palestrina's parody Mass *Assumpta es Maria*, for example, is based on his own motet of that title, and in a similar way the tenth section of Bach's motet *Jesu, meine Freude* might be said to 'parody' the work's second section. But when applied to the vocal music of Bach and his contemporaries the term normally refers to the creation of a new work from existing music in one or other of two ways. The first is largely through the use of contrafactum—the straightforward substitution of a new text for the one originally set to music. In this type of parody the responsibility lies principally with the poet, who must ensure that the rhymes, accentuation, and meaning of the new verses so fit the music that a minimum of recomposition, and preferably none at all, is necessary. The second (and less common) type involves the fitting of old music to an already existing text for which it was not specifically intended. This tests the skill of the composer, firstly in choosing suitable music for the text, and secondly in adapting it to the words so that it will appear, as far as possible, as though music and text had always existed together. In this type of parody some degree of recomposition is normally called for. Bach employed both types, but especially the first.[2] The *St Mark Passion*

---

[1] The collection, consisting of twenty vocal works when it was in the possession of C. P. E. Bach, was later acquired by the Berlin Singakademie; it disappeared during the turmoil of World War II but was rediscovered in 1999 at the Staatsarchiv in Kiev. The majority of the pieces are in the hand of the Arnstadt Kantor Ernst Dietrich Heindorf (1651–1724).

[2] For a complete list of Bach's parodies see W. Neumann, 'Über Ausmass und Wesen des Bachschen Parodierfahrens', *Bach-Jahrbuch*, li (1965), 63–85.

of 1731 is one of numerous examples. Its new text was fashioned by the Leipzig poet Picander, to whom Bach frequently turned both for parodies of this kind and for original texts. Picander may also have written parodies for the three oratorios. To the second type belong the four short Masses, as well as considerable portions of the B minor Mass.

Bach used parody techniques for a number of different reasons. Sometimes it was in order to save time when working under abnormal pressure. During his first year at Leipzig, for example, there was an enormous quantity of new music to be written, and some of the cantatas in the first cycle (e.g. Nos. 134, 173, and 184) use music originally composed for secular cantatas at Cöthen. Again, an important funeral might call for a substantial work, but allow very little time to compose and rehearse it; Bach was able to provide such a piece for Prince Leopold's funeral at Cöthen in 1729 by getting Picander to write new texts to music from the *St Matthew Passion* and the *Trauer Ode*. As already mentioned, parody techniques could give greater permanence to an occasional composition, and for this reason the ephemeral homage and birthday cantatas for the nobility were frequently fitted out with fresh texts. Another reason for using parody may have been to 'sanctify' music by substituting a sacred text for a profane one. It is worth remarking that Bach's works afford no example of a sacred text replaced by a secular one, and in this they follow the oldest traditions of contrafactum.

Bach's three oratorios have little in common with the Italianate genre then being cultivated in Germany, for example by Hasse and Zelenka in Dresden and by Keiser and Mattheson in Hamburg. When he used the term 'Oratorium' for what we now know as the *Christmas, Ascension,* and *Easter Oratorios* Bach was adopting Neumeister's idiosyncratic usage in lectures he gave at Leipzig University in 1695.[3] Neumeister defined oratorio as a literary genre mixing biblical verses, aria texts, and chorales, and he illustrated it with two of his own cantata texts. The *Ascension* and *Christmas Oratorios* of Bach recall the Passions in their use

---

[3] Published by C. F. Hunold in *Die allerneueste Art, zur reinen und galanten Poesie zu gelangen* (Hamburg, 1707).

of Gospel narrative declaimed in recitative by a tenor, but otherwise they are hardly distinguishable from extended sacred cantatas (the *Christmas Oratorio* consisting of six separate but related cantatas). Both works use old material, and one item in the *Ascension Oratorio* (BWV11), the aria 'Ach, bleibe doch, mein liebstes Leben', was later adapted as the Agnus Dei in the B minor Mass. The *Easter Oratorio* (BWV249) has rather more in common with the Italian genre: there are no biblical quotations, no narrator, and no chorales. The story of the discovery of the empty sepulchre on Easter morning is told by Mary the mother of James, Mary Magdalene, and the apostles Peter and John in a sequence of recitative and da capo arias framed by choruses and preceded by a two-movement sinfonia (the initial vocal movement completing a three-movement concerto design). The structure resembles that of a secular homage cantata, and it is not surprising to find that the music was originally composed as an entertainment (*Tafelmusik*) for the birthday of Duke Christian of Weissenfels on 23 February 1725. It was performed as a church cantata the following Easter and as an 'oratorio' probably ten years later. Although less well known than the other two oratorios, it is worth performing for the beguiling 'sleep' aria, 'Sanfte soll mein Todeskummer', for tenor accompanied by recorders and muted strings.

The better-known *Christmas Oratorio* (BWV248) was also compiled mainly from secular cantatas, written this time in homage to the Dresden royal family between September 1733 and October 1734 (BWV213–15); Part VI is mostly from a lost church cantata. New recitatives, *turba* choruses, and chorales were added to the borrowed material, making altogether sixty-four sections unequally divided between the six constituent cantatas. Nothing better illustrates the distrust of parody as a compositional technique than the ambivalent attitude that Bach scholars have adopted towards this work. Spitta (ii, 576–7) argued that Bach's secular works were not really secular in their musical style, and that 'the composer only restored them to their native home when he applied them to church use'; Terry refused to believe that the secular versions came first; and more recently it has been suggested that while Bach did set the secular texts first, it was with the music's eventual place in the *Christmas Oratorio* already in his mind.[4] There is no evidence to support any of these views, which arise from a nineteenth-century confusion of religious aspiration with artistic merit and a modern tendency to disparage arrangements of any kind.

The six parts of the *Christmas Oratorio* were performed at Leipzig in 1734–5 on the first three days of Christmas (25, 26, and 27 December), the Feast of the Circumcision (1 January), the Sunday after New Year (2 January), and the Feast of the Epiphany (6 January). Parts I, II, IV, and VI were heard, as was customary, in both the main churches, but Leipzigers wishing to hear all six parts would have had to attend the Nikolaikirche for Parts III and V. While each cantata is complete in itself and appropriate to its particular day, there can be no doubt that Bach envisaged the cycle as a single, unified work. He had the texts printed together, with a title-page embracing them all, and the cycle has an overall tonal structure carefully built around D major (D—G—D—F—A—D). Moreover, the first chorale melody of the opening cantata is the same as the one that concludes the cycle, but so differently treated that the whole oratorio may be understood as expressing joy in the momentous event that transformed a prayer for Jesus's guidance into a hymn of victory and praise. The melody is Hans Leo Hassler's *Herzlich tut mich verlangen*, well-known today as the 'Passion' chorale, but not used exclusively at Passiontide in the eighteenth century. More closely associated with Christmastide is the chorale *Vom Himmel hoch*, which appears three times in the cantatas for the first two days of Christmas.

The *Christmas Oratorio* may be said to vindicate the use of parody as a compositional process, but it does not place Bach's methods entirely beyond criticism. It is difficult, for instance, to understand why he retained so literally the unison phrases of the opening chorus, which were clearly designed to imitate the drums and trumpets referred to in the text of *Tönet, ihr Pauken! Erschallet, Trompeten!* (BWV214) (Ex. 10.1). Even the simple expedient of putting the first five notes of the sopranos into a higher octave (which was, in fact, done by a later owner of the autograph score) would have made the music better suited to the new text. Also, it must be said that the vocal echoes in the soprano aria

[4] A. Dürr, Preface to Urtext edition (based on *NBA*), published by the Johann-Sebastian-Bach-Institut, Göttingen, and the Bach-Archiv, Leipzig, ix–x.

# Am 1sten Heil. Weyhnacht-Feyertage,

## Frühe zu St. Nicolai und Nachmittage zu St. Thomæ.

Tutti.

Jauchzet! frohlocket! auf! preiset
die Tage,
Rühmet, was heute der Höchste gethan,
Lasset das Zagen, verbannet die Klage,
Stimmet voll Jauchzen und Frölichkeit an:
Dienet dem Höchsten mit herrlichen
Chören
Laßt uns den Nahmen des Höchsten
verehren.

**Da Capo.**

A 2                                    Evan-

6   First page of the printed libretto for Bach's *Christmas Oratorio* (1734)

Ex. 10.1

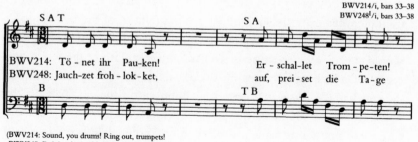

(BWV214: Sound, you drums! Ring out, trumpets!
BWV248: Rejoice, be joyful, rise up, praise the day)

'Flösst, mein Heiland, flösst dein Namen' (Part IV), which were so charmingly appropriate to Hercules's aria 'Treues Echo, dieser Orten' in BWV213, can sound incongruous, if not actually risible, in an oratorio performance. But most of the parodies work extremely well, including the beautiful 'Schlafe, mein Liebster' (Part II), originally sung to Hercules by Sensuality in BWV213, but entirely fitting as the shepherds' lullaby to the infant Christ.

The newly composed items are not less inspired, proving beyond doubt that Bach's use of parody is not to be equated with a decline in inspiration. The well-known Sinfonia ('Pastoral Symphony') that opens Part II is a good example of this. A quartet of oboes (two *d'amore* and two *da caccia*) introduces an appropriately rustic tone into an orchestral tutti of strings and flutes which already shows many of the pastoralisms associated with Christmas music (12/8 metre, lilting dotted rhythms, and parallel thirds). The tradition is familiar from Corelli, Alessandro Scarlatti, Handel, and others, but Bach surpasses all his models in the sheer quality of his invention and the originality of his orchestral textures. Even the conventional drone is presented in a new way: usually in the bass, it is here shared by all four oboes in turn.

While the *Christmas Oratorio* is now one of the most admired of Bach's sacred works, the four *Missae*, or 'short Masses' (BWV233–6), have often earned the disapproval of scholars for their extensive use of parody. Spitta found them generally inferior to the works on which they are based; Schweitzer (ii, 326) called the adaptations 'perfunctory and occasionally quite nonsensical'; and Terry described them as 'laboured and unsatisfactory arrangements of unsuitable material'.[5] It is, of course, true that the parody process in these works presented greater difficulties for the composer than the straightforward contrafacta of the *Christmas Oratorio*; but if the parodies were as unsuccessful as has been claimed, one would expect a wider consensus regarding the origins of the few movements of which earlier versions do not exist. In fact, it can hardly be denied that the *Missa* versions often improve on the originals, or that neglect of these works in the past has robbed choirs of the chance to sing some fine music which is easier to programme, and offers more to the choral singers, than most Bach cantatas. It is gratifying to find that the harsh judgments of Spitta, Schweitzer, and Terry have been largely reversed by more recent Bach scholars, and that the *Missae* are finding a securer place in the repertories of many choral societies.

A striking feature of the four *Missae* is their structural similarity, which points to a single period of composition and perhaps to a common purpose. They all have six sections: No. 1 is a choral Kyrie and Nos. 2–6 a Gloria in which three arias are framed by two choruses. The textual division of the Gloria depends largely on the material to be parodied, but the key relationships between sections are similar in each work (and identical in BWV233 and 236). Earlier versions of all but four of the twenty-four sections have been found, and these are shown in the following table, in which the key of the Mass section is followed in parentheses by the key and BWV number of the original version, where known:

| Section | BWV233 | BWV234 | BWV235 | BWV236 |
|---------|--------|--------|--------|--------|
| 1. Chorus | F (F, 233a) | A (?, ?) | g (g, 102/i) | G (G, 179/i) |
| 2. Chorus | F (?, ?) | A (A, 67/vi) | g (a, 72/i) | G (G, 79/i) |
| 3. Aria | C (?, ?) | f♯ (?, ?) | d (g, 187/iv) | D (D, 138/v) |
| 4. Aria | g (f, 102/iii) | b (a, 179/v) | B♭ (B♭, 187/iii) | a (b, 79/v)[6] |
| 5. Aria | d (g, 102/v) | D (D, 79/ii) | E♭ (E♭, 187/v) | e (e, 179/iii) |
| 6. Chorus | F (F, 40/i) | A (A, 136/i) | g (g, 187/i) | G (A, 17/i) |

It will be noticed that in only seven known cases did Bach have to transpose the original.

[5] C. S. Terry, *J. S. Bach: the Magnificat, Lutheran Masses and Motets* (London, 1929), 27.

[6] This movement is a duet.

Spitta, on the evidence of the cantus firmus intoned by the basses, assigned the original Kyrie of the F major *Missa* to the first Sunday in Advent at Leipzig, but it is now thought to have been written at Weimar.[7] As well as this bass cantus firmus, the music incorporates the Protestant hymn tune *Christe du Lamm Gottes*; this was originally sung by the sopranos but for the *Missa* Bach transferred it to oboes and horns. The movement remains one of the most remarkable in the four *Missae*. The fugue theme of the first Kyrie is inverted for the Christe eleison and then used in original and inverted forms together for the second Kyrie, at the same time combining with the two cantus firmi simultaneously. The other borrowings for which earlier versions are known are all from German church cantatas, and the four sections for which no original has yet been located are almost certainly parodies as well. The 6/8 dance rhythms and the ternary structure of the F major Gloria in excelsis (No. 2) point to a lost secular cantata; the Domine Deus of the same *Missa* (like the corresponding movement of the B minor Mass) is obviously a truncated da capo structure; the extraordinary music of the Christe eleison in the A major *Missa*—a kind of canonic recitative in five parts (the fifth part played by flutes)—was surely not conceived for this text, although it obviously belongs with the second Kyrie eleison, if not with the first; and in the Domine Deus (No. 4) of the same work a conventional da capo aria has been adapted to words that do not naturally suggest such a structure.

When and why Bach composed the four short Masses are questions that remain unanswered. A *terminus post quem* is provided by the cantata movements, which all date from 1723–6. Autograph scores exist for only two of the *Missae* (those in A major and G major) and the evidence they offer suggests a date of about 1738; it seems likely that the other two date from about the same time. Their chronology is, of course, tied up with Bach's reasons for writing them, about which various theories have been advanced. It has been argued that they were written for Leipzig, where the liturgy allowed opportunities for concerted performances of the Kyrie and Gloria; a Leipzig performance of the A major *Missa*, at least, is suggested by the existence of an organ part in G, the Leipzig organs being tuned to *Chorton*, a tone higher in pitch

[7] C. Wolff, *Der stile antico in der Musik Johann Sebastian Bachs*, 71.

than the Baroque woodwind instruments. Spitta, on the other hand, suggested that all four works except the F major, with its Lutheran cantus firmus, were intended for the Dresden court, and this has been widely accepted, Schweitzer (ii, 326) stating categorically that Bach sent them to Dresden 'as tokens of his assiduity'. There is no direct evidence for this, but it might well be true; Bach's name appears in the Dresden lists specifically as 'Kirchen-Compositeur'. A third hypothesis was proposed in 1936 by the German scholar Arnold Schering, who argued that Bach wrote the short Masses for his Bohemian patron, Count Sporck. Sporck had borrowed a set of parts of the Sanctus BWV232$^{III}$ and, Schering supposed, 'once convinced of Bach's ability and interest in writing mass movements, Sporck would have commissioned the four short masses . . . '.[8] Despite being based on faulty chronology (Schering thought the Sanctus was composed in 1733) and lacking any firm evidence to support it, this hypothesis has found general favour among modern Bach scholars; but it is only one possibility among several.

One reason why Schering rejected the Dresden court as recipient of the short Masses was that he considered Bach's ambition (*Ehrgeiz*) would not have allowed him to send parody Masses to such an exalted patron. (Schering's distrust of parody *per se* is everywhere evident.) This, however, ignores the fact that Bach had already plundered his German cantatas for sections of the B minor *Missa* (BWV232$^I$) that accompanied his petition for the title of *Hofcompositeur* in 1733. On a much grander scale, with five-part choral writing and an orchestra including trumpets and drums, these two Mass sections (Kyrie and Gloria) are divided into eleven movements, and Schering must have been aware that Gratias agimus and Qui tollis peccata mundi came from Cantatas 29 and 46, and perhaps that the majestic opening bars of the first Kyrie eleison were adapted from the *Traver Ode*. That several other movements are also parodies of works now lost is easily demonstrated.[9] The complete Mass in B minor was not compiled until the last years of Bach's life, probably in 1748–9. For parts of the Credo (or 'Symbolum Nicenum'

[8] A. Schering, 'Die Hohe Messe in h-moll', *Bach-Jahrbuch*, xxxiii (1936), 29–30.
[9] See K. Häfner: 'Über die Herkunft von zwei Satzen der h-moll-Messe', *Bach-Jahrbuch*, lxiii (1977), 55–74.

as Bach called it) he again drew on earlier compositions: 'Patrem om-
nipotentem' is recognizable in Cantata 171 (?1729), 'Crucifixus' in
Cantata 12 (1714), and 'Et expecto resurrectionem mortuorum' in
Cantata 120 (1729 or earlier). Again, internal evidence suggests that
other parts of the Credo are also parodies, and possibly the only original sections are 'Credo in unum Deum' and 'Confiteor unum baptisma', both of them five-part *stile antico* settings incorporating
plainchant. For the Sanctus Bach used the six-part setting he had written for Christmas 1724, and he completed the Mass with a final section
(Osanna, Benedictus, and Agnus Dei) made up entirely of parodies.
'Osanna in excelsis' is a reworking of music from the secular cantata
*Preise dein Glücke* (BWV 215, 1734, already a parody of a still earlier
piece); for Agnus Dei Bach added a new opening section to an aria
originally included in a wedding cantata of 1725 and re-used in the
*Ascension Oratorio* ten years later; and the final chorus of the Mass,
'Dona nobis pacem', is again a parody of a parody since it repeats the
music used for 'Gratias agimus' in the Gloria. Of the twenty-four sections that form the complete Mass, perhaps only half-a-dozen or so
were composed specially for it.

This must seem to us a curiously haphazard way of composing a
major work, especially one that is widely regarded as Bach's masterpiece,
and that the Swiss publisher Hans Georg Nägeli (who failed to secure
enough subscribers to publish the Mass in 1818) described as 'the
greatest musical work of art of all times and all peoples'. But no other
work more convincingly demonstrates that at the highest level Bach's
process of parody, adaptation, and compilation must be accepted as a
creative act almost on a par with what we normally think of as 'original
composition'. The success of the parody technique here results partly
from the fact that the text is more subdivided than in the short Masses,
and Bach is therefore able to match music and words more carefully. In
some cases there exists a direct parallel between the original text and
the new one, so that the music is equally suitable for each of them: the
chorus 'Wir danken dir, Gott' (We thank Thee, God) in Cantata 29
must have seemed an obvious choice for 'Gratias agimus tibi' (We give
thanks to Thee) in the Gloria. But even when the textual parallel is not
quite as close as this the music can sound just as appropriate. It is

Ex. 10.2

BWV232$^{II}$/v, bars 37–42

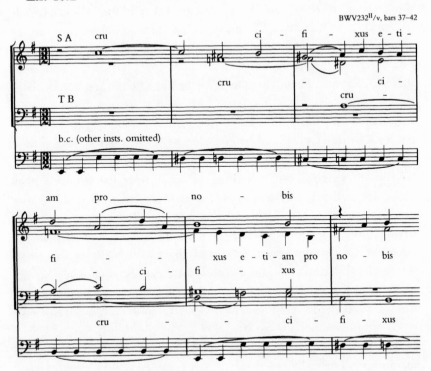

difficult to believe, for example, that the tortured chromatic vocal lines of 'Crucifixus' (Ex. 10.2) were not originally intended to suggest the nails tearing at Christ's flesh on the Cross, but were expressive of a more general feeling of pain in Cantata 12; and there has probably never been a more exultant hymn of praise to God than 'Osanna in excelsis', originally written to celebrate the accession of Augustus III as King of Poland.

The two great *stile antico* choruses that frame the Credo must certainly have been written specially for the Mass and are supreme examples of Bach's late contrapuntal style. They both use portions of the Gregorian plainchant Credo II (*Liber usualis*, 66; *Graduale Romanum*, 62★), but in the somewhat altered version found in Vopelius's *Gesangbuch* (1682), in which the fourth and fifth notes of the Credo intonation are reversed (Ex. 10.3)., Bach makes this the subject of a fugue in five

**Ex. 10.3**

parts, increased to seven by the participation of first and second violins. This is worked out in stretto over an independent crotchet bass and clinched by a single statement of the theme (bass voices) in majestic augmentation. 'Confiteor unum baptisma' is similar in style, but even more astonishing in its contrapuntal resource. The fugue proceeds this time in stretto from the beginning, and on two subjects (one for each clause in the text) heard separately, then together, and finally in combination with the plainchant cantus firmus. Again slightly altered from the Roman version, this appears first in canon at the fifth (basses and altos) and then in augmentation (tenors), resulting in such contrapuntal miracles as Ex. 10.4.

Bach's reason for completing the B minor Mass during the last years of his life has been the subject of much speculation. Among the more convincing arguments in favour of a particular occasion for the work is that put forward by the German scholar Wolfgang Osthoff, who suggested that it may have been intended for the consecration of the new Dresden Hofkirche in 1751.[10] As it turned out, that occasion was celebrated with a new Mass by Johann Adolf Hasse which, however, shows some interesting similarities to Bach's. One of these is the reversal of the fourth and fifth notes of the Credo intonation, which, as mentioned above, may be understood as a Lutheran feature but which is also found, as Osthoff points out, in Catholic Masses intended for special occasions. But it seems just as likely that Bach composed the work not with any idea of performance in mind, but as a kind of monument or summation of his life's work. He was certainly aware

[10] W. Osthoff, 'Das "Credo" der h-moll-Messe: italienische Vorbilder und Anregungen', in *Bach und die italienische Musik/Bach e la musica italiana*, ed. W. Osthoff and R. Wiesend (Venice, 1987), 109–40. For other views on Bach's intention in this regard see Butt, *Bach: Mass in B minor*, 20–4.

**Ex. 10.4**

BWV232<sup>II</sup>/viii, bars 92–101

of the long and distinguished tradition of the Mass Ordinary as a musical genre, and a wish to contribute an example of his own to that tradition is consistent with his embracing of other genres (oratorio and *dramma per musica*) for which his calling provided no real opportunities.

Whatever Bach's intentions were, the B minor Mass raises fundamental questions about the nature of religious music. Those for whom it represents a dedication to God of a whole world of human experience will not be unduly disconcerted by its mixture of the near-*galant* and the deliberately archaic, by its juxtaposition of learned fugue and racy concerto textures, by its mingling of prayer with song and dance, or by the fact that it was compiled from music written during a span of some thirty-five years, much of it for quite different words. The accumulated experience of innumerable performances during the last 150 years or so can leave us in no doubt about the power of this incomparable ecumenical omnium-gatherum to express the deepest aspirations 'of all times and all peoples'. And yet, those for whom stylistic integrity is a *sine qua non* of the highest art, and for whom the setting of 'Et in Spiritum sanctum' in the Credo might seem, more than anything in the short Masses, to merit Schweitzer's description as 'perfunctory and quite nonsensical', will continue to admire the B minor Mass for its parts while acknowledging that, as a unified religious and musical whole, it falls short of Bach's supreme achievement in church music, the *St Matthew Passion*.

## Harpsichord Concertos

The equivalent in instrumental music to the vocal parody is the arrangement, and Bach's reliance on parody in his church music in the years after 1729 is paralleled by a reliance on arrangements for the new music he needed for his *collegium musicum* during the same period. In fact, the process of arrangement in these works is not very different from parody, the aim in each case being to adapt the solo line(s) to the new conditions while preserving the material of the accompaniment with as few changes as possible. Of the fourteen concertos for one, two, three, or four harpsichords that date from the *collegium musicum* years at

Leipzig, only the C major concerto for two harpsichords (BWV1061) seems to have been an original keyboard work (perhaps without accompaniment in the first instance, since the strings contribute little). The others were composed originally for different solo instruments, mainly the violin. It is, of course, possible that other original concertos written at Leipzig have been lost, but it seems unlikely that there were many of these.

Five of the fourteen concertos are known to us both in their original versions and as keyboard arrangements. One of these is the concerto for four violins in B minor by Vivaldi (RV580), arranged by Bach for four harpsichords (BWV1065); the others are the A minor and E major violin concertos, the concerto for two violins in D minor and the fourth Brandenburg Concerto. In each case the music has been transposed down a tone, probably to compensate for the harpsichord's lack of the high *e'''* prominent in violin writing. As far as the other harpsichord concertos are concerned, the identity of the original solo instrument, and even of the original composer, remains a matter for scholarly conjecture, and possibly for this reason some of them are not heard today as often as they should be. The fine D minor concerto (BWV1052) could confidently be attributed to Bach even if its first two movements had not been used (with solo organ) in Cantata 146 (1726–8). The outer movements of the well-known F minor concerto (BWV1056) are thought to have originated in a lost oboe concerto, and Donald Tovey's suggestion that the lovely A major concerto (BWV1055) was originally scored by Bach for oboe d'amore has found general acceptance. (If this is in fact the case, it means that Bach must almost certainly have composed the work at Leipzig and not at Cöthen, since the oboe d'amore was a new instrument and almost unknown before about 1723.) The C minor concerto for two harpsichords (BWV1060) has in recent times achieved popularity in its putative original form for violin and oboe.

Although not originally for harpsichord, these works deserve more attention from keyboard players than they have so far received. They also occupy a position of major importance in the history of the keyboard concerto, and have an even stronger claim than the fifth Brandenburg Concerto to be considered the true originators of the genre.

Bach's eldest sons, Friedemann and Emanuel, took part in performances at Leipzig,[11] and they went on to cultivate the genre as composers in Dresden and Berlin. Johann Christian was, of course, too young
to assist his father at meetings of the *collegium musicum*, but he undoubtedly played and imitated his elder brother's concertos in Berlin
after 1750, and his own piano concertos, published in London, form
the most important link in the development of the genre between J. S.
Bach and Mozart.

### The *Clavier-Übung*

In Leipzig in 1689 Johann Kuhnau, Bach's predecessor as Thomaskantor, published his *Neue Clavier-Übung*, consisting of seven keyboard
suites in major keys. A second volume of seven suites in minor
keys, together with a sonata, followed three years later. When Bach
began issuing his first printed keyboard works he adopted Kuhnau's
general title of *Clavier-Übung* (Keyboard practice) for the series, as well
as his title of 'partita' (or 'Partie') for each of the six suites that make
up the first part. The first five partitas were published, at the average
of one a year, between 1726 and 1730, the complete set appearing as
Op.1 in 1731. However, at least two of them were composed before
this: early versions of No. 3 in A minor and No. 6 in E minor were
included as the opening items in the second *Clavierbüchlein* for Anna
Magdalena Bach, begun in 1725. It seems from an advertisement of 1
May 1730 that Bach originally intended the set to include seven partitas, like Kuhnau's, but he finally decided on six—the more usual
number for published sets of instrumental pieces. As in Kuhnau's partitas, the dances of the classical suite—allemande, courante, sarabande,
and gigue—are always present (except for the omission of the gigue
from No. 2), but Bach goes further than Kuhnau in the addition of
'andern Galanterien', as he calls them on his title-page. Every partita
has at least one, and they include such rarities as the A minor Burlesca,
with its daring parallel octaves and strange harmonies, and the C minor

[11] As also, probably, did their younger brother Gottfried Bernhard, who was an excellent
keyboard player by the time he left Leipzig for Mühlhausen in 1735. The solo harpsichord
concertos date from Bach's second period as director of the *collegium musicum* (1739 to 1741
or later), after his two eldest sons had left Leipzig.

Capriccio, a graveyard for all but the most nimble-fingered executants. A particular feature of the partitas is the variety of their preludial movements, each one having a different title: Praeludium, Sinfonia, Fantasia, Ouverture, Praeambulum, and Toccata. Clearly Bach's intention was to give each partita as distinct an individuality as possible.

Part II of the *Clavier-Übung* (1735) consists of two works which have in common the fact that they each transfer an orchestral genre to the two-manual harpsichord. In other respects they exhibit contrast rather than similarity. One is Italian in style, the other French; one is a concerto, the other a suite; one is in a major key (F) with one flat in its signature, the other in a minor key (B) with a signature of two sharps. In the tonal spectrum they are about as far removed from each other as they could possibly be. The *Italian Concerto* (BWV971) is a brilliant re-creation in keyboard terms of the three-movement Vivaldian solo concerto, one manual representing the soloist and the other (or both together) the tutti. The ritornello structure of the outer movements is so clearly articulated that it would be almost a matter of routine to arrange them orchestrally, while the highly embellished 'solo' line of the central Andante recalls many similar oboe or violin movements in the cantatas and concertos. The *Overture in the French Style* (BWV831) is similarly modelled on the orchestral suites, and like them it begins with an imposing French overture, the outer sections (measured and sonorous) enclosing a fast fugue on concerto lines, just as in the second orchestral suite (also in B minor). As in the orchestral suites, there is no allemande, and although the other dances of the classical suite are there the emphasis is on the *Galanterien*—gavotte, passepied, bourrée (all paired dances, to be played *alternativement*), and a final Echo, liberally supplied with dynamic markings to indicate the echoing of one manual by the other.

While the first part of the *Clavier-Übung* emphasized the singularity of each partita (even to the extent of separate publication) and the second played on dualities and contrasts, Part III (1739) is full of Trinitarian symbolism. Requiring this time two manuals and pedals (i.e. organ, though some of the pieces are to be played *manualiter*— without pedals), it opens with a prelude in E♭ major (BWV552), with a key signature of three flats, whose three quite distinct but thematically interrelated ideas are organized in a spacious rondo structure (A1—B—

A2—C—A3—B+C—A1). The five-part fugue to which this prelude 'belongs' (even though it is separated from it by the volume's other contents) is also in E♭ and again has three subjects.[12] Between these two magnificent pieces comes a sequence of chorale preludes (BWV669–89), the first nine (3 × 3) on the German versions of the Kyrie and Gloria (the Lutheran *Missa*: hence the inaccurate and misleading title of 'Organ Mass' often applied to *Clavier-Übung* III as a whole) and the next twelve on hymns associated with Luther's Catechism. The six catechism hymns, on the Ten Commandments, the Creed, the Lord's Prayer, baptism, penitence, and communion, are each given two settings, a large-scale one with pedals and a less ambitious one without; this is often (and probably correctly) taken to refer to Luther's Greater and Lesser Catechisms. In addition to the prelude and fugue and the chorale preludes (discussed briefly in Chapter 4; see pp. 56–7) there are four enigmatic duets (BWV802–5) for keyboard alone, making altogether twenty-seven (3 × 3 × 3) items. *Clavier-Übung* III went on sale at a price of 3 thalers.

That this collection possesses some esoteric structure beyond these Trinitarian symbols can hardly be doubted. The style of the music—at times verging on the *galant*, at other times most rigorous in its pursuit of the *stile antico*—seems to suggest it, as also does a sense of contrivance in some of the unusually austere chorale preludes and, still more, in the weird duets, with their angular, chromatic, and at times even bitonal lines (Ex. 10.5). The mere presence of the duets still requires explanation, and Bach scholars are not in agreement even about the instrument they were written for. Johann Elias's remark in a letter of 10 January 1739 that the collection was 'chiefly for organists' may be relevant to these pieces, whose style seems more suited to the harpsichord; on the other hand, they remain always within the range of the organ keyboard. Schweitzer (i, 289) was of the opinion that they somehow got into the printed volume by mistake; others have suggested that they were included as communion voluntaries, or simply to make up the total number of pieces to twenty-seven. A not very convincing attempt to relate them thematically to some of the chorale preludes was made by Klaus

---

[12] The fortuitous resemblance of the main subject to the beginning of the well-known hymn tune has earned it the nickname of 'St Anne' in English-speaking countries.

Ex. 10.5

BWV803, bars 53–64

Ericht,[13] and a possible chiastic symbolism was investigated by Gerhard Friedemann.[14] Rudolf Steglich related them to four elements,[15] David Humphreys to Luther's four teaching precepts.[16] Whatever the reason for their inclusion, the 'secret' of *Clavier-Übung* III probably lies behind a remark of Lorenz Mizler, who described the publication in the *Musikalische Bibliothek* (October 1740) as 'a powerful refutation of someone [Scheibe] who has ventured to criticize the composition of the Hof Compositeur'.[17] Certainly *Clavier-Übung* III in some respects anticipates

[13] 'Die zyklische Gestalt und die Aufführungsmöglich des III. Teiles der Klavierübung von Johann Sebastian Bach', *Bach-Jahrbuch*, xxxviii (1949–50), 40–56.

[14] *Bach zeichnet das Kreuz* (Pinneberg, 1963).

[15] *Johann Sebastian Bach* (Potsdam, 1935), 146–7.

[16] *The Esoteric Structure of Bach's Clavierübung* III (Cardiff, 1983), 7–18.

[17] It is possible, however, that some of the pieces in *Clavier-Übung* III were written prior to Scheibe's attack; see G. G. Butler, 'Leipziger Stecher in Bachs Originaldrucken', *Bach-Jahrbuch*, lxvi (1980), 9–26.

the music of Bach's last period, which can be seen as a defence of the fundamental principles of his art.

In view of the contents of *Clavier-Übung* I–III, it might have been expected that the next publication in the series would be motivated by the number 4. That this is not so may explain why Bach called it simply *Clavier-Übung*, adding the individual title *Aria with Divers Variations* (BWV988). The work is now commonly known as the Goldberg Variations because of Forkel's account that it was composed for Bach's insomniac patron Count Keyserlingk at Dresden, who wanted something 'soothing and cheerful' for his harpsichordist Johann Gottlieb Goldberg (1727–56) to play to him during his sleepless nights. According to Forkel, Bach was rewarded with a gold goblet filled with a hundred louis d'or. The story may be doubted, if not because of Goldberg's extreme youth, then at least because the original print contains no dedication; but it is quite possible that Bach did present a copy to Keyserlingk and was rewarded for it. Forkel's statement that Bach's own copy of the print contained some important manuscript corrections was verified in a quite spectacular way in 1974 (see pp. 212–4).

The Goldberg Variations were published by Balthasar Schmid of Nuremberg in 1741 or 1742, but the theme itself, a thirty-two-bar sarabande in binary form, may be earlier. It is found in the second *Clavierbüchlein* for Anna Magdalena (begun in 1725) and may not even be by Bach, although no conflicting attribution is known. As is usual in Baroque variation sets, it is not the theme itself but the harmonies supporting it that form the basis for the variations. Cadences in D major (bar 16), E minor (bar 24), and G major (bar 32) mark the tonal course of the theme, and these remain clearly articulated in all the variations except those in the tonic minor (Nos. 15, 21, and 25), where E♭ major replaces E minor at bar 24. There are thirty variations in all, arranged in groups of three so that every third one up to and including No. 27 is a canon, first at the unison, then at the second, the third, and so on. This makes altogether nine (3 × 3) canons, each one except the last having an independent bass part; Nos. 4 and 5 proceed by inversion.

There is nothing at all dry or 'academic' about these canons, but it is as much the amazing invention that Bach shows in the rest of the work that makes this the greatest of all variation sets between Byrd and

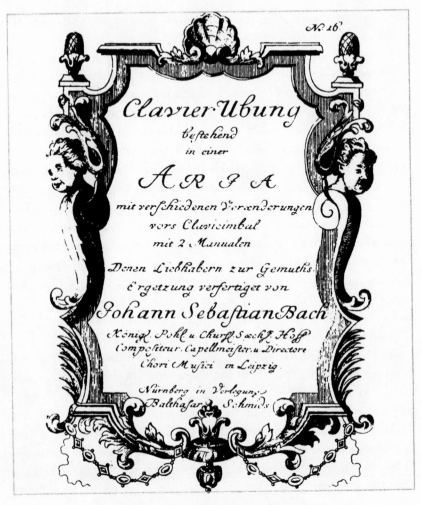

7  Title-page of the Goldberg Variations, original edition (1741–2)

Beethoven. The idea (if Forkel's story is to be believed) was obviously not to send Count Keyserlingk to sleep, but rather to give him and his brilliant young virtuoso something rewarding to occupy their hours awake. Some of the variations are song-like, some dance-like, and some pervaded by an exhilarating wit which can be fully appreciated only by

actually playing them on the two-manual harpsichord for which they
were intended. No. 10 is a fughetta, No. 16 a French overture (inau-
gurating the second half of the set). One of the most remarkable is No.
25 in G minor, where a proliferation of chromatic decoration almost
threatens its tonal stability. No less prophetic, but in a different way, are
variations 28 and 29 which, as Karl Geiringer pointed out,[18] appear to
presage a nineteenth-century style of keyboard writing. Instead of the
expected canon at the tenth for variation 30, Bach writes an ingenuous-
sounding but artfully constructed quodlibet—a mélange of popular
tunes and original material permeated by the first phrase of 'Kraut und
Rüben haben mich vertrieben' (Cabbage and turnips have driven me
away) (Ex. 10.6). 'Kraut and Rüben' is used also idiomatically to mean
'a confused jumble', so perhaps Bach is suggesting that this musical
mélange has driven away the sarabande theme, which he now recalls
in its original form to end the work (or, if wakefulness persists, to begin
it again).

**Ex. 10.6**

BWV988, var. 30, bars 9–12

[18] *Johann Sebastian Bach*, 298.

The Goldberg Variations brought to an end the series of *Clavier-Übung*, and with it the middle period of Bach's creative life at Leipzig. At the same time they ushered in the music of his last years, which was to be dominated by two features that so brilliantly characterize the variations: the systematic use of canon and the building of a large structure from a single theme.

# CHAPTER 11

# *Leipzig*

## (1742–50)

ON 17 MARCH 1739 THE DEPUTY FUNERAL CLERK AT LEIPZIG, aptly named Bienengräber, reported to the town council that he had approached Bach regarding the Passion to be given on Good Friday (27 March) and informed him that the performance could not go ahead without official permission. Bach's reply—that the work had already been done a couple of times, that he would inform the superintendent that it had been forbidden, and that performing the Passion was only a burden to him anyway—signalled another stage in his withdrawal from creative activity as Leipzig's *director musices*. Cantatas 34 and 191 (both of them adapted, and in part parodied, from earlier works) seem to be his only contributions to the regular church services during the last ten years of his life, and even revivals of older pieces are sparsely documented. With the publication in 1741–2 of the last part of the *Clavier-Übung* Bach entered on his final phase as a composer. During these last years he wrote not for the church nor for a princely court, nor even for the more intimate circle of a *collegium musicum*. In works such as the *Musical Offering*, the *Art of Fugue*, and the Canonic Variations he addressed himself at most to a small coterie of connoisseurs; but they are above all works in which Bach, the composer-philosopher, is alone with the impenetrable mysteries of his art.

During this time Bach continued to carry out his duties as Kantor (those, that is, that he was unable to delegate) and, as before, his expertise in organ building and design was frequently called upon. Two

Leipzig organs that came under his inspection during this time were those of the Johanniskirche in 1743 and the Thomaskirche in 1747. In 1746 he examined a new organ by Johann Scheibe at Zschortau and another by Zacharias Hildebrandt at the Wenzelskirche, Naumburg. On this last occasion he was joined by the famous organ builder Gottfried Silbermann, to whom Hildebrandt had been apprenticed in 1713–16. Other professional contacts with Hildebrandt and Silbermann confirm that Bach's practical interest in all aspects of instrument-making remained with him all his life. About 1739, according to a note by J. F. Agricola in Adlung's *Musica mechanica organoedi* (1768), he commissioned Hildebrandt to construct a lute-harpsichord (*Lautenclavicymbel*) to his own specification; it had two rows of gut strings and one of brass sounding an octave higher, and looked like a small harpsichord but could produce a tone exactly like that of a lute. Two such instruments were listed in the inventory of Bach's effects after his death. Silbermann's new-fangled pianos also excited his interest. He had been critical of them in the 1730s, but after their action and tone had been improved (perhaps in response to Bach's remarks) he became more enthusiastic, and seems even to have acted as an agent for them in Leipzig.

Bach continued until the end of his life to accept individual pupils. Some of them were foundationers at the Thomasschule, and others were university students; but several came to Leipzig on purpose to study with him. They included Johann Christian Kittel from Erfurt, the brilliant young harpsichordist Johann Gottlieb Goldberg, and his last pupil, Johann Gottfried Müthel. Another pupil, Johann Christoph Altnickol, entered closely into Bach's last years. While at Leipzig university he assisted the composer as bass singer, violinist, and cellist, and in 1748 Bach successfully petitioned the Naumburg council to secure for him the post of organist at the Wenzelskirche, where he had tested the new organ only two years earlier. Altnickol took up the post in September and four months later he married Bach's second surviving daughter, Elisabeth Juliana Friederica. According to Forkel, it was to Altnickol that Bach, in his blindness, dictated his final composition, the chorale prelude *Vor deinen Thron tret' ich* (BWV 668, actually a reworking of *Wenn wir in höchsten Nöthen sein* from the Weimar *Orgelbüchlein*).

In May 1747 there took place one of the most important and fully documented events in Bach's life. This was his visit to Potsdam, near

Berlin, where his son Carl Philipp Emanuel was harpsichordist to Frederick the Great. Bach had visited his son in Berlin in 1741, as we have seen; he now had further reasons to pay a second visit. In 1744 Emanuel had married Johanna Maria Dannemann (1724–95), the daughter of a wine merchant; their first son, Johann August, was born in December 1745, and at the time of Bach's visit a second child was expected (Anna Carolina Philippina, born September 1747). Hostilities between Prussia and Saxony had until then prevented Bach from making the acquaintance of his daughter-in-law and his first grandchild. A second reason for the Potsdam visit was to attend the soirées at which Frederick the Great delighted in playing the flute. Accounts vary as to the details of Bach's historic meeting with the Prussian monarch. The earliest, and perhaps the most reliable, is a report in a Berlin newspaper, the *Spenersche Zeitung* of 11 May 1747:

> From Potsdam comes the news that last Sunday [7 May] the famous *Kapellmeister* from Leipzig, Herr Bach, arrived with the intention of hearing and enjoying the excellent royal music there. In the evening, at about the time when the customary chamber music in the royal apartments begins, His Majesty was informed that *Kapellmeister* Bach had arrived in Potsdam, and that he was at that very moment in the king's antechamber awaiting His Majesty's permission to listen to the music. The king immediately ordered that he should be allowed to enter, and as he did so His Majesty went to the so-called forte and piano [pianoforte] and condescended, in person and without any preparation, to play to *Kapellmeister* Bach a theme on which to improvise a fugue. This the *Kapellmeister* did so successfully that not only was His Majesty moved to express his most gracious satisfaction with it, but all those present were astonished. Herr Bach found the theme he was given of such unusual beauty that he intends to work it out on paper as a regular fugue and have it engraved on copper. On Monday this famous man played on the organ of the Church of the Holy Ghost in Potsdam, earning general acclaim from the many who heard him. In the evening His Majesty once again commanded him to execute a fugue in six parts, which he did, with the same skill as on the previous occasion, to the king's satisfaction and the admiration of everyone.

Many years later Wilhelm Friedemann, who accompanied his father to Potsdam on this occasion, recalled the visit for Forkel's benefit. Some of the details in Friedemann's account conflict with the newspaper report just quoted, but it is worth quoting also for the new information it contains:

> At this time the King had every evening a private Concert, in which he himself generally performed some Concertos on the flute. One evening, just as he was getting his flute ready, and his musicians were assembled, an officer brought with him a list of the strangers who had arrived. With his flute in his hand he ran over the list, but immediately turned to the assembled musicians, and said with a kind of agitation, 'Gentlemen, old Bach is come.' The flute was now laid aside; and old Bach, who had alighted at his son's lodgings, was immediately summoned to the Palace. . . .
>
> The King gave up his Concert for this evening, and invited Bach, then already called the Old Bach, to try his fortepianos, made by Silbermann, which stood in several rooms of the palace. The musicians went with him from room to room, and Bach was invited everywhere to try and to play unpremeditated compositions. After he had gone on for some time, he asked the King to give him a subject for a Fugue, in order to execute it immediately without any preparation. The King admired the learned manner in which his subject was thus executed extempore; and, probably to see how far such art could be carried, expressed a wish to hear a Fugue with six Obligato Parts. But as it is not every subject that is fit for such full harmony, Bach chose one himself, and immediately executed it to the astonishment of all present in the same magnificent and learned manner as he had done that of the King. His Majesty desired also to hear his performance on the organ. The next day therefore Bach was taken to all the organs in Potsdam, as he had before been to Silbermann's fortepianos. After his return to Leipsig, he composed the subject, which he had received from the King, in three and six parts, added several artificial passages in strict canon to it, and had it engraved, under the title of 'Musicalisches Opfer' (Musical Offering), and dedicated it to the inventor.[1]

The *Musical Offering* was printed by Schübler of Zella and put on sale in time for the Michaelmas fair in Leipzig, which began in 1747 on 1 October. Bach had 100 copies printed; most of these he gave away to

[1] Forkel, 15–17.

friends, and the rest he sold at 1 thaler each, his two eldest sons acting as agents for the publication in Halle and Berlin. In addition, a presentation copy printed on special paper was sent to the monarch whose theme had inspired the composition. The edition was exhausted by October 1748, when Bach had to refuse his cousin Elias's request for a copy, saying that the work would be reprinted before the next New Year fair. Whether or not this was done, and if so how many copies were printed, we do not know.

In June 1747, a month after the Potsdam visit and while he was still working on the *Musical Offering*, Bach became a member of Mizler's Correspondierende Sozietät der Musicalischen Wissenschaften (Corresponding Society of the Musical Sciences). Lorenz Christoph Mizler had studied theology at Leipzig University during Gesner's period as Rektor of the Thomasschule (1731–4); he had at the same time studied music with Bach and probably played the violin and flute in Bach's *collegium musicum*. He was something of a polymath, one of his keenest interests being to find a firm mathematical and philosophical basis for musical science. His master's thesis at Leipzig in 1734 was *Quod musica ars sit pars eruditionis philosophicae* (On whether the art of music is part of philosophic wisdom), and in 1736 he began editing the *Musikalische Bibliothek*, which in 1738 became the official journal of his newly formed society. Among the society's select membership were the composers Telemann, Stölzel, Handel, and Graun, and several theorists with whose views Bach was in sympathy. One of these, Christoph Gottlieb Schröter, had sided with Bach in the controversy with Scheibe, his summary account of the affair appearing in Mizler's periodical in 1746. Possibly it was support of this kind (and perhaps also a personal entreaty from Mizler himself, who was in Leipzig in June–July 1747) that finally persuaded Bach, after much hesitation, to join the society; his portrait in oils by the Leipzig artist Elias Gottlob Haussmann may, however, have been done in anticipation of this.[2] It shows Bach holding the six-part canon (BWV1076) that was later printed and distributed to the

---

[2] Each member was required to present his portrait to the society. Haussmann's 1746 portrait of Bach now hangs in the Museum für Geschichte der Stadt Leipzig, but there is some doubt as to whether it was ever owned by the Mizler society. A second, almost identical portrait, painted by Haussmann in 1748, is in the William H. Scheide Library at Princeton.

members of the society. The Canonic Variations for organ on *Vom Himmel hoch* (BWV769) were also submitted to the society as an example of his musical learning.

The importance to Bach of Mizler's society, and of the ideas that motivated its members, has been generally underestimated. It is true that Carl Philipp Emanuel, replying to Forkel's inquiries, dismissed the reference to Bach's membership that Mizler added to the Obituary: 'the departed was, like me and all true musicians, no lover of dry mathematical stuff'. But one suspects that Emanuel was here expressing his own rather than his father's opinions; his views echo those of his Hamburg colleague, Johann Mattheson, whose opposition to 'mathematical stuff', and to canonic writing in particular, was vehemently expressed. Bach, on the other hand, wrote music after 1746 that was clearly in line with (if not actually influenced by) the ideas current in Mizler's circle, particularly that of music as 'a sounding mathematics'. In the Obituary Mizler mentioned only the presentation canon and the Canonic Variations as works written specifically for the society, but we know from a letter he wrote in September 1747 to Meinrad Spiess (another society member) that Bach intended to include the *Musical Offering* (or part of it) in one of the 'packets' sent regularly to members. Hans Gunter Hoke has argued that the *Art of Fugue* was planned as the last of the *Abhandlungen* (treatises) that Bach, in common with other members, was expected to provide annually up to the age of sixty-five.[3] Whether this is true or not, it is evident that Bach's commitment to the Mizler society was more wholehearted than has usually been thought. That he remained in close touch with at least some of its members is shown by his enlisting, as late as 1749, the help of C. G. Schröter to support his former pupil Johann Friedrich Doles, who was at the time in dispute with the Rektor of the gymnasium at Freiberg, J. G. Biedermann. The critical review of Biedermann's attack on school music, *Programma de vita musica*, that Bach solicited from Schröter led to misunderstandings that were not cleared up before Bach's death the following year.

As far as his own music was concerned, Bach's last years were spent

---

[3] *Zu Johann Sebastian Bachs 'Die Kunst der Fuge'* (Leipzig, 1974).

largely in putting into final form such works as the organ chorales BWV651–67 and the B minor Mass, and in preparing the *Art of Fugue* for publication—a project he did not live to complete. In 1749 his health may have started to decline, for he failed to attend the christening at Naumburg on 6 October of his daughter Elisabeth's first child.[4] Even before this, on 8 June, Gottlob Harrer had travelled from Dresden to perform a *Probe* for the Leipzig cantorate 'in case the Capellmeister and Cantor Herr Sebast: Bach should die', as a Leipzig chronicler reported. This does not necessarily mean, however, that Bach was perilously ill at the time. In 1703 Telemann had been invited in similar circumstances to accept the post of Thomaskantor, although Kuhnau lived for a further nineteen years. Nor should too much be made of the tactlessness of the Leipzig councillors on this occasion. While they were certainly not without blame, it was at the instigation of the powerful First Minister at Dresden, Count Heinrich von Brühl, that Harrer's examination took place. Brühl was Harrer's employer and protector, and, needless to add, it was Harrer who eventually succeeded Bach as Kantor.

Emanuel Bach, who was in Leipzig for a performance of his Magnificat during the months before his father's death, stated in the Obituary that Bach remained vigorous in mind and body up to the time of his eye operations. Certainly he was active enough to take a lively interest in the Biedermann controversy already mentioned, and in the appointment early in 1750 of his son Johann Christoph Friedrich as court musician to Count Wilhelm of Schaumburg-Lippe at Bückerburg. But after this his eyesight began to deteriorate rapidly, and towards the end of March he was treated for cataract by John Taylor, a peripatetic English oculist (or 'ophthalmiater', as he styled himself). There had been some history of blindness in the Bach family (although not among Johann Sebastian's immediate forebears), and according to the Obituary the composer had been born with rather weak eyesight which had worsened as a result of zealous study. The *Vossische Zeitung* for 1 April 1750 reported that Bach recovered his eyesight completely after Taylor operated, but a few days later a second operation was necessary,

---

[4] The child was christened Johann Sebastian after his absent godfather; he lived for less than three months.

and this, together with the prescribed post-operative treatment, resulted in a complete loss of vision.[5] In May Bach was still able to accept into his house his last pupil, J. G. Müthel, and one morning about the middle of July he found his sight suddenly restored. But, as the Obituary states,

> a few hours later he was seized by a stroke; this was followed by a burning fever after which, despite the best attentions of two of the most skilful doctors in Leipzig, on the evening of 28 July 1750 just after a quarter past eight, in the sixty-sixth year of his life, by the will of his Redeemer, he died quietly and peacefully.[6]

Three days later Bach was buried in the graveyard of the Johanniskirche, near the south wall of the church. The precise whereabouts of the grave was soon forgotten, and it was not until 1894 that his remains were exhumed and identified; in 1950, two centuries after his death, they were transferred to their present resting-place in the Thomaskirche. Bach left no will and his estate was therefore divided, according to law, between his widow Anna Magdalena, who received one third, and his nine surviving children, who shared the remainder. An inventory drawn up in the autumn shows that Bach left nineteen musical instruments, including five harpsichords (he had previously presented three other keyboard instruments to Johann Christian), two lute-harpsichords, three violins (one of them a Stainer, another a *violino piccolo*), three violas, a lute, and a spinet. There were also about eighty volumes of theological books, a mining share, cash in the form of gold, silver, and medals, some valuable silverware, household furnishings, and other effects, valued in all at 1,159 thalers 16 groschen. After payment of debts and expenses amounting to nearly 153 thalers, Anna Magdalena's share of the estate would have been valued at some 335 thalers, or about half of her late husband's annual earnings.

[5] The customary treatment after couching for cataract (Taylor's standard operation) was to bathe the eye with a mixture of Peruvian Balsam and warm water, and then to apply a cataplasm of the same with pulp of cassia. 'On the second morning the eye was fomented with "a spirituous Fomentation with Camphire", and the bandage was replaced by a shade. Light diet and gentle evacuations were continued for twenty days.' See R. R. James: *Studies in the History of Ophthalmology in England* (Cambridge, 1933), 175.

[6] According to Terry (264) the symptoms of Bach's last illness point to chronic interstitial nephritis, a form of Bright's disease.

The inventory includes no mention of Bach's manuscripts, or indeed of any music at all. Some cantata parts were made over to the Thomasschule by Anna Magdalena in return for permission to remain in residence at the school for six months after her husband's death (a right which was hers in any case). The bulk of the manuscripts were divided more or less equally between the two eldest sons. Our understanding of Bach's music would be very different today if they had all gone to Carl Philipp Emanuel, who took good care of his share. Wilhelm Friedemann, on the other hand, carelessly gave away or sold many precious manuscripts, and in 1774 the poverty to which a dissolute life had led him forced him to auction a large number of his father's autographs. Emanuel's patrimony, and most of what remained of Friedemann's, eventually found its way to the Königliche Bibliothek in Berlin; it was divided between East and West Berlin after World War II and is now reunited in the Staatsbibliothek zu Berlin—Preussischer Kulturbesitz. The performing parts of the chorale cantatas, donated by Anna Magdalena to the Thomasschule, have never left Leipzig, but isolated autographs are dispersed as widely as Brussels, London, New York, and Tokyo.

After Bach's death the younger male children were looked after by other members of the family, as was customary. Gottfried Heinrich went to live with his married sister and brother-in-law Altnickol in Naumburg, where he died in 1763. Altnickol himself died in 1759, after which Emanuel in Berlin made his widow a regular allowance. Emanuel also looked after and taught his younger half-brother Johann Christian until 1754, when the latter left for Italy, later to achieve fame as a composer and concert promoter in London. Neither Emanuel nor Friedemann seems to have felt any obligation to support his stepmother, left in Leipzig with her unmarried stepdaughter and two younger daughters. She survived her husband for ten years, existing mainly on charity and dying an impoverished almswoman on 27 February 1760.

# CHAPTER 12

# Canons and Counterpoints

IN 1742 BACH TOOK THE UNUSUAL STEP (FOR HIM) OF GOING
again over ground he had trod before, when he completed a second
set of twenty-four keyboard preludes and fugues in all the major and
minor keys (BWV870–93). The title *Well-tempered Clavier* does not this
time appear on Bach's autograph, but it is found in a revised version
copied under his supervision by his future son-in-law J. C. Altnickol
in 1744. Perhaps his main reason for compiling a second book was to
give definitive form to music he had composed many years earlier—a
concern that became increasingly important to him during the 1730s,
as we have seen. Several of the items it contains are known to date
from the Cöthen years; others were composed between 1738 and 1742
to complete the set. Bearing in mind Bach's own use of the '48' as a
teaching manual, another intention behind the new compilation may
have been to reflect some of the stylistic changes that had taken place
in music during the third and fourth decades of the eighteenth century,
and so to provide his young pupils with pieces that might appeal to
them more than those in the earlier volume.

An up-to-date style is, naturally, more apparent in the preludes than
in the fugues of Book II. Whereas only one prelude in Book I (No.
24) used the binary form |: A1 :| |: A2 :|, with each section repeated,
no fewer than ten in Book II employ this structure. Moreover, this is
the binary form not so much of the dance as of the incipient sonata
form, and at least three of the more extended preludes (Nos. 5, 18, and

21) contain in their second (A2) sections a strong element of tonic recapitulation. It is worth remarking, too, that No. 21 is the only prelude among the '48' that calls for hand-crossing in the manner of Domenico Scarlatti, a volume of whose sonatas had appeared in print a few years earlier. The fifth prelude also recalls Scarlatti to some extent, with its arpeggio 'trumpet-calls' at the opening, its frequently *galant* harmony, and its brilliant virtuoso writing.

Unlike those in Book I, all the fugues in Book II are in either three or four parts, but this does not mean that they are less varied in style and expression. No. 9, in E major (with its Fischer-inspired subject; see Ex. 6.11, p. 106) stands at one end of the stylistic spectrum, being the purest example in the '48' of the *stile antico*, while at the other end of the spectrum are the fugues in a modern idiom imbued with the spirit of the dance, such as the gigue-like No. 11 in F major. Among the masterpieces that occupy the middle ground between these two extremes is No. 14, a triple fugue in which first one and then another new theme is introduced on its own and then combined with the main theme. The final page, where all three themes appear in various permutations, is as a *tour de force* of contrapuntal mastery the more remarkable for conveying the impression (perhaps the reality) that it has been achieved with consummate ease.

While in one sense retrospective, the second book of the *Well-tempered Clavier* inaugurates a final period in Bach's output as a composer, a period dominated by the twin genres of fugue and canon. Canon—the derivation of polyphony from a single melodic line through imitation of itself at a fixed interval of pitch and duration—is the strictest of all contrapuntal procedures. We are accustomed to thinking today of canon as a musical piece or passage set out in two or more parts, but the term 'canon' originally referred to the 'rule' itself whereby the polyphony was arrived at from the single line. In this sense the canon *ad hypodiatesseron*, for example, would indicate the pitch interval (a fourth below) and some other term or sign the time interval at which the second part was to begin. A puzzle canon was one in which the canon (rule) itself was incomplete, or in code, or omitted altogether. Because a canon tested the ingenuity of the solver as well as that of the composer, it had become by Bach's time a favourite device for dedications and for greetings between friends. Doubtless there were many canons that Bach inserted into the albums of his students and acquaintances which are lost for ever. Of the half-dozen that remain, the earliest is a perpetual canon in four parts (BWV1073) written at Weimar in 1713 for an unknown recipient (see facing page).[1] Similar canonic tokens of friendship were written for L. F. Hudemann, a law student, in 1727 (BWV1074); for an unidentified godchild in 1734 (BWV1075);[2] for J. G. Fulde, a theology student at Leipzig, in 1747 (BWV1077); and (probably) for Benjamin Gottlob Faber, a medical student who stood proxy for Bach at the baptism of Johann Sebastian Altnickol in 1749 (BWV1078).

While such canons as these were never intended as more than marks of esteem in the form of intriguing musical puzzles, Bach made frequent use of canon in his other works, either in symbolic representation of a text or, more often, simply as a compositional technique (the chorale preludes of the *Orgelbüchlein* furnish examples of both). But with the Goldberg Variations of 1741–2 canon is elevated to a new level of importance in Bach's works, and it permeates his original compositions from then until his death. In the Canonic Variations for organ, the *Musical Offering*, and the *Art of Fugue*, canon at its most intricate achieves a new autonomy, serving not as an esoteric greeting or a dry scholastic exercise, but in the creation of some of the most visionary and profound music ever composed.

The importance of the Goldberg Variations in opening the door to this last phase in Bach's creative life is not confined to the fact that every third variation in that work is a canon. In 1974 an important discovery was made when the composer's *Handexemplar* (working copy) of the variations turned up in Strasbourg. In addition to showing corrections to the printed text in Bach's hand (as reported by Forkel in

---

[1] The notes are to be read in the four different clefs, beginning with the bass; successive entries, separated by a fifth in pitch and a minim in duration, are indicated by signs above the staff in bars 1 and 2. Solutions are in *BG*, xlv, 132–3; *NBA*, VIII/i, 6–7; and *The Bach Reader*, 400–1 (but not in *NBR*). The inscription in the lower right-hand corner reads: 'To enter this trifle as a kindly memento for the possessor of this book was the wish of Joh: Sebast. Bach . . . '.

[2] The dedicatee has sometimes been identified as J. M. Gesner, Rektor of the Thomasschule; but see H.-J. Schulze: 'Johann Sebastian Bachs Kanonwidmungen', *Bach-Jahrbuch*, liii (1967), 87–8.

8    Perpetual canon in four parts, BWV1073

1802), the volume was found to contain on the inside back cover fourteen further canons, also in Bach's hand, 'on the first eight notes of the
preceding aria ground' (BWV1087). One of these supplementary canons
(No. 11) was already familiar as that dedicated to Fulde in 1747; another was the *Canon triplex* printed for the Mizler society and shown in
the Haussmann portraits. In both these canons the 'Goldberg' bass is
clearly stated, but although this similarity between them had been noticed, a more direct connection with the Goldberg Variations had
never previously been suspected.

Bach must have added the fourteen canons to his copy of the variations at some time between 1742 (the probable date of publication)
and 1746 (when Haussmann included the thirteenth canon in his portrait of the composer). There is no reason to suppose that he ever
intended them for performance (although public performances have
been given and recordings made since 1974). The importance to us of
their recovery lies not in their purely musical value, in which they are
inferior to the variations themselves, but rather in the light they shed
on Bach's artistic and spiritual development. We can now understand
more fully the nature of Bach's later contrapuntal works, and the connection, through the *Canon triplex*, with the Mizler society is highly

significant. It has even been suggested that all fourteen canons may have been planned expressly for presentation to the society.[3] Certainly the 'science' they display would have made them appropriate for this purpose, and the idea of fourteen canons by the fourteenth member, whose named expressed in terms of the natural-order number alphabet (see p. 233) totalled fourteen, is something that might have appealed to both Bach and Mizler. But by the time he joined the society Bach apparently had other ideas and submitted instead the no less ingenious but more musically satisfying Canonic Variations for organ on Luther's hymn *Vom Himmel hoch, da komm' ich her* (BWV769).

There are certain resemblances in canonic idiom between the Goldberg canons and the Canonic Variations, and these are strengthened by the similarity of the first line of the hymn tune to the opening of the Goldberg bass. In the early *Partite diverse* (BWV766–8) Bach preceded his variations with a plain harmonization of the chorale melody. In *Vom Himmel hoch* he begins immediately with Variation 1, and this should warn us against making extravagant attempts to find correspondences between the variations and the chorale text. The descending-scale motif of Variation 1, however, obviously refers to its first line ('From highest heaven I come'); it is found also in an earlier arrangement of the same chorale (BWV738). Four of the variations treat the chorale melody as a cantus firmus (c.f.) in conjunction with two canonic parts (and in two cases a further free part); in the other variation it is the chorale melody itself that is treated canonically, at four different intervals. The order of the variations in the original print is as follows:

1. Canon at the octave, c.f. in pedals
2. Canon at the fifth, c.f. in pedals
3. Canon at the seventh in two lowest parts, c.f. in upper part, free middle part
4. Canon at the octave in augmentation, c.f. in pedals, free middle part
5. Sequence of four canons by inversion (a) at the sixth, (b) at the third, (c) at the second, (d) at the ninth; coda

The autograph (probably earlier than the print) places the variations in a different order: 1, 2, 5, 3, 4. Although this is 'perhaps more to

[3] N. Kenyon, 'A Newly Discovered Group of Canons by Bach', *Musical Times*, cxvii (1976), pp. 391–3.

a composer's taste than a performer's',[4] it is, paradoxically, the autograph rather than the print that has the appearance of a performing version, the canons being fully worked out on three staves. In Variations 1–3 of the printed edition only the first few notes of the second canonic voice are shown, so that only a performer of extraordinary intellectual skill (perhaps only Bach himself) could hope to play them directly from the page. Both *BG* and *NBA* follow the order of the original print (with, of course, the canons fully written out), and this is the version normally performed. It has the advantage of a climactic (if hand-stretching) coda, with all four lines of the chorale melody sounding together and (as some see it) Bach's 'signature' in the final bar (Ex. 12.1).[5]

**Ex. 12.1**

BWV769, Variatio 5, bars 54–6

[Figures in circles identify lines of the chorale melody.]

Dating from about the same time as *Vom Himmel hoch*, the *Musical Offering* (BWV1079) goes even further in its exploration of erudite canonic procedures. Bach's homage to the Prussian monarch took the form of two fugues (or 'ricercars'), ten canons (one of them a canonic fugue) and a trio sonata, all incorporating the memorable theme (the *thema regium* that Frederick the Great had given him for improvisation during the Potsdam visit of 1747 (see pp. 202–5). The order in which Bach intended the items to be presented (not necessarily performed)

---

[4] P. Williams, *The Organ Music of J. S. Bach*, ii, 319.

[5] In German nomenclature B stands for B♭ and H for B♮. The 'signature' is to be found also towards the end of Variation 4 (the final variation in the manuscript version), but it should be added that this sequence of notes is in any case quite likely to occur towards the end of a piece in C major.

has been a subject of much speculation and controversy, and it raises fundamental questions about the nature of the work itself. Only the six-part ricercar exists in Bach's own hand, and the original print, engraved mainly by J. G. Schübler of Zella but assembled and printed by Breitkopf in Leipzig, is inconsistent in both format and pagination, the six-part fugue being printed in score, the sonata and one of the canons in separate instrumental parts, and the other canons in abbreviated form, like the first three in *Vom Himmel hoch*. No fewer than five printer's units can be observed, consisting of folios (single leaves) and bifolios (folded to form two leaves), some vertical and some horizontal; they were sold unstitched and unbound.

The presentation copy that Bach had printed for Frederick the Great shows a number of minor differences, and also contains handwritten inscriptions in the margin next to the augmentation and modulating canons (Nos. 3d and 3e):

*Notulis crescentibus crescat Fortuna* ⎫
*Ascendenteque Modulatione ascendat Gloria* ⎭   *Regis*

As the notes grow, so may the Fortune ⎫
And as the modulation rises, so may the Glory ⎭   of the King

The title-page, dedication, and three-part ricercar in this *de luxe* edition were later bound together, by which time the trio sonata and the six-part ricercar had evidently been mislaid and were replaced by ordinary copies. From the state of the presentation copy as he knew it, Spitta drew certain conclusions which led him to propose the following layout for the work:

| Printer's Unit (Wolff) | Pagination | BG and BWV1079 | Item(s) | Presentation Copy |
|---|---|---|---|---|
| A (oblong) | None | — | Title-page, dedication | Superior paper, bound with unit B |
| B (oblong) | 1–4 | 1 | Ricercar à 3 | Superior paper, bound with unit A |
|  |  | 2 | *Canon perpetuus* |  |

| | | | | |
|---|---|---|---|---|
| D (upright) | None | 3 | *Canones diversi:* | Superior paper, |
| | | | (a) à 2 *(cancrizans)* | unbound |
| | | | (b) à 2 (2 violins) | |
| | | | (c) à 2 (contrary motion) | |
| | | | (d) à 2 (augmentation and contrary motion) | MS inscription |
| | | | (e) à 2 (modulating canon) | MS inscription |
| | | 4 | *Fuga canonica* | |
| E (oblong) | 1–7 | 5 | Ricercar à 6 | Ordinary paper, unbound |
| | | 6 | Canon à 2 *Quaerendo invenietis* (puzzle canon) | |
| | | 7 | Canon à 4 (puzzle canon) | |
| C (upright) | 1–4 (each part) | 8 | Trio sonata (parts) | Ordinary paper, unbound |
| | | 9 | *Canon perpetuus* (untilted) | |

While Spitta (iii, 293) regarded the *Musical Offering* as 'a strange conglomerate of pieces, wanting not only internal connection but external uniformity', his findings influenced the shape given to the work in Alfred Dörffel's edition for *BG* (vol. xxxi/2), which was accepted by Schmieder for BWV. Since the 1930s, however, several Bach scholars, notably Hans T. David, Christoph Wolff, and Ursula Kirkendale, have challenged Spitta's findings and put forward new theories about Bach's intentions.

H. T. David suggested that the disorganized appearance of the original print was largely the result of Schübler's having first engraved the two ricercars and the trio sonata, and then inserted the canons wherever there was room for them on the plates. He argued for an 'arch' structure, with the trio sonata at the centre supported on each side by five canons and a ricercar:[6]

|  | BWV1079 |
|---|---|
| ricercar à 3 | 1 |
| 5 canons, with royal theme as cantus firmus | 2, 3(b–e) |
| trio sonata | 8 |
| 5 canons, elaborations of royal theme | 9, 3(a), 6, 7, 4 |
| ricercar à 6 | 5 |

This has an appealing symmetry which is consistent with what we know of Bach's methods in other works, but it relies to some extent on hypothesis and, as Christoph Wolff pointed out, leaves certain questions about the original print unanswered. Wolff, after careful diplomatic investigations using all available exemplars of the original print (many of which had previously been overlooked), proposed an arrangement in which the five printer's units (see the above table) were arranged in three fascicles in the order A+B—C—D+E, the bifolios A and D serving as wrappers for B and E respectively;[7] the question of a higher order in Bach's mind is left open, although Wolff argues against cyclic performance as part of his intentions. His writings have been vigorously opposed by Ursula Kirkendale, who claims to have discovered the esoteric structure of the *Musical Offering* in Quintilian's *Institutio oratoria*. She believes Bach designed the work to correspond to the sections of a forensic oration as set out by Quintilian.[8] The close parallels she draws between Bach and Quintilian make her arguments seem very plausible, but we lack any corroboration from Bach's contemporaries to convince us of their truth. Theories, like people, should not hang on circumstantial evidence alone. Meanwhile, the fact that the order adopted by

[6] *J. S. Bach's Musical Offering* (New York, 1945, republished 1972), 45.

[7] 'New Research on Bach's *Musical Offering*', *Musical Quarterly*, lvii (1971), 379–408.

[8] 'The Source for Bach's *Musical Offering*: the *Institutio oratoria* of Quintilian', *Journal of the American Musicological Society*, xxxiii (1980), 88–141. It was in a footnote to his 1738 edition of Quintilian that J. M. Gesner praised Bach's ability at playing the organ while directing his choir and orchestra (see pp. 163–4). See also Kirkendale's review of Wolff's facsimile edition in *Music and Letters*, lxii (1981), 91–5.

the *BG*, although determined by largely erroneous assumptions, should be confirmed by Quintilian must seem an extraordinary coincidence.

Faced with a mass of scholarship and speculation from these and other writers on the subject, it is easy to forget that anyone who knocked on Bach's door in Leipzig in October 1747 and exchanged his thaler for a copy of the *Musical Offering* would have been given a sheaf of unbound and unstitched leaves, possibly in a loose wrapper or with the title-page bifolio acting as a temporary cover for the rest. If the purchaser had the misfortune to slip as he left Bach's house and to scatter the pages of his copy over the cobbles of the Thomaskirchhof, he would have found some difficulty in rearranging them when he got home. The pagination and other clues would have enabled him to restore the five units, but (except, of course, for the title-page) he would not have been able to tell what order they were in when he bought them, even if he had read his Quintilian.

Nor, perhaps, would he have cared. The question of a fixed order does not arise until we wish to bind the work under one cover or to perform it complete, and there is no evidence that Bach envisaged either course. Our imaginary Leipziger would have found his purchase to consist of music for a variety of uses: a fugue to play at the keyboard,[9] another in six parts for study and contemplation, a sonata to perform with friends, and canons to occupy the musical intellect. He would read in the dedication Bach's reference to Frederick the Great as a man famed for his 'greatness and strength in all the sciences of war and peace, and especially in music', and he would see how the composer had demonstrated the comparable versatility of the royal theme in a variety of styles, from the severest *stile antico* of the sometimes overrated six-part ricercar to the *galant*, dance-like finale of the sonata, the brightest gem in the compendium. And above all he would recognize that the work's (or works') 'internal connection' resides (as Spitta well knew) in the admirable royal theme itself and its many guises, from the shadowy reference at the opening of the sonata (basso continuo) to such rhythmic transformations as shown in Ex. 12.2.

[9] Perhaps a considered recollection of the one Bach improvised for Frederick on one of Silbermann's fortepianos.

**Ex. 12.2**

(a)    BWV1079/i, bars 1–9

(b)    BWV1079/vii, bars 1–8

(c) Allegro   fl.    BWV1079/viii (finale), bars 1–9

(d)   fl    tr    BWV1079/ix, bars 1–9

The problem of determining Bach's intentions in these late works is no less acute in the case of the final monument to his contrapuntal art, the so-called *Art of Fugue* (BWV 1080). (The title was not Bach's, and he might perhaps not have approved of it since he himself used the term *contrapunctus* (counterpoint) for the pieces it contains.) In this case it is not the absence of an autograph that causes the difficulty (if anything, the autograph material only adds to the problems), but rather the fact that Bach died during the engraving process. When the edition was completed (by his elder sons) and published in 1751 it included seventeen fugues and four canons. Ignorant of the composer's final intentions, or perhaps misunderstanding them, the editors included an early, shorter version of Contrapunctus X and arrangements for two claviers of both versions of the three-part mirror fugue, and they compensated purchasers for the incomplete state of the final fugue by adding to the print the G major chorale prelude *Wenn wir in höchsten Nöthen sein* (BWV668a, a slightly different version of the incomplete BWV668). This last, in particular, has no place in the *Art of Fugue*, which is otherwise in D minor and based on a single theme. The theme itself is in this instance Bach's own, and better suited than the royal theme of the *Musical Offering* to contrapuntal manipulation (especially in stretto and inversion), and therefore to his intentions in this work.

The order of the items in the *Art of Fugue*, as we find them in the original print and in editions (including *BG*) derived from it, becomes increasingly bewildering as the work proceeds. It begins, logically enough, with four straightforward four-part fugues, Nos. 3 and 4 using the inversion of the theme; these form a unit within the larger whole, each fugue beginning with a different 'voice', in the order: alto, bass, tenor, soprano. Then follows a group of three so-called counter-fugues (one might have expected four) in which the normal answer is replaced by an inversion of the subject, that of No. 6 showing also diminution, and No. 7 diminution and augmentation; the order of initial entries is again alto, bass, tenor. All three fugues show a pervading use of stretto, and another feature of the group is that the texture of each fugue becomes thicker towards the end, increasing from four to five, six, or (in the final bar) even seven parts. Contrapuncti VIII–XI form a group of four fugues on newly invented subjects which combine with the 'Art of Fugue' theme. No. 8, one of the most attractive in the work, is a three-part fugue on three subjects which are heard separately and then in combination, their final conjunctions placing them at the pitch (although not at the octave) at which they first appeared (Ex. 12.3). In No. 9 the 'Art of Fugue' theme appears as a cantus firmus in long notes, combining with the new theme in double counterpoint at the twelfth; and in No. 10 it is heard in stretto and inversion against another new theme in double counterpoint at the tenth. Both of these fugues

**Ex. 12.3**

are in four parts. No. 11 is one of the miracles of the *Art of Fugue*: the three subjects of No. 8 (see Ex. 12.3) are all inverted, re-ordered, and finally combined, in a four-part fugue of amazing resource and ingenuity. All the fugues in this third group lead off with the alto part. Contrapuncti XII and XIII (the latter not actually numbered in the print) are mirror fugues designed to be played either *rectus* or *inversus*, so that between them they produce another group of four fugues. Bach's manuscript has the two versions placed one immediately above the other, making the mirror construction clear, but, no doubt for practical reasons, they were printed one after the other.

Up to this point (certainly as far as Contrapunctus XI) it is possible to detect Bach's hand in the ordering of the pieces, as well as in some of the engraving, but the remaining items in the print are unnumbered and seem to have been assembled in a haphazard way. The mirror fugues are followed by an earlier and shorter version of Contrapunctus X, supererogatory to any definitive edition of the work. Then come four canons, of which the first, by reason of its complexity (it proceeds by inversion and augmentation and then repeats itself with the two voices interchanged), might have been expected to come last; the other three, at the octave, tenth, and twelfth respectively, are more straightforward, although Nos. 2 and 3 also display invertible counterpoint.

More problematic still is the final, unfinished fugue, headed in the printed edition (but not in the autograph) 'Fuga a 3 Soggetti'. The first of its three subjects is a measured, ricercare-style theme, and this is worked out in stretto and inversion. The second, mainly in quavers, is more 'modern' in style; it is exposed and then combined with the first subject, again with some stretto. Both of these subjects show a striking kinship to the 'Art of Fugue' theme (Ex. 12.4) The third subject is Bach's own 'signature' in minims, and this is developed in a short but concentrated passage of counterpoint, again employing stretto and inversion. At this point the print breaks off, probably because the engraver had filled the plate, but the autograph continues for a further seven bars, showing the first of what was presumably to have been several different ways of combining the three fugue subjects (see Plate 13). A note added later to the manuscript by C. P. E. Bach states: 'NB While working on this fugue, where the name BACH is introduced as a countersubject, the author died'.

Bach's autograph of this fugue exists as a separate *Beilage* (appendix) to the main body of the work, and Spitta (iii, 205) took the view that, because the 'Art of Fugue' theme does not appear in it, it does not belong with the rest and should not have been included in the 1751 publication. In 1881, however, the Beethoven scholar Gustav Nottebohm demonstrated that the three existing subjects combine well with the main theme, and since then the torso has been generally accepted

Ex. 12.4

as belonging with the rest. Several scholars have completed Bach's work for him, the most skilful perhaps being Donald Tovey in his edition of 1931; Tovey also supplied a complete mirror fugue on four subjects (including the 'Art of Fugue' theme), following the somewhat imprecise statement of Bach's intentions in the Obituary. The problem of the final fugue has by no means been resolved, however. Spitta's views have found belated support among several modern scholars and performers, including Gustav Leonhardt, who was at one time opposed to them.[10] Leonhardt rejects Nottebohm's discovery as 'mere coincidence', but finds significance in the fact that the second book of the '48' contains exactly the same number of bars (2,135) as the *Art of Fugue* without the unfinished movement—an observation based on faulty arithmetic and which, in any case, places altogether too much confidence in the 1751 print as representing Bach's intentions, with or without the final fugue.[11]

An interesting theory about the incomplete fugue was advanced by Christoph Wolff.[12] He suggested that, despite Carl Philipp Emanuel's *nota bene* (which cannot in any case be taken literally, since Bach's blindness would have prevented him from writing down music during the months before his death), Bach did in fact complete the piece. He postulates the existence at one time of a 'fragment x' on which the combination of the four themes (the three existing ones and the 'Art of Fugue' theme) had been worked out in advance. According to Wolff, if Bach had ever intended to fill what is now the final page he would not have selected such a faulty sheet of manuscript paper (see especially the third staff from the bottom in Plate 15): 'he stopped at m[easure] 239 . . . because the continuation of the piece was already written down elsewhere, namely in fragment x'. This might seem very plausible, but while it is likely that Bach would try out the four themes in combination in advance of composing the fugue, it seems unlikely that he would

[10] Insert notes to recording on Harmonia mundi 1C 165–99 793/94 (1969). Cf. his *The Art of Fugue: Bach's Last Harpsichord Work* (The Hague, 1952), 4.

[11] The total of 2,135 bars for the *Art of Fugue* is arrived at by omitting the shortened version of Contrapunctus X; the number of bars in Book II of the '48' is about 3,040, or about 1,676 in the fugues alone (the numbers vary slightly between different sources).

[12] 'Bach's *Art of Fugue*: an Examination of the Sources', *Current Musicology*, xix (1975), 47–77.

have brought the final section to a finished state before composing the rest. The evidence of other autographs suggests that it was Bach's normal practice to compose a piece in its essential details from beginning to end.[13] Besides, if 'fragment x' really did exist we might expect Bach to have left some written instructions directing the copyist or engraver to it, or at least to have completed bar 239 and inserted the usual continuation signs to indicate the notes that immediately follow.

Another much debated question raised by the *Art of Fugue* (and by other late works, too) is the fundamental one of Bach's purpose in writing it. Is it a theoretical work, a piece of 'abstract' music, a scientific treatise for the Mizler society,[14] a practical exploration of musical temperaments,[15] or simply a collection of pieces to be performed like any other? Such questions entail some consideration also of the instrument(s) for which the music was conceived. Its appearance in the original print, with the fugues set out in score and with no mention at all of instrumentation, led most early writers to consider it a theoretical work. Even Carl Philipp Emanuel, who was largely responsible for seeing it through the press and who kept the original plates in his possession, stressed above all its didactic value: 'every student of the art . . . cannot fail to learn from it how to compose a good fugue and will therefore need no oral teacher, who often charges dearly enough for passing on the secrets of fugue'.[16] Spitta (iii, 199) also thought Bach's intention was primarily to instruct; for him the *Art of Fugue* was a work of artistic example, like the Inventions, Sinfonias, *Welltempered Clavier* and other works of the Cöthen period. Schweitzer (i, 427) echoed this view: 'his purpose in this work being a purely theoretical one, Bach writes the fugues out in score, and calls them "counterpoints" '.

In 1756 C. P. E. Bach reported that only thirty copies of the *Art of Fugue* had been sold, and in 1880, despite the fact that several editions (mainly for keyboard) were published during the nineteenth century, Spitta (iii, 203) was moved to lament that

[13] See R. L. Marshall, *The Compositional Process of J. S. Bach*, especially i, 234–41.

[14] H. G. Hoke, *Zu Johann Sebastian Bachs 'Die Kunst der Fuge'* (Leipzig, 1974).

[15] C. L. van Panthaleon van Eck, *J. S. Bach's Critique of Pure Music* (Waalre, 1981).

[16] F. W. Marpurg, *Historisch-Kritische Beyträge*, ii (Berlin, 1756), 576.

few, perhaps, have the ability and the inclination to understand it as a whole. The obscure state in which it has hitherto lain has rendered this task all the harder, and it has thus come about that a composition of incomparable perfection and depth of feeling, although it has always been mentioned with especial reverence as being Bach's last great work, has never yet formed part of the life of the German nation.

Modern acceptance of the *Art of Fugue* as a concert work has been achieved mainly through the efforts of well-meaning but misguided editors who have taken the layout of the original score as an excuse for all kinds of arrangements for orchestra or instrumental ensemble. Wolfgang Graeser's edition of 1926 was in this respect of enormous influence, and although Donald Tovey was arguing as early as 1931 for keyboard performance it is only comparatively recently that keyboard players have taken up the work in concerts and recordings.[17] The case for harpsichord performance has been thoroughly investigated in the writings of Gustav Leonhardt already cited, but it should be pointed out that the evidence he draws from earlier keyboard works published in score fails to take into account the immense difficulty of printing complex keyboard music on two staves using movable type. On the other hand, Leonhardt might have mentioned two further pieces of evidence to support the view that Bach wrote the *Art of Fugue* with a keyboard instrument in mind. One is that both the autograph and the original print use the *chevron* symbols for ornaments that Bach elsewhere reserved almost exclusively for keyboard music;[18] the other is that the first edition was engraved in such a way as to facilitate the turning of the pages during performance.[19]

The *Art of Fugue* is better known today than it was to Spitta's generation a century ago, but it does not follow that it is better understood. We can see now that 'abstract' and 'theoretical' are inappropriate epithets for music that has been imagined in keyboard terms and in which at least the *possibility* of performance is an important dimension. We can see, too, that to orchestrate the *Art of Fugue* is no more to fulfil Bach's

---

[17] Only three of the artists who perform the work on the sixty complete recordings listed in M. Elste, *Bachs Kunst der Fuge auf Schallplatten* (Frankfurt, 1981), play it on the harpsichord.

[18] F. Neumann, *Ornamentation in Baroque and Post-Baroque Music* (Princeton, 1978), 314–15.

[19] See especially p. 49, presumably designed to occupy a *recto* position.

intentions than to orchestrate the *Well-tempered Clavier* or the *Italian Concerto*. And yet, not to recognize that the music of the *Art of Fugue*, the Canonic Variations, and the *Musical Offering* is a fundamentally different kind of music from that of the *Well-tempered Clavier* or the *Italian Concerto*, and that the notation is one sign of this difference, is to misunderstand the nature of these late works. It may even be that the laudable and successful attempts to remove them from dusty shelves and make them regularly available in recital programmes has actually obscured their real nature. For while it may be true that Bach wrote them with particular instruments in mind, this does not mean that performance is intrinsic to the music, as it is, for example, to the English Suites or the flute sonatas. Indeed, performance alone can never result in a complete apprehension of Bach's last-period works. Even with the most thoughtful performance and the most attentive listening the augmentation canons in the *Musical Offering* and the *Art of Fugue* will sound dry, academic, and even ungainly if experienced in the same way as one might experience the *Orgelbüchlein* or the '48'. But to the score reader, able to follow and ponder on their cold logic, they offer an insight into the mysteries of infinity every bit as teasing in its mathematical beauty as Zeno's paradox of Achilles and the tortoise. Similarly, through the mirror fugues (especially in the form in which Bach first notated them) we can enter a new dimension of musical space, a world whose strange beauties can never be realized in performance.[20] One would not, of course, willingly forgo the degree of comprehension and enjoyment that performance of this music can offer, but only through study can we hope to arrive at a complete perception of it, and after study contemplation; for it exists in a world far removed from the *musica humana* of our own, where music, mathematics, and philosophy are one.

[20] For an absorbing and highly personal expansion of these views, see D. R. Hofstadter, *Gödel, Escher, Bach: an Eternal Golden Braid* (New York and Brighton, 1979).

# CHAPTER 13

# The Bach Heritage

W HILE BACH'S MUSIC HAS NEVER BEEN MORE WIDELY STUD-
ied and performed than it is today, the picture we have of the
composer himself remains incomplete and in some ways enigmatic.
Even his physical appearance largely eludes us. Only one of the several
portraits said to be of Bach—that painted by Haussmann in 1746—can
be considered as authentic. It hangs now in the old town hall, the
Museum für Geschichte der Stadt Leipzig; a second version, also by
Haussmann and presumably copied from the first, is in the William H.
Scheide Library, Princeton (see Plate 14). The portrait suggests a com-
manding though benign presence, perhaps the most striking physical
attributes being a slight podginess in the hand holding the *Canon triplex*
and a certain severity about the eyes and mouth (more pronounced in
the later version). At the same time it must be borne in mind that the
Haussmann portraits (particularly the 1746 one) have been retouched
since the eighteenth century, and that, as Stephen Daw has pointed
out,[1] the most expressive features (the eyes and mouth) probably reflect
Haussmann's general style of portraiture as much as what the painter
actually saw.

We need to be cautious, too, in attempting to form a picture of
Bach's personality and temperament, for here again the evidence is slen-
der. What we lack most are the personal letters that so vividly bring to

---

[1] *The Music of Johann Sebastian Bach: The Choral Works*, 14.

life other great composers of the past, for example Mozart and Beethoven. It is to be regretted that, as C. P. E. Bach informed Forkel in a letter dated 13 January 1775: 'with his numerous commitments he had scarcely time for the most pressing correspondence, and consequently could not engage in extensive conversations in writing'. Except for the two letters to Georg Erdmann (see pp. 118–21) and a few notes to his kinsman Elias, very little remains in Bach's hand to throw light on his domestic and social life. Contemporary accounts speak of him as a musician, rarely (and only in the most general terms) as a private person; they tell us nothing, for example, about his religious convictions or about his views on the burning philosophical debates of his day. The evidence of his music might have suggested the opposite to those of his contemporaries who found it 'erudite' and devoid of any 'deep feeling for expression',[2] but Bach seems to have been warm-hearted, generous, and hospitable in his own home. A man who enjoyed a pipe, who liked his wine and beer, and who fathered twenty children cannot have been indifferent to sensual pleasures, and during the period of his greatest celebrity in Leipzig he was always ready to receive the many visitors who sought him out. C. P. E. Bach, in the letter to Forkel mentioned above, described Bach's dwelling in the Thomaskirchhof as a *Taubenhaus* (dovecot), and in his autobiography (1773) he wrote:

> In my youth . . . no master of music was likely to travel through this place [Leipzig] without making my father's acquaintance and playing before him. My father's greatness as a composer, organist and keyboard player *sui generis* was much too renowned for a musician of standing not to get to know the great man better when the opportunity arose.

Among such visitors were the organist of the Gnadenkirche at Hirschberg, Johann Balthasar Reimann, who later recalled Bach's cordiality towards him, and the composer Conrad Friedrich Hurlebusch, who was impressed by his 'politeness and kindly reception'.

Forkel devoted the eighth chapter of his biography to a study of Bach's character, but apart from the composer's amiability and selfless devotion to his art and his family, the only personal quality he remarked

[2] J. F. Reichardt, quoted in *The Bach Reader*, 455 (not included in *NBR*).

on was his modesty. As an example of this he mentioned Bach's reluctance to speak about his contest with Marchand in 1717, and he also retold the story of Hurlebusch's visit, first related anonymously in the *Allgemeine deutsche Bibliothek*, 1788. The author there (possibly C. P. E. Bach) gives the following account:

> Bach once received a visit from Hurlebusch, a clavier player and organist very well known at the time. The latter was asked to be seated at the harpsichord; and what did he play for Bach? A printed minuet with variations. Afterwards Bach played very seriously, as was his way. The visitor, impressed by Bach's politeness and kindly reception, made Bach's children a present of his printed sonatas which he said they should study, unaware that Bach's sons were already capable of playing things of quite a different kind. Bach smiled inwardly, remaining modest and friendly.

The composer and theorist G. A. Sorge, a fellow member of Mizler's society, also praised Bach for his modesty when he dedicated to him the third part of his first *Clavier-Übung* (*c.* 1745):

> Many will perhaps be surprised at my boldness in dedicating the present sonatinas to Your Honour, so great and world-famous a virtuoso and prince of clavier players. But they will not be aware that the great musical skill [*Virtu*] that Your Honour possesses is adorned with a genial disposition and unfeigned love of your neighbour. It is true that here and there one encounters an excellent artist and a worthy virtuoso; but many of them are so full of conceit and noxious self-regard that they count as nothing all those they can look down on, and set aside completely that love of one's neighbour which is so much needed. I am sure of something altogether different and better from Your Honour.

While amiability, modesty, and neighbourly concern seem to have motivated much of Bach's private life, he could show a very different side to his temperament when he came into conflict with anyone in authority. It is impossible not to admire the single-mindedness and dedication to his art that Bach manifested in his dealings with the consistory at Arnstadt and with Ernesti and the town council at Leipzig. But his determination could easily harden into obstinacy when he failed to get his way. Patience was certainly not among his chief virtues, as we may infer from his unsatisfactory relationship with the choristers at Arnstadt and Leipzig. On the other hand, those who were gifted enough to be taught individually by him seem to have been devoted to him as both a teacher and a person.

The traditional picture of Bach as a deeply religious man, dedicated to serving God and the church, has been subject to much re-examination in the light of research undertaken since World War II. Using Spitta's chronology it was possible to understand Bach's early ambitions for a 'well-regulated church music' as something he pursued most of his life and finally achieved with the remarkable series of chorale cantatas during the years 1735–44; the secular works, no matter how excellent their quality, could be seen as incidental to this main aim. When he became *Kapell-meister* at Cöthen Bach thus 'surrendered the declared object of his life, and divorced his art from the exalted purpose to which he had dedicated it' (Terry, 116), while his acceptance of the cantorate at Leipzig was a 're-turn to the pastures whence he had strayed' ibid., 117). The chronology of the vocal works established in the 1950s by Alfred Dürr, who studied the papers and copyists in the surviving sources, and Georg van Dadelsen, whose research was directed mainly towards Bach's own handwriting, modified this view of Bach considerably, opening the door to a great deal of speculation (much of it prompted by ideologies of one kind or another) regarding Bach's religious beliefs and artistic convictions. His involvement in secular music, not only at Cöthen but also, from 1729, at Leipzig, could no longer be seen as incidental to some greater artistic destiny, and his ambitions for church music could now be understood as springing from artistic as much as from religious motives, and to be one manifestation of an encyclopedic artistic nature which sustained itself by setting new goals and then achieving them.

While the lack of autograph material has left the chronology of some of Bach's music, notably most of the organ works, impossible to determine, some progress has been made in refining the dating of other sections of his output. Yoshitake Kobayashi's close study of the sources has led to several new datings, particularly for the late works,[3] and after Christoph Wolff's and Robert Marshall's investigations into the Leipzig

---

[3] See especially Y. Kobayashi, 'Zur Chronologie der Spätwerke Johann Sebastian Bachs: Kompositions- und Aufführungstätigkeit von 1736 bis 1750', *Bach-Jahrbuch*, lxxiv (1988), 7–72.

manuscripts it is no longer possible to assume that the violin concertos, flute sonatas, and other chamber works are products of the Cöthen period. All this has tended to reinforce the picture of Bach in Leipzig as an enterprising, entrepreneurial musician, ready to engage in a multiplicity of compositional tasks, and we know already that he was involved at the same time in several other spheres of musical activity: as a teacher, as an organizer and director of a music society, as an agent for instrument makers and for other composers' music, as an adviser on church organs, and as the inventor of the *viola pomposa*.

This is not, of course, to deny that Bach was also a devout Christian who thought deeply about the orthodox Lutheran convictions with which he was brought up and to which he clung throughout his life. The inclusion in the 1750 inventory of Bach's effects of a large number of theological books can tell us very little about his religious convictions until we learn more about how and when he acquired them and what use he made of them, but the discovery in the USA in 1934 of his copy of the Calov Bible, with annotations and underlinings in Bach's hand, has shown that he studied at least some of these writings very closely. The theological background to the composer's life and works has since then assumed enormous importance in writings on Bach, and in 1976 the Internationale Arbeitsgemeinschaft für theologische Bachforschung was founded by Walter Blankenburg and Christoph Trautmann in Berlin to lead and co-ordinate research into this aspect of Bach studies. The closer relevance of theology to the structure and interpretation of particular Bach works has also been a source of fruitful investigation, not least on the part of such distinguished American scholars as Eric Chafe and Michael Marissen, who have found religious significance not only in the vocal church music, where one might expect to find it, but also in a number of purely instrumental works.[4] The difficulty with such lines of investigation is to know how far to go. Some commentators have found the music to be so rich in theological symbolism that even a three-part invention can be understood as expressing the composer's

---

[4] See especially E. Chafe, *Tonal Allegory in the Vocal Music of J. S. Bach*; M. Marissen, *The Social and Religious Designs of J. S. Bach's Brandenburg Concertos*; idem., 'The Theological Character of J. S. Bach's *Musical Offering*', in *Bach Studies* 2, 85–106.

personal belief in Christ's crucifixion and redemption.[5] This could not, however, have been the experience of Bach's own audiences and congregations, and one may question whether, in composing the cantatas and Passions, he had any other aim than to set the text in the most effective (and affective) way he could, and to produce a finished work of art. If the result was that Bach wrote greater sacred music than did any of his contemporaries, this was because he was a greater and more skilful composer, not because he believed more deeply than they did.

Another area of inquiry into esoteric interpretations of Bach's music has entailed a study of its number symbolism. Bach's interest in the symbolism of numbers is shown, on the simplest level, in such straightforward equations between text and music as the tenfold entry of the fugue subject in the organ chorale *Dies sind die heil'gen zehn Gebot* (These are the holy ten commandments, BWV679) and the eleven repetitions (one for each of the disciples except Judas) of 'Herr, bin ich's?' (Lord, is it I?) in No. 9c of the *St Matthew Passion*. Less obvious, but still unmistakable, is the Trinitarian symbolism of the Sanctus in the B minor Mass and of *Clavier-Übung* III. Much more problematic is Bach's use (or supposed use) of the natural-order number alphabet (often referred to as numerology or gematria), in which each letter of the alphabet is paired with a number from 1 to 24, so that $A = 1$, $B = 2$, $C = 3$, and so on (the letter I counting the same as J, and U the same as V). From this it will be seen that BACH $(2 + 1 + 3 + 8) = 14$, and J. S. BACH $(9 + 18 + 14) = 41$, and it thus becomes possible for the number of notes, rests, or bars in a particular movement or passage to take on a significance not apparent from a simple reading or hearing of the music.

A pioneer work in the study of this aspect of Bach's music was Friedrich Smend's *Johann Sebastian Bach: Kirchen-Kantaten* (Berlin, 1947–9; 2nd ed., 1950), which was followed three years later by his *Johann Sebastian Bach bei seinem Namen gerufen*. Smend investigated several instances of numerical significance in the *Canon triplex* of the Haussmann

---

[5] U. Siegele, 'Erfahrungen bei der Analyse Bachscher Musik', *Bachforschung und Bachinterpretation heute: Bericht über das Bachfest-Symposium 1978 der Philipps-Universität Marburg* (Leipzig, 1981), pp. 142–4. See also W. Mellers, *Bach and the Dance of God*, pp. 247–50.

portraits (see Plate 14), drawing attention to, among other things, the fourteen notes of the two canonic parts. He also found numerological significance in the cantus firmus of the 'deathbed' chorale, *Vor deinen Thron tret' ich*, which has fourteen notes in its first line and forty-one in all. Smend's evidence for the significance of the numbers 14 and 41 in Bach's music is persuasive, coming as it does mainly from dedication canons and from works of the late period when Bach's involvement with Lorenz Mizler's Sozietät der Musikalischen Wissenschaften might have inclined him towards investing his music with such hidden meanings, and his hypothesis has been bolstered by at least two further pieces of evidence since he wrote. The composer's *Handexemplar* of the Goldberg Variations, which came to light in 1974 (see pp. 212–14), was found to include fourteen canons in Bach's hand which were quite possibly intended for Mizler's society. And both Wolfgang Wiemer and Gregory Butler have identified the unfinished fugue in the *Art of Fugue* (the one containing Bach's musical 'signature') as constituting Contrapunctus 14 in Bach's original scheme for the work.[6]

The problem, again, is to know where to stop (or even, in this case, whether to start); Smend's ideas were pursued, especially in the 1970s and '80s, with more vigour than discretion by commentators who saw the natural-order number alphabet as a direct hermeneutical pathway to Bach's intentions in specific works. A not untypical example is provided by the following commentary on Cantata No. 148, *Bringet dem Herrn Ehre seines Namens*:

> The Gospel of the day is taken from St. Luke 14, which might be the origin of the following: the first fugal subject [of the opening chorus] has twice 14 notes; the trumpet theme, equally, 14 notes. A melisma on the word 'name' in measures 53–62 has 41 notes in the Soprano—the Alto, 18 notes for the same word; the Tenor, only 40 notes, and the Bass, 29 notes in two melismas. The four vocal parts have 1440 notes altogether. In the alto aria, 'See My Heart Lord, Open, Loving' (*Mund und Herz stehn dir offen*), one of Bach's most beautiful inspirations, the number of notes is particularly striking:

[6] W. Wiemer, *Die wiederhergestellte Ordnung in Johann Sebastian Bachs 'Kunst der Fuge* (Weisbaden, 1977), 54–6; G. Butler, 'Ordering Problems in J. S. Bach's *Art of Fugue* Resolved', *Musical Quarterly*, lxix (1983), 44–61.

| | | |
|---|---|---|
| Oboe 1 and Oboe 3 | 700 notes | |
| Oboe 2 and Continuo | 700 notes | = 1400 notes |
| Alto in Main Part | 110 notes | |
| Alto in Middle Section | 100 notes | = 210 notes |

During the *Ritornello*, the instruments play 220 notes, and during the vocal parts, they play 960 notes.[7]

What is most troublesome here is not the faulty arithmetic, but rather the supposition that Bach could possibly have encumbered his 'most beautiful inspirations' with preliminary note-counts of this nature. The advisability of exercising caution in such matters was put forward in 1991 by Ruth Tatlow,[8] who pointed out the lack of any historical evidence for Bach's use of the natural-order number alphabet and provided details of other number alphabets that he might have used, and even preferred, if he had been so inclined. Number symbolism seems unlikely now to provide fresh insights into Bach's mind and his music, though the natural-order number alphabet will no doubt continue to provide innocent amusement for writers and editors, as it has done in the past.[9]

One may wonder why it is that Bach's music has given rise to so much speculative analysis of this kind. We do not, after all, look for chiastic structures in Purcell's anthems, or for religious symbolism in Vivaldi's concertos, or for the workings of number alphabets in Handel's oratorios. One reason must be that Bach himself had little to say about his own music (or indeed about music in general), and so left the way open for others to propose what he might have said about a particular work. But another, more fundamental, reason lies in the nature of the music itself, which has a weightiness and complexity of texture, harmony, and counterpoint that encourage one to look for layers of meaning even in works that make a direct appeal to the listener. The richness and complexity of the music is, in fact, one measure of its greatness.

[7] A. Hirsch, 'Number Symbolism in Bach's First Cantata Cycle: 1723–1724', *Bach*, vi/3 (1975), 11–19; vi/4 (1975), 14–19; vii/1 (1976), 27–32.

[8] *Bach and the Riddle of the Number Alphabet.*

[9] See, for example, N. Kenyon, 'A Newly Discovered Group of Canons by Bach', *Musical Times*, cxvii (1976), 391–3, in which the author, or his editor, contrived to include fourteen footnotes.

Another is its originality. This is not to be judged by the extent to which Bach anticipated, or helped to initiate, the musical idiom of a succeeding generation. He was not, in this sense, an innovator or what is often called a 'historically important figure'. In fact, his musical style, particularly in the late works, might be considered in a very real sense reactionary. Yet not even Scheibe criticized the music for lack of originality, and while Bach may have chosen not to keep pace with the latest styles in music (the 'usual lirumlarum' as he once described it to Kirnberger), he brought new ideas to every genre he worked in, and his own artistic growth far outstripped that of more up-to-date composers, as we can see by comparing his earliest works with the sublime masterpieces of his last years.

Bach's early years and his subsequent moves from one place of employment to another—Arnstadt, Mühlhausen, Weimar, Cöthen, Leipzig—provide obvious points of division in any biography of the composer. But while these coincide to some extent with Bach's concentration on particular genres (as the organization of the present volume has tried to show), the development of his musical style cuts across them. It is difficult to support Manfred Bukofzer's endorsement of Wilibald Gurlitt's view that 'in the creative development of Bach five periods can be distinguished that roughly correspond to the positions he held during his life'.[10] The growth and development of Bach's musical style is as complex as the music itself, since it was constantly fed by an avid, if critical, interest in the music of other composers, past and present. But there were two watersheds of crucial importance in this process, one occurring about 1713 and the other about 1739–40. These mark off three broad stylistic periods which, like the three periods into which it is customary to divide Beethoven's output, might be described as apprenticeship, mastery, and transcendence. In the music he wrote before about 1713 (mainly organ and clavier works and a few cantatas) Bach built on the developments his compatriots had made in instrumental and church music during the later seventeenth century. Replying to questions from Forkel in 1775, C. P. E. Bach listed the composers

[10] *Music in the Baroque Era* (New York, 1947), 271. W. Gurlitt, in *J. S. Bach: der Meister und sein Werk* (Berlin, 1936), makes the following divisions: (1) 1703–8; (2) 1708–17; (3) 1717–23; (4) 1723–45; (5) 1745–50.

his father had 'loved and studied' at about this time, and apart from Frescobaldi and 'some old good Frenchmen' the list consisted entirely of Germans, most of whom excelled in these two genres and were 'strong fugue writers'. These composers had already absorbed stylistic influences from France and Italy, and even from England, but not the modern Italian operatic styles of Venice and Naples.

The beginning of Bach's second stylistic period coincides with his direct exposure to the latest Italian music, and in particular the concerto, at Weimar from about 1713 onwards. To the melodic clarity and rhythmic zest of the new Italian style, with its 'modern' approach to tonality and its structures clearly shaped by a strong feeling for cadence, Bach brought the sobriety of the Lutheran chorale, a richness of inner texture, and a northern delight in complex counterpoint. The result was a style at once unmistakably his own and adaptable to all kinds of music (except perhaps theatre music, in which he was not engaged). The works of the Cöthen and early Leipzig periods show an ever-increasing technical command and reflect a deepening experience, but there is no fundamental widening of stylistic parameters until we reach the inward-looking music of the last decade, beginning with *Clavier-Übung* III (1739). The new works (as distinct from the parodies) of this final period, which is analogous to Beethoven's in the way the music reflects 'the years that bring the philosophic mind', are predominantly (and significantly) instrumental, and even when words are involved (as in the 'Credo in unum Deum' and 'Confiteor unum baptisma' of the B minor Mass) they are not set in the 'affective' manner of the earlier church music. Their composition coincides with Bach's involvement in the Mizler society and, just as significantly, with the publication of Mizler's German translation of Fux's treatise on strict counterpoint, *Gradus ad Parnassum* (Leipzig, 1742).

The stylistic development briefly summarized here is impressive, but a broad outline such as this cannot take into account, for example, the stylistic differentiation that exists between sacred and secular works (for the boundaries were there, even if they were not rigidly drawn and could be crossed in parodies and transcriptions) or the infiltration of *style galant* elements into Bach's later works.[11] Nor does it say anything

[11] See R. L. Marshall, 'Bach the Progressive: Observations on his Later Works', *Musical Quarterly*, lxii (1976), 313–57.

about the nature of Bach's individuality as a composer. A gift for melody—not typically of the flowing, vocal kind that we associate with
his great contemporary, Handel–and a distinctive command of harmonic resource, from the sturdiest diatonicism to the boldest chromaticism, were both part of Bach's endowment as a composer. But of no
other music is it truer to say that melody and harmony as stylistic constituents are inseparable. Bach's artistry is often shown in the way that
melody and harmony complement each other in a consistent euphony,
but not infrequently one of these elements pursues its own logical
course in the teeth of the other, creating a type and level of dissonance
that is a distinctive part of the Bach style. Some familiar examples occur
in the slow movement of Brandenburg Concerto No. 1 (Ex. 13.1).
Active and motivic middle parts, such as those in this example, frequently heighten the incidence of dissonance in the music and give it
a density—a high 'specific gravity'—that no other music of the period
possesses.

It is a commonplace of Bach and Handel criticism to draw compar-

**Ex. 13.1**

isons between these two giants of the late Baroque. They were born in the same year and within less than 100 miles of each other; they were both members of the Mizler society; they were both operated on by the same oculist with equally damaging results; and they shared the acquaintance of some of the leading musicians of the time. Perhaps they regretted not meeting each other (Bach certainly did), and yet it was appropriate in one way that they never did meet. Their music shares very little common ground. Handel excelled in those genres (opera, oratorio, and the Corelli type of concerto) that Bach left untouched; Bach's greatest music is to be found in genres (church cantata, oratorio Passion, Mass, and the Vivaldi type of concerto) uncultivated by Handel. Secular music was as central to Handel's activities as church music was to Bach's. Their compositions overlap only in the relatively minor genres of the keyboard suite and instrumental sonata, and even here their styles are radically different. Handel's music, to take a general view, is empirical in structure, vocal in idiom, melody-dominated, and essentially Italianate; Bach's is carefully crafted, instrumental in idiom, contrapuntally orientated, and unmistakably German.

Even in the matter of 'borrowings', where the two composers are frequently paired, their practices were very different. Both, it is true, borrowed freely from their own earlier compositions, rearranging whole movements for different combinations of voices or instruments, or adapting them to new texts. Bach's re-workings of other composers' music, however, are few and entirely confined to his early period (up to about 1712 at the latest); they may be thought of as compositional exercises and were certainly intended only for private use. The opportunist Handel, on the other hand, appropriated throughout his life whatever in the music of others suited his needs; usually he improved on what he took, but sometimes he made little material alteration to it. His methods have sometimes been defended as being widespread among his contemporaries, but it is questionable whether this was in fact the case, at least as far as the major composers were concerned. One looks in vain for similar borrowings by Purcell, Corelli, Vivaldi, and the two Scarlattis, for example. This is not to question the ethics of Handel's working methods, merely to point out that in this particular also they were different from Bach's.

What also distinguishes Bach's music from Handel's is its technical difficulty; as his contemporaries were not slow to point out, his music is much harder to perform than any other music of the eighteenth century. In some works, including the early organ pieces, the solo violin sonatas, the fifth Brandenburg Concerto (with its long and showy cadenza), and some of the Goldberg Variations, virtuosity is cultivated for its own sake. Others test the stamina of the performer: cantata arias, for example, in which (as Scheibe correctly observed) 'he expects singers and players to do with their throats and instruments what he can play on the clavier'. But the essential difficulty of Bach's music (and one that applies even more to the keyboard works than to the others) lies in the intrinsic complexity of the musical thought. It is not that the music is awkwardly laid out or that it tests the dexterity of the performer, but rather that its figuration (to some extent interchangeable between voices and instruments, and more violin-orientated than is generally recognized) has a logic that is directed not by the fingers but by the brain. Advances in instrumental technique during the past two centuries have tended to remove the difficulties of earlier music, but Bach's works continue to test the player and to challenge the sight-reader.

It was no doubt partly because of its complexity and technical difficulty that Bach's music was not more widely disseminated during his lifetime, and was to some extent neglected after his death. The story of its rediscovery and revival has been told many times,[12] but the romantic picture of a self-effacing genius whose music was unrecognized during his lifetime and neglected after his death, only to be rediscovered by a much later generation, is one that persists. Even had this been the case, it would have meant only that Bach, after his death, shared the fate of still better-known composers, such as Vivaldi and Telemann, whose music fell into even deeper oblivion and for a longer time. Handel was in this respect exceptional, his music kept alive after his death because of its accessibility (in every sense), because of the conservatism of English tastes, and because the king found it to his liking. But even Handel's fame was perpetuated by a relatively small number of major works.

Popular notions about Bach's reputation stand in need of revision in

---

[12] See especially F. Blume, *Two Centuries of Bach* (London, 1950; translated from the German original of 1947).

a number of respects. First, it is not true to say that his contemporaries admired him only as an executant. Certainly there are numerous accounts that stress his extraordinary skill as an organist and keyboard player, but the earliest reference to Bach in print—a passage in Mattheson's *Das beschützte Orchestre* (Hamburg, 1717)—extols the music, not the playing, of the 'famous organist at Weimar'. By the time the publication of the *Clavier-Übung* was complete, in 1741–2, Bach was widely recognized as one of the finest composers of his time. Writing from Bologna to a correspondent in Fulda only three months before Bach's death, the great Italian musician Padre Martini, who had certainly never heard him play, could say: 'I consider it unnecessary to describe the singular merit of Sig. Bach since it is too well known and admired not only in Germany but all over Italy. I will say only that I hold it difficult to find a better *Professore* since every day he can claim to be among the finest in Europe.' Bach may never have enjoyed the popular success that could come to an opera composer of international repute, such as Handel and Hasse, but his music was eulogized in terms similar to Padre Martini's throughout the rest of the eighteenth century. Mozart and Beethoven knew and admired it, and by the time Beethoven died, in 1827, Bach had taken his place in the German consciousness alongside Handel, Haydn, and Mozart as one of music's immortals, as Grillparzer's funeral oration makes clear.

Until then, however, his reputation rested almost entirely on the keyboard works. It was these that Baron van Swieten made known to Viennese musical circles in the 1780s, and it was these that particularly interested an active 'Bach junto' (Wesley's term) in England, a coterie that included A. F. C. Kollmann, K. F. Horn, George Pinto, and Samuel Wesley himself. In Forkel's biography of 1802 (dedicated to Baron van Swieten and translated into English, probably by Kollmann, in 1820) it was again only the clavier and organ music that received any detailed consideration. All Forkel's music examples are taken from these works, and it is unlikely that he knew much of the vocal music at first hand. This should come as no surprise. There was no particular reason why a Kantor in Germany should perform the cantatas and Passions of his predecessor, especially those as difficult as Bach's and at a time when the cantata and the oratorio Passion were, in any case, in decline as part of the Lutheran liturgy. Since there was simply no other occasion on which to perform them, there was also no possibility of reviving Bach's sacred choral works until public interest in oratorio as a concert genre gained momentum, stimulated largely by the English example. Mendelssohn's historic performance of the *St Matthews Passion* on 11 March 1829 (for which his teacher Carl Friedrich Zelter, who had cleared the ground in his rehearsals of the work during the preceding years, should share the credit) took place not in a church, but in the hall of the Berlin Singakademie. Its success, which resulted in two repeat performances, opened the door to concert revivals of the other major choral works soon afterwards.

The next important step in recovering the Bach heritage was the formation of a Bach-Gesellschaft (Bach society) in 1850 (the centenary of the composer's death), with the aim of publishing a complete edition of his music. This great venture occupied the next half-century, during which time Philipp Spitta completed a critical biography which served as a cornerstone for Bach studies during the following three-quarters of a century and set new standards for the conduct of musicological research in general. It also showed unmistakably, as Forkel's book had done, how the Bach revival in the nineteenth century served as a focal point for a re-awakening of German national pride.

German scholars have remained in the forefront of Bach studies during the twentieth century, and have played a leading part in disseminating his music, largely through the activities of the Neue (new) Bach-Gesellschaft, formed from the ashes of the old in 1900. Of all the numerous life-and-works studies that have appeared since Spitta's, none has been more influential than Albert Schweitzer's *J. S. Bach, le musicien-poète* (1905, revised German translation, 1908). The aesthetics of Bach's music were further explored by the French scholar André Pirro (1907), and the English writer C. S. Terry brought to light much new material in his biography of 1928 (which should be read in one of its later revised editions) and in other writings on the composer. Meanwhile, deficiencies in the *BG* edition, particularly in its editors' use and interpretation of manuscript sources, were being noticed. In 1950 (the bicentenary of Bach's death) Wolfgang Schmieder's thematic catalogue, the *Bach-Werke-Verzeichnis*, brought a century of Bach research to a close. Five years later there appeared the first volume in a new collected edition, the

*Neue Bach-Ausgabe*, a venture that has brought with it a new era in Bach studies, a revised chronology of his works, and fresh insight into the nature of the man and his music. Bach research in Germany today is centred at the Bach-Archiv in Leipzig and the Bach-Institut at Göttingen, both of them headquarters for the new edition. The former has rendered a service of inestimable value to students and scholars by publishing three volumes of source material in accurate transcriptions and another of pictures, all relating to Bach's life (*Bach-Dokumente*, i–iv, 1963–79).[13] A new thematic catalogue, the *Bach Compendium* in course of preparation under the editorship of Hans-Joachim Schulze and Christoph Wolff, will serve the new edition as Schmieder's catalogue served the old one.

Alongside this scholarly activity have come new concepts in performing Bach's music. Much research has been directed towards the interpretation of rhythms, ornaments, continuo accompaniments, and so on, with results that have been both revolutionary and controversial. The revival of Bach's Masses, cantatas, and Passions in the nineteenth century came on a wave of enthusiasm for mammoth choral and orchestral performances in large halls. Mendelssohn's choir for the 1829 revival of the *St Matthew Passion* has been estimated at 158, but even such a modest total (for the time) would have been at least six times (and perhaps as much as sixteen times) the size of Bach's choir at the Thomaskirche a century earlier. The tendency since 1950 has been to revive eighteenth-century conditions of performance as far as possible, with small choirs accompanied by instruments of the period (or exact copies of them). Again, the results have been controversial, not least in the epoch-making recordings by Telefunken of the complete cantatas in performances directed by Gustav Leonhardt and Nikolaus Harnoncourt; but the revelatory nature of such recordings has given them an enormous and beneficial influence on the present-day performance of Bach's music. The quest continues, not for that complete 'authenticity' in performance which is unattainable and probably undesirable, but to

---

[13] Two very useful and inexpensive handbooks abstracted from these are a *Kalendarium zur Lebensgeschichte Johann Sebastian Bachs* (Leipzig, 2nd ed., 1979) and *Johann Sebastian Bach: Leben und Werk in Dokumenten* (Leipzig, 2nd ed., 1975).

establish what conditions are indispensable for any performance that hopes to capture the true essence of Bach's art. Possibly the most revealing discoveries still to be made await a more thorough application than has so far been attempted of the temperaments (tunings) in use during Bach's time.

Schweitzer (i, 3) recognized in Bach's music the perfection and culmination of all that his predecessors had been striving towards: 'Bach is thus a terminal point. Nothing comes from him; everything merely leads up to him.' Bach's influence as a composer on the immediately succeeding generations was indeed minimal, except in the case of his eldest sons and some of his pupils. His music, insofar as it was known, was a thing of the past, and its impact even on Mozart and Beethoven, for whom a direct influence can be claimed, has often been exaggerated. Its craftsmanship, on the other hand, was universally acknowledged, and the pedagogical value of the chorale harmonizations and the keyboard fugues, in particular, was soon recognized. Two volumes of chorales were published as models of their kind by F. W. Birnstiel of Berlin in 1765–9, and a better, more complete edition of 371 (including some duplicates) was edited by Kirnberger and C. P. E. Bach and published in four volumes by Breitkopf in 1784–7. Extracts from the fugues, and in some cases whole pieces, appeared in treatises on counterpoint by Marpurg (1753–4), Kirnberger (1771), Kollmann (1799), and others. Since then generations of music students have been nurtured on Bach's music, and the 'Bach style' has entered into the subconscious of Western music, to surface in isolated works of the nineteenth century, and then as a rallying point for the neo-classicism of the twentieth. Composers as different as Busoni, Bartók, Schoenberg, Webern, Hindemith, and Stravinsky acknowledged their debt to Bach, either verbally or just as explicitly in their music. Far from being a 'terminal point', Bach's music has been a source of inspiration for all kinds of new developments and for countless individual works.

It is not really surprising that the compositional mastery of Bach's music should inspire the creative artist, that its philological and other problems should fascinate the scholar, or that its technical challenges should be taken up by the performer. What *is* astonishing, and in the end inexplicable, is that music which makes so few concessions to the listener should enjoy an immense popular following. Today a performance of the B minor Mass or of the Brandenburg Concertos can be relied on to fill a cathedral or a concert hall, and festivals devoted largely or exclusively to Bach are a commonplace in the musical calendar. Every generation of music lovers seems to find in the works of this incomparable artist that *Gemütsergötzung,* that 'refreshment of the spirit', which his title-pages promised, and which his music so richly provides.

# APPENDIX A

# *Calendar*

(Figures in parenthesis denote the age reached by the person mentioned during the year in question.)

| Year | Age | Life | Contemporary Musicians |
|---|---|---|---|
| 1685 | | Johann Sebastian Bach born, 21 March, at Eisenach. Youngest child of Johann Ambrosius Bach, town and court musician, and his wife Maria Elisbetha, née Lämmerhirt. Bapt., 23 March. | Handel born, 23 Feb; D. Scarlatti born, 26 Oct. Albinoni aged 14; Biber 41; Blow 36; Böhm 24; G. Bononcini 15; Buxtehude 48; Caldara *c.* 15; Charpentier *c.* 40; Corelli 32; Couperin 17; Fux 25; Graupner 2; Grigny 13; Heinichen 2; Keiser 11; Kerll 58; J. P. Krieger 36; Kuhnau 25; Lalande 28; Legrenzi 59; Lully 53; A. Marcello 1; Marchand 16; Mattheson 4; Pachelbel 32; Pasquini 48; Purcell 26; Rameau 2; Reincken 62; A. Scarlatti 25; Steffani 31; Telemann 4; Torelli 27; Vivaldi 7; J. G. Walther 1; Zelenka 6. |
| 1686 | 1 | Sister, Johanna Juditha (6), dies; buried 3 May. | B. Marcello born, 24 June; Porpora born, 17 Aug; S. L. Weiss born, 12 Oct. |
| 1687 | 2 | | Geminiani bapt. 5 Dec; Lully (54) dies, 22 March; Pisendel born, 26 Dec. |

| Year | Age | Life | Contemporary Musicians |
|------|-----|------|------------------------|
| 1688 | 3 | | Fasch born, 15 April. |
| 1689 | 4 | | Boismortier born, 23 Dec. |
| 1690 | 5 | | Legrenzi (63) dies, 27 May. |
| 1691 | 6 | | |
| 1692 | 7 | Enters Lateinschule, Eisenach. | Kerll (65) dies, 13 Feb; Tartini born, 8 April |
| 1693 | 8 | | |
| 1694 | 9 | Mother (50) dies, 1 May. Father marries Barbara Margaretha Keul, 27 Nov. | |
| 1695 | 10 | Father (49) dies, 20 Feb. Bach leaves Eisenach to live with brother, Johann Christoph (24), in Ohrdruf. Enters lyceum there. | Locatelli born, 3 Sept; Purcell (36) dies, 21 Nov. |
| 1696 | 11 | | |
| 1697 | 12 | | Quantz born, 30 Jan; Leclair born, 10 May. |
| 1698 | 13 | | |
| 1699 | 14 | | Hasse bapt. 25 March. |
| 1700 | 15 | Leaves Ohrdruf for Lüneburg. Enrols in Michaelisschule there. | G. B. Sammartini born (or 1701) |
| 1701 | 16 | | |
| 1702 | 17 | Applies unsuccessfully for organist's post at Jakobikirche, Sangerhausen. | |
| 1703 | 18 | Court musician at Weimar, March–Sept. Appointed organist at Neue Kirche, Arnstadt, 9 Aug. | C. H. Graun born (or 1704); Harrer born, 8 May; Grigny (41) dies, 30 Nov. |
| 1704 | 19 | | Charpentier (c. 59) dies, 24 Feb; Biber (59) dies, 3 May. |
| 1705 | 20 | Granted 4 weeks' leave of absence to visit Lübeck in ?Oct, but stays away longer. | |
| 1706 | 21 | Returns to Arnstadt, Jan/Feb. Appears before the consistory to answer for length of absence. | Pachelbel (52) buried, 9 March; Martini born, 24 April. |
| 1707 | 22 | Apppointed organist at Blasiuskirche, Mühlhausen, 15 June. Marries Maria Barbara Bach (23) at Dornheim, 17 Oct. | Buxtehude (c. 70) dies, 9 May. |
| 1708 | 23 | Appointed organist and chamber musician to Duke Wilhelm Ernst at Weimar, June. First child, Catharina Dorothea, bapt., 29 Dec. | Blow (59) dies, 1 Oct. |

| Year | Age | Life | Contemporary Musicians |
|------|-----|------|------------------------|
| 1709 | 24 | | Torelli (50) dies, 8 Feb; F. Benda bapt., 22 Nov. |
| 1710 | 25 | Second child, Wilhelm Friedemann, born, 22 Nov. | Pergolesi born, 4 Jan; Arne bapt., 28 May; Pasquini (72) dies, 21 Nov. |
| 1711 | 26 | | Boyce born, Sept. |
| 1712 | 27 | | |
| 1713 | 28 | Visits Weissenfels, Feb. Third and fourth children (twins), Johann Christoph and Maria Sophia, born 23 Feb, and die, 23 Feb and *c.* 13 March. Bach competes for organist's post at Halle, Dec. | Corelli (59) dies, 8 Jan; J. L. Krebs bapt., 12 Oct. |
| 1714 | 29 | Declines offer of Halle post, Feb, and is promoted to *Konzertmeister* at Weimar, 2 March. Fifth child, Carl Philipp Emanuel, born, 8 March. | Gluck born, 2 July; Jommelli born, 10 Sept. |
| 1715 | 30 | Sixth child, Johann Gottfried Bernhard, born, 11 May. | Wagenseil born, 29 Jan; Doles born, 23 April. |
| 1716 | 31 | Examines new organs at Liebfrauenkirche, Halle, 29 April– 2 May, and Augustinerkirche, Erfurt, July. | |
| 1717 | 32 | Directs performance of a Passion at Gotha, 26 March. Appointed *Kapellmeister* to Prince Leopold at Cöthen, 5 Aug, but is at first prevented by Duke Wilhelm Ernst from taking up the post. Visits Dresden and accepts invitation to take part in contest with Marchand. Is imprisoned by Wilhelm Ernst, 6 Nov, but then allowed to leave Weimar, 2 Dec. Examines organ in Paulinerkirche, Leipzig, 16 Dec. | J. Stamitz bapt., 19 June. |
| 1718 | 33 | Visits Carlsbad with Prince Leopold, May–June. Seventh child, Leopold Augustus, bapt., 17 Nov. | |
| 1719 | 34 | Death of son, Leopold Augustus (10 months), 26 Sept. | L. Mozart born, 14 Nov. |

| Year | Age | Life | Contemporary Musicians |
|------|-----|------|------------------------|
| 1720 | 35 | Visits Carlsbad, May–July. Wife (35) dies; buried, 7 July. Bach visits Hamburg, Nov, and is offered post as organist at the Jakobikirche, which he declines. | Altnickol bapt., 1 Jan; J. F. Agricola born, 4 Jan. |
| 1721 | 36 | Brother, Johann Christoph (49), dies, 22 Feb. Brandenburg Concertos dedicated to Margrave Christian Ludwig, 24 March. Marries Anna Magdalena (20) at Cöthen, 3 Dec. Prince Leopold (27) marries Friederica Henrietta von Anhalt-Bernburg (19) at Bernburg, 11 Dec. | Kirnberger bapt., 24 April. |
| 1722 | 37 | Brother, Johann Jacob (40), dies, 16 April. Bach enters candidature for cantorate at Leipzig, Dec. | G. Benda bapt., 30 June; Kuhnau (62) dies, 5 June; Reincken dies, 24 Nov. |
| 1723 | 38 | Eighth child, Christiana Sophia Henrietta, born. Bach signs contract as Thomaskantor in Leipzig, 5 May. Arrives in Leipzig with family, 22 May. Cantata 75 performed in Nikolaikirche, 30 May. Examines organ at Störmthal, Nov. Magnificat (BWV243a) performed in Thomaskirche, 25 Dec. | Gassmann born, 3 May. |
| 1724 | 39 | Ninth child, Gottfried Heinrich, born, 26 Feb. *St. John Passion* performed in Nikolaikirche, 7 April. Examines organ in Johanniskirche, Gera, 25 June. | |
| 1725 | 40 | Tenth child, Christian Gottlieb, bapt., 14 April. Bach gives organ recitals in Sophienkirche, Dresden, 19–20 Sept. Visits Cöthen, 15 Dec. | J. P. Krieger (75) dies, 6 Feb; A. Scarlatti (65) dies, 22 Oct. |
| 1726 | 41 | Eleventh child, Elisabeth Juliana Friederica, bapt., 5 April. Daughter, Christiana Sophia Henrietta (3), dies, 29 June. Partita I (BWV825) published, Michaelmas. | Lalande (68) dies, 18 June. |

| Year | Age | Life | Contemporary Musicians |
|------|-----|------|------------------------|
| 1727 | 42 | *St Matthew Passion* performed in Thomaskirche, 11 April (?). *Trauer Ode* (BWV198) performed, 17 Oct, at memorial ceremony for Electress Christiane Eberhardine (died, 5 Sept). Bach's twelfth child, Ernestus Andreas, bapt., 30 Oct; dies, 1 Nov. | Traetta born, 30 March. |
| 1728 | 43 | Son, Christian Gottlieb (3), dies, 21 Sept. Thirteenth child, Regina Johanna, bapt., 10 Oct. Prince Leopold of Anhalt-Cöthen (33) dies, 19 Nov. Bach's sister, Marie Salome Wiegand (née Bach) (51), dies in Erfurt; buried 27 Dec. | Piccinni born, 16 Jan; Steffani (73) dies, 12 Feb. |
| 1729 | 44 | Bach visits Weissenfels, Feb. Visits Cöthen to perform funeral music for Prince Leopold, 23–4 March. *St Matthew Passion* performed (for ?second time) in Thomaskirche, 15 April. Disputes with council over admission of unmusical pupils to Thomasschule. Bach assumes direction of *collegium musicum*. Illness prevents his visiting Handel in Halle, June. Rektor of Thomasschule, J. H. Ernesti (77), dies, 16 Oct. | Heinichen (46) dies, 16 July. |
| 1730 | 45 | Fourteenth child, Christiana Benedicta Louisa, bapt., 1 Jan; dies, 4 Jan. Bach addresses memorandum on church music to town council, 23 Aug, and letter to Erdmann seeking possible employment in Danzig, 28 Oct. J. M. Gesner appointed Rektor of the Thomasschule, 8 Sept. | |
| 1731 | 46 | Clavier-Übung I (BWV825–30) published. Fifteenth child, Christiana Dorothea, bapt., 18 March. *St Mark Passion* performed in Thomaskirche, 23 March. Bach gives organ recitals in Dresden, 14–21 Sept. Examines organ at Stöntzsch, 12 Nov. | Cannabich bapt., 28 Dec. |

| Year | Age | Life | Contemporary Musicians |
|------|-----|------|------------------------|
| 1732 | 47 | Sixteenth child, Johann Christoph Friedrich, born, 21 June. Daughter, Christiana Dorothea (1), dies, 31 Aug. Bach examines organ in Martinskirche, Cassel, 22–8 Sept. | Marchand (63) dies, 17 Feb; J. Haydn born, 31 March. |
| 1733 | 48 | Daughter, Regina Johanna (4), dies 25 April. Son, Wilhelm Friedemann (23), appointed organist at Sophienkirche, Dresden, 23 June. Bach visits Dresden, July, and presents *Missa* (BWV232¹) to Elector Friedrich August II. Seventeenth child, Johann August Abraham, bapt., 5 Nov; dies, 6 Nov. | Böhm (71) dies, 18 May; Couperin (64) dies, 11 Sept. |
| 1734 | 49 | J. A. Ernesti (27) appointed Rektor of the Thomasschule. *Christmas Oratorio* parts I–III performed, 25, 26, 27 Dec. | Gossec born, 17 Jan. |
| 1735 | 50 | *Christmas Oratorio* parts IV–VI performed, 1, 2, 6 Jan. *Clavier-Übung* II (BWV971, 831) published, May. Bach examines organ in Marienkirche, Mühlhausen, June, where his son Gottfried Bernhard (20) is appointed organist, 16 June. Bach's eighteenth child, Johann Christian, bapt., 7 Sept. | |
| 1736 | 51 | 'Battle of the prefects' with Ernesti begins, July. Appointed *Hofcompositeur* to the Elector of Saxony, 19 Nov. Gives organ recital in Frauenkirche, Dresden, 1 Dec. | Pergolesi (26) dies, 16 March; Caldara (*c.* 66) dies, 28 Dec. |
| 1737 | 52 | Son, Johann Gottfried Bernhard (22), appointed organist at the Jakobikirche, Sangerhausen, 4 April. Bach temporarily relinquishes directorship of the *collegium musicum,* spring. J. A. Scheibe publishes adverse criticism of Bach's music. Johann Elias Bach joins Bach's household as tutor and secretary, ?Oct. Nineteenth child, Johanna Carolina, bapt., 30 Oct. | Mysliveček born, 9 March; M. Haydn born, 14 Sept. |

| Year | Age | Life | Contemporary Musicians |
|------|-----|------|------------------------|
| 1738 | 53 | Son, Carl Philipp Emanuel (24), appointed harpsichordist to crown prince Frederick of Prussia. Bach visits Dresden, May. Son, Johann Gottfried Bernhard (23), contracts debts at Sangerhausen and absconds. | |
| 1739 | 54 | Son, Johann Gottfried Bernhard (24), dies, 27 May. Bach gives organ recital in the Schlosskirche, Altenburg. *Clavier-Übung* III published, Sept. Resumes as director of the *collegium musicum,* 2 Oct. Visits Weissenfels with Anna Magdalena, 7–14 Nov. | Vanhal born, 12 May; B. Marcello (52/53) dies, 24 July; Keiser (65) dies, 12 Sept; Dittersdorf born, 2 Nov. |
| 1740 | 55 | Visits Halle, April. | Paisiello born, 9 May. |
| 1741 | 56 | Visits son, Carl Philipp Emanuel, in Berlin, Aug. Anna Magdalena seriously ill. Bach visits Dresden, Nov. *Clavier-Übung* IV published (or 1742). | Grétry born, 8 Feb; Fux (*c.* 80) dies, 13 Feb; Vivaldi (63) dies, 28 July |
| 1742 | 57 | Twentieth child, Regina Susanna, bapt., 22 Feb. Johann Elias Bach leaves Leipzig, 31 Oct. | |
| 1743 | 58 | Examines organ in Johanniskirche, Leipzig, Dec. | Boccherini born, 19 Feb. |
| 1744 | 59 | Son, Carl Philipp Emanuel (30), marries Johanna Maria Dannemann (20) in Berlin. | |
| 1745 | 60 | First grandchild, Johann August Bach, born 30 Nov. | Zelenka (66) dies, 23 Dec. |
| 1746 | 61 | Son, Wilhelm Friedemann (36), appointed organist at the Liebfrauenkirche, Halle, 16 April. Bach examines organs in Zschortau, 7 Aug, and Wenzelskirche, Naumburg, 27 Sept. | |
| 1747 | 62 | Visits court of Frederick the Great at Potsdam, 7–8 May, and gives organ recital in the Heiliggeistkirche there, 8 May. Composes and publishes (Sept) the *Musical Offering*. Joins Mizler's Society of Musical Sciences, June, for which he com- | A. Marcello (63) dies, 19 June; Bononcini (76) dies, 9 July. |

| Year | Age | Life | Contemporary Musicians |
|------|-----|------|------------------------|
| | | poses the Canonic Variations (BWV769). | |
| 1748 | 63 | Grandson, Johann Sebastian Bach, born, 24 Sept. | J. G. Walther (63) dies, 23 March; Cimarosa born, 17 Dec. |
| 1749 | 64 | Daughter, Elisabeth Juliana Friederica (23), marries Johann Christoph Altnickol (29) in Leipzig, 20 Jan. Harrer performs *Probe* in Leipzig, with a view to succeeding Bach as Thomaskantor, 8 June. Grandson, Johann Sebastian Altnickol, born, 4 Oct, buried 21 Dec. Bach completes B minor Mass. | |
| 1750 | 65 | Son, Johann Christoph Friedrich (18), appointed court musician at Bückeburg, Jan. Bach occupied engraving the *Art of Fugue*. Operated on by oculist, John Taylor, March–April. Takes final communion, 22 July, and dies, 28 July. Buried in graveyard of the Johanniskirche, 31 July. | S. L. Weiss (64) dies, 12 Oct. Agricola aged 30; Albinoni 79; Altnickol 30; Arne 40; F. Benda 41; G. Benda 28; Boccherini 7; Boismortier 61; Boyce 39; Dittersdorf 11; Doles 35; Fasch 62; Gassmann 27; Geminiani 63; Gluck 36; Gossec 16; C. H. Graun *c.* 47; Graupner 67; Grétry 9; Harrer 47; Hasse 51; J. L. Haydn 18; M. Haydn 13; Jommelli 36; Kirnberger 29; J. L. Krebs 37; Leclair 53; Locatelli, 55; Martini 44; L. Mozart 31; Mysliveček 13; Paisiello 10; Piccinni 22; Pisendel 63; Porpora 64; Quantz 53; Rameau 67; Sammartini *c.* 50; J. Stamitz 33; Tartini 58; Telemann 69; Traetta 23; Vanhal 11; Wagenseil 35. |

# List of Works

This list of J. S. Bach's extant works adopts the numbering and, in outline, the arrangement of the standard *Bach-Werke-Verzeichnis* (BWV) by W. Schmieder (Leipzig, 1950, 2nd ed., 1990). For the vocal works the numbering of the *Bach Compendium (BC)* by Hans-Joachim Schulze and Christoph Wolff is also shown. It is divided into the following categories:

1 Church Cantatas [with alphabetical index]
2 Motets, Passions, Oratorios
3 Latin Church Music
4 Secular Cantatas
5 Chorales, Sacred Songs etc.
6 Organ Music
  (a) preludes/toccatas/fantasias and fugues
  (b) concerto arrangements
  (c) other 'free' compositions
  (d) chorale settings [with alphabetical index]
  (e) chorale variations (Partite)
7 Instrumental and Chamber Music
  (a) original clavier works
  (b) clavier arrangements of concertos
  (c) other instrumental and chamber works
8 Concertos and Orchestral Suites
9 Canons and Late Contrapuntal Works

*Notes*

Dates refer (a) in categories 1–4 (except for BWV232) to the earliest known or presumed performance in the form to which the BWV number applies; (b) in the case of published (pubd) works, to the date of publication; and (c) in all other cases to the period of composition. Dates are expressed according to British usage; e.g. 7.2.1723 = 7 February 1723.

Advent/Lent 1 (etc.) = 1st (etc.) Sunday in Advent/Lent; Easter/Epiphany/Trinity 1 (etc.) = 1st (etc.) Sunday after Easter/Epiphany/Trinity.

Keys: capitals indicate major keys, lower-case minor keys (C = C major; c = C minor).

Works of doubtful authenticity are indicated by an asterisk (*); spurious works are summarized at the end of each main category.

Editions: the relevant volume number of the two complete editions (for details, see p. xix) is given for each entry.

## 1 Church Cantatas

| BWV | BC | Text incipit (author) | Occasion | Date | BG; NBA vol. |
|---|---|---|---|---|---|
| 1 | A 173 | Wie schön leuchtet der Morgenstern | Annunciation | 25.3.1725 | i; I/28.2 |
| 2 | A 98 | Ach Gott, vom Himmel sieh darein | Trinity 2 | 18.6.1724 | i; I/16 |
| 3 | A 33 | Ach Gott, wie manches Herzeleid | Epiphany 2 | 14.1.1725 | i; I/5 |
| 4 | A 54 | Christ lag in Todes Banden | Easter | ?1707–8 | i; I/9 |
| 5 | A 145 | Wo soll ich fliehen hin | Trinity 19 | 15.10.1724 | i; I/24 |
| 6 | A 57 | Bleib bei uns, denn es will Abend | Easter Monday | 2.4.1725 | i; I/10 |
| 7 | A 177 | Christ unser Herr zum Jordan kam | St John | 24.6.1724 | i; I/29 |
| 8 | A 137 | Liebster Gott, wenn werd ich sterben? | Trinity 16 | 24.9.1724 | i; I/23 |
| 9 | A 107 | Es ist das Heil uns kommen her | Trinity 6 | c 1732–5 | i; I/17.2 |
| 10 | A 175 | Meine Seele erhebt den Herren | Visitation | 2.7.1724 | i; I/28.2 |
| 11 | D 9 | Lobet Gott in seinen Reichen [Ascension Oratorio] | Ascension | 19.5.1735 | ii; II/8 |
| 12 | A 68 | Weinen, Klagen, Sorgen, Zagen (S. Franck) | Easter 3 | 22.4.1714 | ii; I/11.2 |
| 13 | A 34 | Meine Seufzer, meine Tränen (G. C. Lehms) | Epiphany 2 | 20.1.1726 | ii; I/5 |
| 14 | A 40 | Wär Gott nicht mit uns diese Zeit | Epiphany 4 | 30.1.1735 | ii; I/6 |
| 16 | A 23 | Herr Gott, dich loben wir (Lehms) | New Year | 1.1.1726 | ii; I/4 |

| BWV | BC | Text incipit (author) | Occasion | Date | BG; NBA vol. |
|---|---|---|---|---|---|
| 17 | A 131 | Wer Dank opfert, der preiset mich | Trinity 14 | 22.9.1726 | ii; I/21 |
| 18 | A 44 | Gleichwie der Regen und Schnee (E. Neumeister) | Sexagesima | 1713–15 | ii; I/7 |
| 19 | A 180 | Es erhub sich ein Streit | St Michael | 29.9.1726 | ii; I/30 |
| 20 | A 95 | O Ewigkeit, du Donnerwort | Trinity 1 | 11.6.1724 | ii; I/15 |
| 21 | A 99 | Ich hatte viel Bekümmernis (?Franck) | Trinity 3 | 17.6.1714 | v/1; I/16 |
| 22 | A 48 | Jesus nahm zu sich die Zwölfe | Quinquagesima | 7.2.1723 | v/1; I/8.1 |
| 23 | A 47 | Du wahrer Gott und Davids Sohn | Quinquagesima | 7.2.1723 | v/1; I/8.1 |
| 24 | A 102 | Ein ungefärbt Gemüte (Neumeister) | Trinity 4 | 20.6.1723 | v/1; I/17.1 |
| 25 | A 129 | Es ist nichts Gesundes an meinem Leibe | Trinity 14 | 29.8.1723 | v/1; I/21 |
| 26 | A 162 | Ach wie flüchtig, ach wie nichtig | Trinity 24 | 19.11.1724 | v/1; I/27 |
| 27 | A 138 | Wer weiss, wie nahe mir mein Ende | Trinity 16 | 6.10.1726 | v/1; I/23 |
| 28 | A 20 | Gottlob! nun geht das Jahr zu Ende (Neumeister) | Sunday after Christmas | 30.12.1725 | v/1; I/3 |
| 29 | B8 | Wir danken dir, Gott | council election | 27.8.1731 | v/1; I/32.2 |
| 30 | A 178 | Freue dich, erlöste Schar (?Picander) | St John | ?1738–42 | v/1; I/29 |
| 31 | A 55 | Der Himmel lacht! (Franck) | Easter | 21.4.1715 | vii; I/9 |
| 32 | A 31 | Liebster Jesu, mein Verlangen (Lehms) | Epiphany 1 | 13.1.1726 | vii; I/5 |
| 33 | A 127 | Allein zu dir, Herr Jesu Christ | Trinity 13 | 3.9.1724 | vii; I/21 |
| 34 | A 84 | O ewiges Feuer, O Ursprung der Liebe | Whitsunday | c. 1746–7 | vii; I/13 |
| 34a | B 13 | O ewiges Feuer, O Ursprung der Liebe | wedding | 1726 | xli; I/33 |
| 35 | A 125 | Geist und Seele wird verwirret (Lehms) | Trinity 12 | 8.9.1726 | vii; I/20 |
| 36 | A 3 | Schwingt freudig euch empor (?Picander) | Advent 1 | 2.12.1731 | vii; I/1 |

| BWV | BC | Text incipit (author) | Occasion | Date | BG; NBA vol. |
|---|---|---|---|---|---|
| 37 | A 75 | Wer da gläubet und getauft wird | Ascension | 18.5.1724 | vii; I/12 |
| 38 | A 152 | Aus tiefer Not schrei ich zu dir | Trinity 21 | 29.10.1724 | vii; I/25 |
| 39 | A 96 | Brich dem Hungrigen dein Brot | Trinity 1 | 23.6.1726 | vii; I/15 |
| 40 | A 12 | Darzu ist erschienen der Sohn Gottes | 2nd day of Christmas | 26.12.1723 | vii; I/3 |
| 41 | A 22 | Jesu, nun sei gepreiset | New Year | 1.1.1725 | x; I/4 |
| 42 | A 63 | Am Abend aber desselbigen Sabbats | Easter 1 | 8.4.1725 | x; I/11.1 |
| 43 | A 77 | Gott fähret auf mit Jauchzen | Ascension | 30.5.1726 | x; I/12 |
| 44 | A 78 | Sie werden euch in den Bann tun | Sunday after Ascension | 21.5.1724 | x; I/12 |
| 45 | A 113 | Es ist dir gesagt, Mensch | Trinity 8 | 11.8.1726 | x; I/18 |
| 46 | A 117 | Schauet doch und sehet | Trinity 10 | 1.8.1723 | x; I/19 |
| 47 | A 141 | Wer sich selbst erhöhet (Helbig) | Trinity 17 | 13.10.1726 | x; I/23 |
| 48 | A 144 | Ich elender Mensch | Trinity 19 | 3.10.1723 | x; I/24 |
| 49 | A 150 | Ich geh und suche mit Verlangen | Trinity 20 | 3.11.1726 | x; I/25 |
| 50 | A 194 | Nun ist das Heil und die Kraft | St Michael | ? | x; I/30 |
| 51 | A 134 | Jauchzet Gott in allen Landen! | Trinity 15 | 17.9.1730 | xii/2; I/22 |
| 52 | A 160 | Falsche Welt, dir trau ich nicht | Trinity 23 | 24.11.1726 | xii/2; I/26 |
| 54 | A 51 | Widerstehe doch der Sünde (Lehms) | ?Lent 3 | ?24.3.1715 | xii/2; I/18 |
| 55 | A 157 | Ich armer Mensch, ich Sündenknecht | Trinity 22 | 17.11.1726 | xii/2; I/26 |
| 56 | A 146 | Ich will den Kreuzstab gerne tragen | Trinity 19 | 27.10.1726 | xii/2; I/24 |
| 57 | A 14 | Selig ist der Mann (Lehms) | 2nd day of Christmas | 26.12.1725 | xii/2; I/3 |
| 58 | A 26 | Ach Gott, wie manches Herzeleid | Sunday after New Year | 5.1.1727 | xii/2; I/4 |
| 59 | A 82 | Wer mich liebet (Neumeister) | Whitsunday | ?16.5.1723 | xii/2; I/13 |
| 60 | A 161 | O Ewigkeit, du Donnerwort | Trinity 24 | 7.11.1723 | xii/2; I/27 |

| BWV | BC | Text incipit (author) | Occasion | Date | BG; NBA vol. |
|------|------|------------------------|-----------|--------|---------------|
| 61 | A 1 | Nun komm, der Heiden Heiland (Neumeister) | Advent 1 | 2.12.1714 | xvi; I/1 |
| 62 | A 2 | Nun komm, der Heiden Heiland | Advent 1 | 3.12.1724 | xvi; I/1 |
| 63 | A 8 | Christen, ätzet diesen Tag (?J. M. Heineccius) | Christmas | 25.12.1714 | xvi; I/2 |
| 64 | A 15 | Sehet, welch eine Liebe (Knauer) | 3rd day of Christmas | 27.12.1723 | xvi; I/3 |
| 65 | A 27 | Sie werden aus Saba alle kommen | Epiphany | 6.1.1724 | xvi; I/5 |
| 66 | A 56 | Erfreut euch, ihr Herzen | Easter Monday | 10.4.1724 | xvi; I/10 |
| 67 | A 62 | Halt im Gedächtnis Jesum Christ | Easter 1 | 16.4.1724 | xvi; I/11.1 |
| 68 | A 86 | Also hat Gott die Welt geliebt (Ziegler) | Whit Monday | 21.5.1725 | xvi; I/14 |
| 69 | B 10 | Lobe den Herrn | council election | 1743–8 | xvi; I/32 |
| 69a | A 123 | Lobe den Herrn (Knauer) | Trinity 12 | 15.8.1723 | xvi; I/20 |
| 70 | A 165 | Wachet! betet! betet! wachet! (Franck, adapted) | Trinity 26 | 21.11.1723 | xvi; I/27 |
| 71 | B 1 | Gott ist mein König (? G. C. Eilmar) | council election | 4.2.1708 | xviii; I/32.1 |
| 72 | A 37 | Alles nur nach Gottes Willen (Franck) | Epiphany 3 | 27.1.1726 | xviii; I/6 |
| 73 | A 35 | Herr, wie du willt, so schicks mit mir | Epiphany 3 | 23.1.1724 | xviii; I/6 |
| 74 | A 83 | Wer mich liebet (Ziegler) | Whitsunday | 20.5.1725 | xviii; I/13 |
| 75 | A 94 | Die Elenden sollen essen | Trinity 1 | 30.5.1723 | xviii; I/15 |
| 76 | A 97 | Die Himmel erzählen die Ehre Gottes | Trinity 2 | 6.6.1723 | xviii; I/16 |
| 77 | A 126 | Du sollt Gott, deinen Herren, lieben (Knauer) | Trinity 13 | 22.8.1723 | xviii; I/21 |
| 78 | A 130 | Jesu, der du meine Seele | Trinity 14 | 10.9.1724 | xviii; I/21 |
| 79 | A 184 | Gott der Herr ist Sonn und Schild | Reformation festival | 31.10.1725 | xviii; I/31 |

| BWV | BC | Text incipit (author) | Occasion | Date | BG; NBA vol. |
|---|---|---|---|---|---|
| 80 | A 183 | Ein feste Burg ist unser Gott (Franck) | Reformation festival | ?c. 1735–9 | xviii; I/31 |
| 81 | A 39 | Jesus schläft, was soll ich hoffen? | Epiphany 4 | 30.1.1724 | xx/1; I/16 |
| 82 | A 169 | Ich habe genung | Purification | 2.2.1727 | xx/1; I/28.1 |
| 83 | A 167 | Erfreute Zeit im neuen Bunde | Purification | 2.2.1724 | xx/1; I/28.1 |
| 84 | A 43 | Ich bin vergnügt mit meinem Glücke (?Picander) | Septuagesima | 9.2.1727 | xx/1; I/7 |
| 85 | A 66 | Ich bin ein guter Hirt | Easter 2 | 15.4.1725 | xx/1; I/11.1 |
| 86 | A 73 | Wahrlich, wahrlich, ich sage euch | Easter 5 | 14.5.1724 | xx/1; I/12 |
| 87 | A 74 | Bisher habt ihr nichts gebeten (Ziegler) | Easter 5 | 6.5.1725 | xx/1; I/12 |
| 88 | A 105 | Siehe, ich will viel Fischer aussenden | Trinity 5 | 21.7.1726 | xx/1; I/17.2 |
| 89 | A 155 | Was soll ich aus dir machen, Ephraim? | Trinity 22 | 24.10.1723 | xx/1; I/26 |
| 90 | A 163 | Es reisset euch ein schrecklich Ende | Trinity 25 | 14.11.1723 | xx/1; I/27 |
| 91 | A 9 | Gelobet seist du, Jesu Christ | Christmas | 25.12.1724 | xxii; I/2 |
| 92 | A 42 | Ich hab in Gottes Herz und Sinn | Septuagesima | 28.1.1725 | xxii; I/7 |
| 93 | A 104 | Wer nur den lieben Gott lässt walten | Trinity 5 | 9.7.1724 | xxii; I/17.2 |
| 94 | A 115 | Was frag ich nach der Welt | Trinity 9 | 6.8.1724 | xxii; I/19 |
| 95 | A 136 | Christus, der ist mein Leben | Trinity 16 | 12.9.1723 | xxii; I/23 |
| 96 | A 142 | Herr Christ, der einge Gottessohn | Trinity 18 | 8.10.1724 | xxii; I/24 |
| 97 | A 189 | In allen meinen Taten | ? | 1734 | xxii; I/34 |
| 98 | A 153 | Was Gott tut, das ist wohlgetan | Trinity 21 | 10.11.1726 | xxii; I/25 |
| 99 | A 133 | Was Gott tut, das ist wohlgetan | Trinity 15 | 17.9.1724 | xxii; I/22 |
| 100 | A 191 | Was Gott tut, das ist wohlgetan | ? | c. 1734 | xxii; I/34 |
| 101 | A 118 | Nimm von uns, Herr, du treuer Gott | Trinity 10 | 13.8.1724 | xxiii; I/19 |
| 102 | A 119 | Herr, deine Augen sehen nach dem Glauben | Trinity 10 | 25.8.1726 | xxiii; I/19 |

| BWV | BC | Text incipit (author) | Occasion | Date | BG; NBA vol. |
|---|---|---|---|---|---|
| 103 | A 69 | Ihr werdet weinen (Ziegler) | Easter 3 | 22.4.1725 | xxiii; I/11.2 |
| 104 | A 65 | Du Hirte Israel, höre | Easter 2 | 23.4.1724 | xxiii; I/11.1 |
| 105 | A 114 | Herr, gehe nicht ins Gericht | Trinity 9 | 25.7.1723 | xxiii; I/19 |
| 106 | B 18 | Gottes Zeit ist die allerbeste Zeit ('Actus tragicus') | funeral | c. 1708 | xxiii; I/34 |
| 107 | A 109 | Was willst du dich betrüben | Trinity 7 | 23.7.1724 | xxiii; I/18 |
| 108 | A 72 | Es ist euch gut (Ziegler) | Easter 4 | 29.4.1725 | xxiii; I/12 |
| 109 | A 151 | Ich glaube, lieber Herr | Trinity 21 | 17.10.1723 | xxiii; I/25 |
| 110 | A 10 | Unser Mund sei voll Lachens (Lehms) | Christmas | 25.12.1725 | xxiii; I/2 |
| 111 | A 36 | Was mein Gott will, das g'scheh allzeit | Epiphany 3 | 21.1.1725 | xxiv; I/6 |
| 112 | A 67 | Der Herr ist mein getreuer Hirt | Easter 2 | 8.4.1731 | xxiv; I/11.1 |
| 113 | A 122 | Herr Jesu Christ, du höchstes Gut | Trinity 11 | 20.8.1724 | xxiv; I/20 |
| 114 | A 139 | Ach, lieben Christen, seid getrost | Trinity 17 | 1.10.1724 | xxiv; I/23 |
| 115 | A 156 | Mache dich, mein Geist, bereit | Trinity 22 | 5.11.1724 | xxiv; I/26 |
| 116 | A 164 | Du Friedefürst, Herr Jesu Christ | Trinity 25 | 26.11.1724 | xxiv; I/27 |
| 117 | A 187 | Sei Lob und Ehr dem höchsten Gut | ? | c.1728-31 | xxiv; I/34 |
| 119 | B 3 | Preise Jerusalem, den Herrn | council election | 30.8.1723 | xxiv; I/32.1 |
| 120 | B 6 | Gott, man lobet dich in der Stille | council election | 1728/9 | xxiv; I/32.2 |
| 120a | B 15 | Herr Gott, Beherrscher aller Dinge | wedding | 1729 | xli; I/33 |
| 121 | A 13 | Christum wir sollen loben schon | 2nd day of Christmas | 26.12.1724 | xxvi; I/3 |
| 122 | A 19 | Das neugeborne Kindelein | Sunday after Christmas | 31.12.1724 | xxvi; I/3 |
| 123 | A 28 | Liebster Immanuel, Herzog der Frommen | Epiphany | 6.1.1725 | xxvi; I/5 |
| 124 | A 30 | Meinen Jesum lass ich nicht | Epiphany 1 | 7.1.1725 | xxvi; I/5 |

| BWV | BC | Text incipit (author) | Occasion | Date | BG; NBA vol. |
|------|------|------|------|------|------|
| 125 | A 168 | Mit Fried und Freud ich fahr dahin | Purification | 2.2.1725 | xxvi; I/28.1 |
| 126 | A 46 | Erhalt uns, Herr, bei deinem Wort | Sexagesima | 4.2.1725 | xxvi; I/7 |
| 127 | A 49 | Herr Jesu Christ, wahr' Mensch und Gott | Quinquagesima | 11.2.1725 | xxvi; I/8.1 |
| 128 | A76 | Auf Christi Himmelfahrt (Ziegler) | Ascension | 10.5.1725 | xxvi; I/12 |
| 129 | A 93 | Gelobet sei der Herr, mein Gott | Trinity | ?16.6.1726 | xxvi; I/15 |
| 130 | A 179 | Herr Gott, dich loben alle wir | St Michael | 29.9.1724 | xxvi; I/30 |
| 131 | B 25 | Aus der Tiefen rufe ich, Herr | ? | 1707 | xxviii; I/34 |
| 132 | A 6 | Bereitet die Wege, bereitet (Franck) | Advent 4 | 22.12.1715 | xxviii; I/1 |
| 133 | A 16 | Ich freue mich in dir | 3rd day of Christmas | 27.12.1724 | xxviii; I/3 |
| 134 | A 59 | Ein Herz, das seinen Jesum lebend weiss | Easter Tuesday | 11.4.1724 | xxviii; I/10 |
| 135 | A 100 | Ach Herr, mich armen Sünder | Trinity 3 | 25.6.1724 | xxviii;1/16 |
| 136 | A 111 | Erforsche mich, Gott, und erfahre | Trinity 8 | 18.7.1723 | xxviii; I/18 |
| 137 | A 124 | Lobe den Herren, den mächtigen | Trinity 12 | 19.8.1725 | xxviii; I/20 |
| 138 | A 132 | Warum betrübst du dich, mein Herz | Trinity 15 | 5.9.1723 | xxviii, I/22 |
| 139 | A159 | Wohl dem, der sich auf seinen Gott | Trinity 23 | 12.11.1724 | xxviii; I/26 |
| 140 | A 166 | Wachet auf, ruft uns die Stimme | Trinity 27 | 25.11.1731 | xxviii; I/27 |
| *143 | — | Lobe den Herrn, meine Seele | New Year | ?1708–14 | xxx; I/4 |
| 144 | A 41 | Nimm was dein ist, und gehe hin | Septuagesima | 6.2.1724 | xxx; I/7 |
| 145 | A 60 | Auf, mein Herz! Des Herren Tag [= Ich lebe, mein Herze] (Picander) | Easter Tuesday | ?19.4.1729 | xxx; I/10 |
| 146 | A 70 | Wir müssen durch viel Trübsal | Easter 3 | ?1726 or 1728 | xxx; I/11.2 |

| BWV | BC | Text incipit (author) | Occasion | Date | BG; NBA vol. |
|---|---|---|---|---|---|
| 147 | A 174 | Herz und Mund und Tat und Leben (Franck, adapted) | Visitation | 2.7.1723 | xxx; I/28.2 |
| 148 | A 140 | Bringet dem Herrn Ehre (Picander, adapted) | Trinity 17 | ?19.9.1723 | xxx; I/23 |
| 149 | A 181 | Man singet mit Freuden (Picander) | St Michael | 1728/9 | xxx; I/30 |
| 150 | B 24 | Nach dir, Herr, verlanget mich | ? | ?before 1708 | xxx; I/41 |
| 151 | A 17 | Süsser Trost, mein Jesus kömmt (Lehms) | 3rd day of Christmas | 27.12.1725 | xxxii; I/3 |
| 152 | A 18 | Tritt auf die Glaubensbahn (Franck) | Sunday after Christmas | 30.12.1714 | xxxii; I/3 |
| 153 | A 25 | Schau, lieber Gott, wie meine Feind | Sunday after New Year | 2.1.1724 | xxxii; I/4 |
| 154 | A 29 | Mein liebster Jesus ist verloren | Epiphany 1 | 9.1.1724 | xxxii; I/5 |
| 155 | A 32 | Mein Gott, wie lang, ach lange (Franck) | Epiphany 2 | 19.1.1716 | xxxii; I/5 |
| 156 | A 38 | Ich steh mit einem Fuss im Grabe (Picander) | Epiphany 3 | ?23.1.1729 | xxxii; I/6 |
| 157 | A170 | Ich lasse dich nicht (Picander) | funeral | 6.2.1727 | xxxii; I/34 |
| 158 | A 61 | Der Friede sei mit dir | Easter Tuesday | ?after 1722 | xxxii; I/10 |
| 159 | A 50 | Sehet, wir gehn hinauf (Picander) | Quinquagesima | ?27.2.1729 | xxxii; I/8,1 |
| 161 | A 135 | Komm, du süsse Todesstunde (Franck) | Trinity 16 | ?27.9.1716 | xxxiii; I/23 |
| 162 | A 148 | Ach! ich sehe, itzt, da ich zu Hochzeit gehe (Franck) | Trinity 20 | 25.10.1716 | xxxiii; I/25 |
| 163 | A 158 | Nur jedem das Seine (Franck) | Trinity 23 | 24.11.1715 | xxxiii; I/26 |
| 164 | A 128 | Ihr, die ihr euch von Christo nennet (Franck) | Trinity 13 | 26.8.1725 | xxxiii; I/21 |
| 165 | A 90 | O heiliges Geist- und Wasserbad (Franck) | Trinity | 16.6.1715 | xxxiii; I/15 |
| 166 | A 71 | Wo gehest du hin? | Easter 4 | 7.5.1724 | xxxiii; I/12 |
| 167 | A 176 | Ihr Menschen, rühmet Gottes Liebe | St John | 24.6.1723 | xxxiii; I/29 |

| BWV | BC | *Text incipit (author)* | *Occasion* | *Date* | *BG; NBA vol.* |
|-----|-----|-----|-----|-----|-----|
| 168 | A 116 | Tue Rechnung! Donnerwort (Franck) | Trinity 9 | 29.7.1725 | xxxiii; I/19 |
| 169 | A 143 | Gott soll allein mein Herze haben | Trinity 18 | 20.10.1726 | xxxiii; I/24 |
| 170 | A 106 | Vergnügte Ruh, beliebte Seelenlust (Lehms) | Trinity 6 | 28.7.1726 | xxxiii; I/17.2 |
| 171 | A 24 | Gott, wie dein Name, so ist auch dein Ruhm (Picander) | New Year | ?1.1.1729 | xxxv; I/4 |
| 172 | A 81 | Erschallet, ihr Lieder (?Franck) | Whitsunday | 20.5.1714 | xxxv; I/13 |
| 173 | A 85 | Erhöhtes Fleisch und Blut | Whit Monday | ?29.5.1724 | xxxv; I/14 |
| 174 | A 87 | Ich liebe den Höchsten (Picander) | Whit Monday | 6.6.1729 | xxxv; I/14 |
| 175 | A 89 | Er rufet seinen Schafen mit Namen (Ziegler) | Whit Tuesday | 22.5.1725 | xxxv; I/14 |
| 176 | A 92 | Es ist ein trotzig, und verzagt Ding (Ziegler) | Trinity | 27.5.1725 | xxxv; I/15 |
| 177 | A 103 | Ich ruf zu dir, Herr Jesu Christ | Trinity 4 | 6.7.1732 | xxxv; I/17.1 |
| 178 | A 112 | Wo Gott, der Herr, nicht bei uns hält | Trinity 8 | 30.7.1724 | xxxv; I/18 |
| 179 | A 121 | Siehe zu, dass deine Gottesfurcht | Trinity 11 | 8.8.1723 | xxxv; I/20 |
| 180 | A 149 | Schmücke dich, o liebe Seele | Trinity 20 | 22.10.1724 | xxxv; I/25 |
| 181 | A 45 | Leichgesinnte Flattergeister | Sexagesima | 13.2.1724 | xxxvii; I/7 |
| 182 | A 53 | Himmelskönig, sei willkommen (?Franck) | Palm Sunday | 25.3.1714 | xxxvii; I/8.2 |
| 183 | A 79 | Sie werden euch in den Bann tun (Ziegler) | Sunday after Ascension | 13.5.1725 | xxxvii; I/12 |
| 184 | A 88 | Erwünschtes Freudenlicht | Whit Tuesday | 30.5.1724 | xxxvii; I/14 |
| 185 | A 101 | Barmherziges Herze der ewigen Liebe (Franck) | Trinity 4 | 14.7.1715 | xxxvii; I/17.1 |

| BWV | BC | Text incipit (author) | Occasion | Date | BG; NBA vol. |
|-----|-----|-----------------------|----------|------|--------------|
| 186 | A 108 | Ärgre dich, o Seele, nicht (Franck, adapted) | Trinity 7 | 11.7.1723 | xxxvii; I/18 |
| 187 | A 110 | Es wartet alles auf dich | Trinity 7 | 4.8.1726 | xxxvii; I/18 |
| 188 | A 154 | Ich habe meine Zuversicht (Picander) | Trinity 21 | ?17.10.1728 | xxxvii; I/25 |
| 190 | A 21 | Singet dem Herrn (incomplete) | New Year | 1.1.1724 | xxxvii; I/4 |
| 191 | E 16 | Gloria in excelsis Deo | Christmas | c. 1743–6 | xli; I/2 |
| 192 | A 188 | Nun danket alle Gott (incomplete) | ? | ?1730 | xli; I/34 |
| 193 | B 5 | Ihr Tore zu Zion (incomplete) | council election | 25.8.1727 | xli; I/32.1 |
| 194 | B 31, A 91 | Höchsterwünschtes Freudenfest | dedication of church and organ | 2.11.1723 | xxix; I/31 |
| 195 | B 14 | Dem Gerechten muss das Licht | wedding | 1727–31 | xii/1; I/33 |
| 196 | B 11 | Der Herr denket an uns | wedding | ?1708 | xiii/1; I/33 |
| 197 | B 16 | Gott ist unsre Zuversicht | wedding | c. 1736–7 | xiii/1; I/33 |
| 197a | A 11 | Ehre sei Gott in der Höhe (Picander) (incomplete) | Christmas | ?25.12.1728 | xli; I/2 |
| 199 | A 120 | Mein Herze schwimmt im Blut (Lehms) | Trinity 11 | ?27.8.1713 | —; I/20 |
| 200 | A 192 | Bekennen will ich seinen Namen (incomplete) | ? | c. 1742 | —; I/28.1 |
| 223 | A 186 | Meine Seele soll Gott loben (fragment) | ? | ?c. 1707–8 | —; — |

## Alphabetical index to church cantatas

*Spurious:* BWV15, Denn du wirst meine Seele (by J. L. Bach); BWV53, Schlage doch, gewünschte Stunde (by Hoffmann); BWV141, Das ist je gewisslich wahr (by Telemann); BWV142, Uns ist ein Kind geboren; BWV160, Ich weiss, dass mein Erlöser lebt (by Telemann); BWV189, Meine Seele rühmt und preist (by Hoffmann).

## 2 Motets, Passions, Oratorios

| BWV | BC | Title (author) | Date | BG; NBA vol. |
|---|---|---|---|---|
| 118 | B 23 | Motet: O Jesu Christ, mein Lebens Licht | 1736–7 | xxiv; III/1 |
| 225 | C 1 | Motet: Singet dem Herrn | 1726–7 | xxxix; III/1 |
| 226 | C 2 | Motet: Der Geist hilft unser Schwachheit auf | 20.10.1729 | xxxix; III/1 |
| 227 | C 5 | Motet: Jesu, meine Freude | ? | xxxix; III/1 |
| 228 | C 4 | Motet: Fürchte dich nicht | ? | xxxix; III/1 |
| 229 | C 3 | Motet: Komm, Jesu, komm! (P. Thymich) | ?1730 | xxxix; III/1 |
| 230 | C 6 | Motet: Lobet den Herrn alle Heiden | ? | xxxix; III/1 |
| Anh. III 159★ | C 9 | Motet: Ich lasse dich nicht | before 1714 | — |
| 244 | D 3 | St Matthew Passion (Picander) | 11.4.1727 or 15.4.1729 | iv; II/5 |
| 245 | D 2 | St John Passion | 7.4.1724 | xii/1; II/4 |
| 11 | D 9 | Ascension Oratorio [see 'Church Cantatas'] | | |

| BWV | BC | Title (author) | Date | BG; NBA vol. |
|---|---|---|---|---|
| 248 | D 7 | Christmas Oratorio (?Picander) | 1734–5 | v/2; II/6 |
| 249 | D 8 | Easter Oratorio (?Picander) | 1.4.1725 | xxi/3; II/7 |

*Spurious:* BWV246 (St Luke Passion)

## 3 Latin Church Music

| BWV | BC | Title | Date | BG; NBA vol. |
|---|---|---|---|---|
| 232 | E 1 | Mass in b | 1724–c. 1749 | vi; II/1 |
| 233 | E 6 | Missa in F | ?1735–40 | viii; II/2 |
| 234 | E 3 | Missa in A | ?1735–40 | viii; II/2 |
| 235 | E 5 | Missa in g | ?1735–40 | viii; II/2 |
| 236 | E 4 | Missa in G | ?1735–40 | viii; II/2 |
| 237 | E 10 | Sanctus in C | ?24.6.1723 | xi; II/2 |
| 238 | E 11 | Sanctus in D | ?25.12.1723 | xi/1; II/2 |
| 239* | | Sanctus in d | c. 1735–46 | xi/1; II/9 |
| 240 | | Sanctus in G | c. 1742 | xi/1; II/9 |
| 241 | | Sanctus in D | c. 1747–8 | xli; II/9 |
| 242 | E 8 | Christe eleison (for Mass in c by Durante) | ?1727–31 | xli; II/2 |
| 1081 | E 9 | Credo (for Mass in F by Bassani) | 1747–8 | —; II/2(KB) |
| 243a | E 13 | Magnificat in E♭ | 25.12.1723 | —; II/3 |
| 243 | E 14 | Magnificat in D | c. 1732–5 | xi/1; II/3 |

## 4 Secular Cantatas

| BWV | BC | Incipit (occasion) | Author | Date | BG; NBA vol. |
|---|---|---|---|---|---|
| 30a | G 31 | Angenehmes Wiederau (homage to J. C. von Hennicke) | Picander | 28.9.1737 | v/1, xxxiv; I/39 |
| 36b | G 38 | Die Freude reget sich (homage to ?J. F. Rivinus) | ?Picander | ?1735 | xxxiv; I/38 |
| 36c | G 35 | Schwingt freudig euch empor (birthday) | ?Picander | 1725 | xxxiv; I/39 |
| 134a | G 5 | Die Zeit, die Tag und jahre macht (New Year) | Hunold | 1.1.1719 | xxix; I/35 |
| 173a | G 9 | Durchlauchtster Leopold (birthday of Prince Leopold) | ? | ?10.12.1722 | xxxiv; I/35 |

| BWV | BC | Incipit (occasion) | Author | Date | BG; NBA vol. |
|---|---|---|---|---|---|
| 198 | G 34 | Lass, Fürstin, lass noch [Trauer Ode] (commemorative service for Electress Christiane Eberhardine) | J. C. Gottsched | 17.10.1727 | xiii/3; I/38 |
| 201 | G 46 | Geschwinde, ihr wirbelnden Winde [Der Streit zwischen Phoebus und Pan] | Picander | 1729 | xi/2; I/40 |
| 202 | G 44 | Weichet nur, betrübte Schatten (wedding) | | before 1731 | xi/2; I/40 |
| *203 | G 51 | Amore traditore | ? | ? | xi/2; I/41 |
| 204 | G 45 | Ich bin in mir vergnügt | Hunold | 1726–7 | xi/2; I/40 |
| 205 | G 36 | Zerreisset, zersprenget (name-day of A. F. Müller) | Picander | 3.8.1725 | xi/2; I/38 |
| 206 | G 23, 26 | Schleicht, spielende Wellen (birthday of Elector Friedrich August II) | ?Picander | 7.10.1736 | xx/2; I/36 |
| 207 | G 37 | Vereinigte Zwietracht der wechselnden Saiten (installation of Professor G. Kortte) | ? | 11.12.1726 | xx/2; I/38 |
| 207a | G 22 | Auf, schmetternde Töne (name-day of Friedrich August II) | ?Picander | ?3.8.1735 | xx/2; I/37 |
| 208 | G 1,3 | Was mir behagt (birthday of Duke Christian of Weissenfels) | Franck | ?23.2.1713 | xxix; I/35 |
| 209 | G 50 | Non sa che sia dolore | ? | ? | xxix; I/41 |
| 210 | G 44 | O holder Tag, erwünschte Zeit (wedding) | ? | c. 1738–41 | xxix; I/40 |

| BWV | BC | Incipit (occasion) | Author | Date | BG; NBA vol. |
|---|---|---|---|---|---|
| 211 | G 48 | Schweigt stille, plaudert nicht [Coffee Cantata] | Picander | *c.* 1734 | xxix; I/40 |
| 212 | G 32 | Mer hahn en neue Oberkeet [Peasant Cantata] (homage to C. H. von Dieskau) | Picander | 30.8.1742 | xxix; I/39 |
| 213 | G 18 | Lasst uns sorgen, lasst uns wachen [Hercules auf dem Scheidewege] (birthday of Prince Friedrich Christian of Saxony) | Picander | 5.9.1733 | xxxiv; I/36 |
| 214 | G 19 | Tönet, ihr Pauken! Erschallet Trompeten! (birthday of Electress Maria Josepha) | ? | 8.12.1733 | xxxiv; I/36 |
| 215 | G 21 | Preise dein Glücke, gesegnetes Sachsen (anniversary of accession of Augustus III to Polish throne) | J. C. Clauder | 5.10.1734 | xxxiv; I/37 |
| 216 | G 43 | Vergnügte Pleisenstadt (wedding) [incomplete] | Picander | 5.2.1728 | —; I/40 |

## 5 Chorales, Sacred Songs etc.

| BWV | Item, date | BG; NBA vol. |
|---|---|---|
| 250–52 | 3 wedding chorales | xiii/1; III/2.1 |
| 253–438 | 186 harmonized chorales, pubd Leipzig, 1784–7, ed. J. P. Kirnberger and C. P. E. Bach | xxxix; III/2.1–2 |
| 439–507 | 69 hymns for voice and continuo, in Schemelli's *Musicalisches Gesang-Buch,* pubd Leipzig, 1736 [in most cases only figured bass is by Bach] | xxxix; III/2.1 |
| 509–18 | Vocal pieces in Clavierbüchlein, ii, for Anna Magdalena Bach, 1725 [some doubtful] | xxxix; V/4 |
| 524 | Quodlibet, SATB [incomplete], *c.* 1707 | |

*Spurious:* BWV 508 (Bist du bei mir), 519–23

## 6 Organ Music

### (a) Preludes/toccatas/fantasias and fugues (BG xv [except BWV549–51, 562: xxxviii]; NBA IV/5 [except BWV551, 564–6: IV/6])

| BWV | Title, key (date) |
|---|---|
| 531 | Prelude and Fugue, C (?before 1707) |
| 532 | Prelude and Fugue, D (?1708–17) |
| 533 | Prelude and Fugue, e (?c. 1704) |
| 534 | Prelude and Fugue, f (?1708–17) |
| 535 | Prelude and Fugue, g (?1705–17) |
| 536 | Prelude and Fugue, A (?1708–17) |
| 537 | Fantasia and Fugue, c (?1708–17, or later) |
| 538 | Toccata and Fugue, d (1708–17) |
| 539 | Prelude and Fugue, d (after 1720) |
| 540 | Toccata and Fugue, F (?1708–17) |
| 541 | Prelude and Fugue, G (?1708–17) |
| 542 | Fantasia and Fugue, g (1708–23) |
| 543 | Prelude and Fugue, a (?1708–17) |
| 544 | Prelude and Fugue, b(1727–31) |
| 545 | Prelude and Fugue, C (1708–17) |
| 546 | Prelude and Fugue,c (?after 1722) |

| BWV | Title, key (date) |
|---|---|
| 547 | Prelude and Fugue, C (?c. 1740) |
| 548 | Prelude and Fugue, e (1727–31) |
| 549 | Prelude and Fugue, c (?1703–7) |
| 550 | Prelude and Fugue, G (?before 1708) |
| 551 | Prelude and Fugue, a (?before 1708) |
| 552 | Prelude and Fugue, E♭ [see BWV 669–89] |
| 562 | Fantasia and Fugue, c (?1730–c. 1745) |
| 564 | Toccata, Adagio and Fugue, C (1708–17) |
| ★565 | Toccata and Fugue, d (?before 1708) |
| 566 | Prelude and Fugue, E (?before 1708) |

### (b) Concerto arrangements ?1713–14 (BG xxxviii; NBA IV/8)

| BWV | Key | Original composer |
|---|---|---|
| 592 | G | Prince Johann Ernst |
| 593 | a | Vivaldi, RV522 |
| 594 | C | Vivaldi, RV208 |

| BWV | Key | Original composer |
|---|---|---|
| 595 | C | Prince Johann Ernst |
| 596 | d | Vivaldi, RV565 |
| ★597 | E♭ | ? |

### (c) Other 'free' compositions

| BWV | Title, key | Date | BG; NBA vol. |
|---|---|---|---|
| 525–30 | 6 trio sonatas, E♭, c, d, e, C, G | c. 1730 | xv; IV/7 |
| ★563 | Fantasia, b | before 1707 | xxxviii; IV/6 |
| ★568 | Prelude, G | ?before 1708 | xxxviii; IV/6 |
| 569 | Prelude, a | ?before 1708 | xxxviii; IV/6 |
| 570 | Fantasia, C | ?before 1707 | xxxviii; IV/6 |
| 572 | Pièce d'orgue, G | before 1708 | xxxviii; IV/7 |
| 573 | Fantasia, C [incomplete] | c. 1722 | xxxviii; IV/6 |
| 574 | Fugue on theme by Legrenzi, c | ?before 1708 | xxxviii; IV/6 |
| 575 | Fugue, c | ?1708–17 | xxxviii; IV/6 |
| 578 | Fugue, g | ?before 1707 | xxxviii; IV/6 |
| 579 | Fugue on theme by Corelli, b | ?before 1708 | xxxviii; IV/6 |

| BWV | Title, key | Date | BG; NBA vol. |
|------|-----------|------|--------------|
| 582 | Passacaglia and Fugue, c | 1708–12 | xv; IV/7 |
| 583 | Trio, d | 1723–9 | xxxviii; IV/7 |
| 588 | Canzona, d | ?1704–7 | xxxviii; IV/7 |
| *589 | Alla breve, D | ? | xxxviii; IV/7 |
| 590 | Pastorella, F | ?after 1720 | xxxviii; IV/7 |
| 802–5 | 4 duets, e, F, G, a [see BWV669–89] | | |

## (d) Chorale settings

| BWV | Title | BWV | Title |
|------|-------|------|-------|

*Orgel-Büchlein, c.1713–16 (except BWV613: ?after 1724) (BG xxv/2; NBA IV/1)*

| BWV | Title | BWV | Title |
|------|-------|------|-------|
| 599 | Nun komm, der Heiden Heiland | 624 | Hilf Gott, dass mir's gelinge |
| 600 | Gott, durch deine Güte | 625 | Christ lag in Todesbanden |
| 601 | Herr Christ, der ein'ge Gottes-Sohn | 626 | Jesus Christus, unser Heiland |
| | | 627 | Christ ist erstanden |
| 602 | Lob sei dem allmächtigen Gott | 628 | Erstanden ist der heil'ge Christ |
| 603 | Puer natus in Bethlehem | 629 | Erschienen ist der herrliche Tag |
| 604 | Gelobet seist du, Jesu Christ | | |
| 605 | Der Tag, der ist so freudenreich | 630 | Heut' triumphiret Gottes Sohn |
| 606 | Vom Himmel hoch, da komm' ich her | 631 | Komm, Gott Schöpfer, heiliger Geist |
| 607 | Vom Himmel kam der Engel Schaar | 632 | Herr Jesu Christ, dich zu uns wend |
| 608 | In dulci jubilo | 633 | Liebster Jesu, wir sind hier |
| 609 | Lobt Gott, ihr Christen allzugleich | 634 | Liebster Jesu, wir sind hier |
| 610 | Jesu, meine Freude | 635 | Dies sind die heil'gen zehn Gebot' |
| 611 | Christum wir sollen loben schon | 636 | Vater unser im Himmelreich |
| 612 | Wir Christenleut' | 637 | Durch Adams Fall ist ganz verderbt |
| 613 | Helft mir Gottes Güte preisen | | |
| 614 | Das alte Jahr vergangen ist | 638 | Es ist das Heil uns kommen her |
| 615 | In dir ist Freude | | |
| 616 | Mit Fried' und Freud' ich fahr dahin | 639 | Ich ruf' zu dir, Herr Jesu Christ |
| 617 | Herr Gott, nun schleuss den Himmel auf | 640 | In dich hab' ich gehoffet, Herr |
| 618 | O Lamm Gottes, unschuldig | 641 | Wenn wir in höchsten Nöthen sein |
| 619 | Christe, du Lamm Gottes | | |
| 620 | Christus, der uns selig macht | 642 | Wer nur den lieben Gott lässt walten |
| 621 | Da Jesus an dem Kreuze stund | | |
| 622 | O Mensch, bewein' dein' Sünde gross | 643 | Alle Menschen müssen sterben |
| 623 | Wir danken dir, Herr Jesu Christ | 644 | Ach wie nichtig, ach wie flüchtig |

| BWV | Title | BWV | Title |
|---|---|---|---|

'Schübler' chorales, pubd 1748/9 (BG xxv/2; NBA IV/1)

| BWV | Title | BWV | Title |
|---|---|---|---|
| 645 | Wachet auf, ruft uns die Stimme | 649 | Ach bleib bei uns, Herr Jesu Christ |
| 646 | Wo soll ich fliehen hin | | |
| 647 | Wer nur den lieben Gott lässt walten | 650 | Kommst du nun, Jesu, vom Himmel |
| 648 | Meine Seele erhebt den Herren | | |

'Leipzig' chorales, mostly 1708–17, revised c. 1739–42 and later (BG xxv/2; NBA IV/2)

| BWV | Title | BWV | Title |
|---|---|---|---|
| 651 | Komm, heiliger Geist | 661 | Nun komm, der Heiden Heiland |
| 652 | Komm, heiliger Geist | | |
| 653 | An Wasserflüssen Babylon | 662 | Allein Gott in der Höh' sei Ehr' |
| 654 | Schmücke dich, o liebe Seele | 663 | Allein Gott in der Höh' sei Ehr' |
| 655 | Herr Jesu Christ, dich zu uns wend | 664 | Allein Gott in der Höh' sei Ehr' |
| | | 665 | Jesus Christus, unser Heiland |
| 656 | O Lamm Gottes, unschuldig | 666 | Jesus Christus, unser Heiland |
| 657 | Nun danket alle Gott | 667 | Komm, Gott Schöpfer, heiliger Geist |
| 658 | Von Gott will ich nicht lassen | | |
| 659 | Nun komm, der Heiden Heiland | 668 | Vor deinen Thron tret' ich (incomplete) |
| 660 | Nun komm, der Heiden Heiland | | |

Clavier-Übung III, pubd 1739 [includes also Prelude and Fugue BWV552 and 4 duets BWV802–5] (BG iii; NBA IV/4)

| BWV | Title | BWV | Title |
|---|---|---|---|
| 669 | Kyrie, Gott Vater in Ewigkeit | 680 | Wir glauben all' an einen Gott |
| 670 | Christe, aller Welt Trost | 681 | Wir glauben all' an einen Gott |
| 671 | Kyrie, Gott heiliger Geist | 682 | Vater unser im Himmelreich |
| 672 | Kyrie, Gott Vater in Ewigkeit | 683 | Vater unser im Himmelreich |
| 673 | Christe, aller Welt Trost | 684 | Christ, unser Herr, zum Jordan kam |
| 674 | Kyrie, Gott heiliger Geist | | |
| 675 | Allein Gott in der Höh' sei Ehr' | 685 | Christ, unser Herr, zum Jordan kam |
| 676 | Allein Gott in der Höh' sei Ehr' | | |
| 677 | Allein Gott in der Höh' sei Ehr' | 686 | Aus tiefer Not schrei ich zu dir |
| 678 | Dies sind die heil'gen zehn Gebot | 687 | Aus tiefer Not schrei ich zu dir |
| | | 688 | Jesus Christus unser Heiland |
| 679 | Dies sind die heil'gen zehn Gebot | 689 | Jesus Christus unser Heiland |

Miscellaneous chorales, ?c. 1708–17, unless otherwise stated (BG xl; NBA IV/3 (except * doubtful works: IV/9))

| BWV | Title | BWV | Title |
|---|---|---|---|
| 690 | Wer nur den lieben Gott lässt walten | 696 | Christum wir sollen loben schon |
| | | 697 | Gelobet seist du, Jesu Christ |
| 691 | Wer nur den lieben Gott lässt walten | 698 | Herr Christ, der ein'ge Gottes Sohn |
| 694 | Wo soll ich fliehen hin | 699 | Nun komm, der Heiden Heiland |
| 695 | Christ lag in Todesbanden | | |

| BWV | Title | BWV | Title |
|---|---|---|---|
| 700 | Vom Himmel hoch, da komm' ich her (before 1708; revised 1740s) | ★723 | Gelobet seist du, Jesu Christ |
| | | 724 | Gott, durch dein Güte/Gottes Sohn ist kommen (before 1708) |
| 701 | Vom Himmel hoch, da komm' ich her | 725 | Herr Gott, dich loben wir |
| ★702 | Das Jesulein soll doch mein Trost | 726 | Herr Jesu Christ, dich zu uns wend |
| 703 | Gottes Sohn ist kommen | 727 | Herzlich thut mich verlangen |
| 704 | Lob sei dem allmächtigen Gott | 728 | Jesus, meine Zuversicht (1722) |
| ★705 | Durch Adams Fall ist ganz verderbt | 729 | In dulci jubilo |
| 706 | Liebster Jesu, wir sind hier | 730 | Liebster Jesu, wir sind hier |
| ★707 | Ich hab' mein' Sach' | 731 | Liebster Jesu, wir sind hier |
| ★708 | Ich hab' mein' Sach' | 732 | Lobt Gott, ihr Christen, allzugleich (1703–17) |
| 709 | Herr Jesu Christ, dich zu uns wend | 733 | Meine Seele erhebt den Herren |
| 710 | Wir Christenleut' | 734 | Nun freut euch, lieben Christen/ Es ist gewisslich an der Zeit |
| 711 | Allein Gott in der Höh' sei Ehr' | 735 | Valet will ich dir geben (1703–9) |
| 712 | In dich hab' ich gehoffet, Herr | 736 | Valet will ich dir geben |
| 713 | Jesu meine Freude | 737 | Vater unser im Himmelreich (1703–9) |
| 714 | Ach Gott und Herr | | |
| 715 | Allein Gott in der Höh' sei Ehr' | 738 | Vom Himmel hoch, da komm' ich her |
| ★716 | Allein Gott in der Höh' sei Ehr' | 739 | Wie schön leuchtet der Morgenstern [not in *NBA*] |
| 717 | Allein Gott in der Höh' sei Ehr' | | |
| 718 | Christ lag in Todesbanden (1703–9) | 741 | Ach Gott, vom Himmel sieh' darein (?*c.* 1705, revised 1740s) |
| 719 | Der Tag, der ist so freudenreich | | |
| 720 | Ein' feste Burg ist unser Gott (?1709) | 742 | Ach Herr, mich armen Sünder |
| | | 764 | Wie schön leuchtet der Morgenstern [incomplete; not in *NBA*] |
| 721 | Erbarm' dich mein, o Herre Gott (1703–9) | | |
| 722 | Gelobet seist du, Jesu Christ (1703–17) | | |

*'Neumeister' chorales*, before 1710 (*NBA* V/9)

| | | | |
|---|---|---|---|
| 957 | Machs mit mir, Gott, nach deiner Güt | 1098 | Wir glauben all an einen Gott |
| 1090 | Wir Christenleut | 1099 | Aus tiefer Not schrei ich zu dir |
| 1091 | Das alte Jahr vergangen ist | 1100 | Allein zu dir, Herr Jesu Christ |
| 1092 | Herr Gott, nun schleuss den Himmel auf | 1101 | Durch Adams Fall ist ganz verderbt |
| 1093 | Herzliebster Jesu, was hast du verbrochen | 1102 | Du Friedefürst, Herr Jesu Christ |
| 1094 | O Jesu, wie ist dein Gestalt | 1103 | Erhalt uns, Herr, bei deinem Wort |
| 1095 | O Lamm Gottes unschuldig | 1104 | Wenn dich Unglück tut greifen an |
| 1097 | Ehre sei dir, Christe | 1105 | Jesu, meine Freude |

**Alphabetical index to chorale settings:**

## (e) chorale variations (Partite)

| BWV | Title | Date | BG; NBA vol. |
|-----|-------|------|--------------|
| 766 | Christ, der du bist der helle Tag | ?c. 1700 | xl; IV/1 |
| 767 | O Gott, du frommer Gott | ?c. 1700 | xl; IV/1 |
| 768 | Sei gegrüsset, Jesu gütig | ?c. 1700 | xl; IV/1 |
| 769 | Vom Himmel hoch, da komm' ich her | pubd 1747 | xl; IV/2 |
| 770 | Ach, was soll ich Sünder machen | ? | xl; IV/1 |

*Doubtful or spurious:* BWV553–60 (Eight short preludes and fugues), 561, 567, 577, 580–81, 584–5, 591 (Kleines harmonisches Labyrinth), 692–3, 740, 743–52, 754–63, 765, 771.

## 7 Instrumental and Chamber Music

## (a) Original clavier works

| BWV | Title, key | Date | BG; NBA vol. |
|-----|------------|------|--------------|
| 772–86 | 15 two-part Inventions, C,c,D,d,E♭,E,e,F,f,G,g,A,a,B♭,b | 1723 | iii; V/3, x/v, V/5 |
| 787–801 | 15 three-part Sinfonias [Inventions], C,c,D,d,E♭,E,e,F,f,G, g,A,a,B♭,b | 1723 | iii; V/3, V/5 |
| 806–11 | 6 English Suites, A,a,g,F,e,d | ?c. 1715 or later | xlv/1; V/7 |
| 812–17 | 6 French Suites, d,c,b,E♭,G,E | c. 1722 | xlv/1; V/8 |
| 818 | Suite, a | c. 1722 | xxxvi; V/8 |
| 819 | Suite, E♭ | c. 1722 | xxxvi; V/8 |
| ★821 | Suite, B♭ | — | xlii |
| 825–30 | *Clavier-Übung* I: 6 Partitas, B♭,c,a,D,G,e, | pubd 1726–31 | iii; V/1, V/4 |
| | *Clavier-Übung* II: | pubd 1735 | iii; V/2 |
| 831 | Ouverture, b | | |
| 971 | Italian Concerto, F | | |
| 846–69 | Well-tempered Clavier [24 preludes and fugues] | 1722 | xiv; V/6.1 |
| 870–93 | 24 Preludes and Fugues ['Well-tempered Clavier', ii] | 1738–42 | xiv; V/6.2 |
| 894 | Prelude and fugue, a | c. 1715–25 | xxxvi; V/9.2 |
| 895 | Prelude and fugue, a | — | xxxvi; V/9.2 |
| ★896 | Prelude and fugue, A | c. 1709 | xxxvi (fugue); V/9.2 |
| ★899 | Prelude and fughetta, d | ?c. 1720 | —; V/12 |
| 900 | Prelude and fughetta, e | ?c. 1720 | xxxvi; V/6.2 |
| 901 | Prelude and fughetta, F | ?c. 1720 | xxxvi; V/6.2 |
| 902 | Prelude and fughetta, G | ?c. 1720 | xxxvi; V/6.2 |
| 903 | Chromatic fantasia and fugue, d | ?c. 1720 | xxxvi; V/9.2 |
| 904 | Fantasia and fugue, a | ?c. 1730 | xxxvi; V/9.2 |

| BWV | Title, key | Date | BG; NBA vol. |
|---|---|---|---|
| 906 | Fantasia and fugue, c [incomplete] | c. 1728, rev. c. 1738 | xxxvi; V/9.2 |
| *909 | Concerto and fugue, c | — | xlii; V/12 |
| 910–11 | 2 Toccatas, f♯,c | c. 1709–12 | iii; V/9.1 |
| 912–16 | 5 Toccatas, D,d,e,g,G | c. 1706–10 | xxxvi; V/9.1 |
| 917–20 | 4 Fantasias, g,c,c*,g* | — | xxxvi, xlii; V/9.2 |
| 921–2 | 2 Preludes, c,a* | — | xxxvi; V/9.2 |
| 933–8 | 6 Little preludes, C,c,d,D,E,e | ?1717–23 | xxxvi; V/9.2 |
| 939–43 | 5 Preludes, C,d,e,a,C | ?1717–23 | xxxvi; V/9.2 |
| 944 | Fantasia and Fugue, a | c. 1708 | iii; V/9.2 |
| 946, 950–1 | 3 Fugues, C,A,b on themes from Albinoni's Suonate a tre, op. 1, nos. 1,2,3, and 8 | ?c. 1710 | xxxvi; V/9.2 |
| 947–9 | 3 Fugues, a,d,A | — | xxxvi; V/9.2 |
| 952 | Fugue, C | ?c. 1720 | xxxvi; V/9.1 |
| 956–7 | 2 Fugues e*,G (see also 'Neumeister Chorales') | — | xlii; IV, supplement |
| *958–9 | 2 Fugues, a,a | — | xlii; V/9.2 |
| 961 | Fughetta,c | — | xxxvi; V/9.2 |
| 963 | Sonata, D | c. 1704 | xxxvi; V/10 |
| 988 | *Clavier-Übung* [IV: Goldberg Variations] | pubd 1741 | iii; V/2 |
| 989 | Aria variata, a | before 1714 | xxxvi; V/10 |
| 992 | Capriccio sopra la lontananza del fratello dilettissimo | c. 1703–6 | xxxvi; V/10 |
| 993 | Capriccio, E | before 1705 | xxxvi; V/10 |

Miscellaneous pieces in Clavier-Büchlein for W. F. Bach (*BG* xxxvi; *NBA* V/5) and Clavierbüchlein, i and ii, for Anna Magdalena Bach (*BG* xliii; *NBA* V/4)

**(b) Clavier arrangements of concertos,** ?1713–14 (*BG* xlii; *NBA* V/11)

| BWV | Key | Original composer | BWV | Key | Original composer |
|---|---|---|---|---|---|
| 972 | D | Vivaldi, RV230 | 981 | c | B. Marcello, |
| 973 | G | Vivaldi, RV299 | | | Op. 1 No. 2 |
| 974 | d | A. Marcello | 982 | B♭ | Prince Johann Ernst, Op. 1 |
| 975 | g | Vivaldi, RV316 | | | No. 1 |
| 976 | C | Vivaldi, RV265 | 983 | g | ? |
| 977 | C | ? | 984 | C | Prince Johann Ernst |
| 978 | F | Vivaldi, RV310 | 985 | g | Telemann |
| 979 | b | Torelli | 986 | G | ? |
| 980 | G | Vivaldi, RV381 | 987 | d | Prince Johann Ernst, Op. 1 No. 4 |

## (c) Other instrumental and chamber works

| BWV | Title, key, scoring | Date | BG; NBA vol. |
|---|---|---|---|
| 995 | Suite, g, lute | 1727–31 | —; V/10 |
| 996 | Suite, e, lute | c. 1708–17 | xlv/1; V10 |
| 997 | Suite, c, lute | 1737–41 | xlv; V/10 |
| 998 | Prelude, fugue and allegro, E♭, lute | 1740s | xlv/1; V/10 |
| 999 | Prelude, c, lute | c. 1720 | xxxvi; V/10 |
| 1000 | Fugue, g, lute | ?c. 1725 | —; V/10 |
| 1001–6 | 3 Sonatas, g,a,C, and 3 Partitas, b,d,E, violin | 1720 | xxvii/1; VI/1 |
| 1007–12 | 6 Suites, G,d,C,E♭,c,D, cello | c. 1720 | xxvii/1; VI/2 |
| 1013 | Partita, a, flute | ?1718 | —; VI/3 |
| 1014–19 | 6 Sonatas, b,A,E,c,f,G, violin and harpsichord | ?1717–23 | ix; VI/1 |
| 1021 | Sonata, G, violin and continuo | ?c. 1732 | —; VI/1 |
| ★1023 | Sonata, e, violin and continuo | ?1714–17 | xliii/1; VI/1 |
| ★1024 | Sonata, c, violin and continuo | — | —; VI/4 |
| 1025 | Trio, A, violin and harpsichord (after S.L. Weiss) | — | ix; VI/5 |
| ★1026 | Fugue, g, violin and harpsichord | — | xliii/1: VI/4 |
| 1027–9 | 3 Sonatas, G,D,g, bass viol and harpsichord | before c. 1741 | ix; VI/4 |
| 1030 | Sonata, b, flute and harpsichord | ?, revised c. 1735 | ix; VI/3 |
| ★1031 | Sonata, E♭, flute and harpsichord | ?1730–33 | ix |
| 1032 | Sonata, A, flute and harpsichord | 1717–23, re-vised c.1735 | ix; VI/3 |
| ★1033 | Sonata, C, flute and continuo | ?c.1736 | xliii/1 |
| 1034 | Sonata, e, flute and continuo | ?c.1717–24 | xliii/1; VI/3 |
| 1035 | Sonata, E, flute and continuo | ?c. 1741 | xliii/1; VI/3 |
| 1039 | Sonata, G, 2 flutes and continuo | ?c. 1720 | ix; VI/3 |
| 1040 | Trio, F, violin, oboe and continuo | 1713 | xxix; I/35 |

*Spurious:* BWV820, 822–4, 832–5, 838–40, 844–5, 897–8, 905, 907–8, 923, 945, 960, 962, 964, 968–70, 1020, 1022, 1036–8

## 8 Concertos and Orchestral Suites

| BWV | Title, key | Date | BG; NBA vol. |
|---|---|---|---|
| 1041 | Violin concerto, a | ? | xxi/1; VII/3 |
| 1042 | Violin concerto, E | ? | xxi/1; VII/3 |
| 1043 | Concerto for 2 violins, d | ? | xxi/1; VII/3 |
| 1044 | Concerto for flute, violin and harpsichord, a | after 1726 | xvii; VII/3 |

| BWV | Title, key | Date | BG; NBA vol. |
|---|---|---|---|
| 1046a | Sinfonia, F, 2 horns, 3 oboes, bassoon, strings and continuo | ?1713 | xxxi/1; VII/2 |
| | 6 Bradenburg Concertos: | ?1713–21 | xix; VII/2 |
| 1046 | No. 1, F, 2 horns, 3 oboes, bassoon, violino piccolo, strings and continuo | | |
| 1047 | No. 2, F, trumpet, recorder, oboe, violin, strings and continuo | | |
| 1048 | No. 3, strings and continuo | | |
| 1049 | No. 4, G, violin, 2 recorders, strings and continuo | | |
| 1050 | No. 5, D, flute, violin, harpsichord, strings and continuo | | |
| 1051 | No. 6, B♭, 2 violas, 2 bass viols, cello and continuo | | |
| 1052–9 | 8 Harpsichord concertos, d, E,D,A,f,F,g,d [arrangements of earlier concertos, some lost] | c. 1738 | xvii; VII/4 |
| 1060–2 | 3 Concertos for 2 harpsichords c,C,c [mostly arrangements of earlier concertos] | c. 1732–42 | xxi/2; VII/5 |
| 1063–4 | 2 Concertos for 3 harpsichords, d,C [arrangements of earlier concertos, lost] | c. 1730 | xxxi/3; VII/6 |
| 1065 | Concerto for 4 harpsichords, a [arrangement of Vivaldi, RV580] | c.1730 | xliii/1; VII/6 |
| 1066–9 | 4 Orchestral Suites, C,b,D,D | ?c.1717–40 | xxxi/1; VII/1 |

*Spurious:* BWV1070 (Orchestral suite, g)

## 9 Canons and Late Contrapuntal Works

| BWV | Title | Date | BG; NBA vol. |
|---|---|---|---|
| 769 | Canonic Variations [see 'Organ Works, (e) chorale variations'] | | |
| 1072 | Canon trias harmonica | — | xlv/1; VIII/1 |
| 1073 | Canon a 4 perpetuus | 2.8.1713 | xlv/1; VIII/1 |
| 1074 | Canon a 4 | 1727 | xlv/1; VIII/1 |
| 1075 | Canon a 2 perpetuus | 10.1.1734 | —; VIII/1 |
| 1076 | Canon triplex | c. 1746 | xlv/1; VIII/1 |
| 1077 | Canone doppio sopr'il soggetto | 15.10.1747 | —; VIII/1 |
| 1078 | Canon super fa mi a 7 | 1.3.1749 | xlv/1; VIII/1 |
| 1079 | Musical Offering | pubd 1747 | xxxi/2; VIII/1 |

| BWV | Title | Date | BG; NBA vol. |
|---|---|---|---|
| 1080 | Art of Fugue | ?c. 1742–9, pubd 1751 | xxv/1; VIII/2.1–2 |
| 1086 | Canon concordia discors | — | —; VIII/1 |
| 1087 | 14 Canons on first 8 bass notes of BWV988 | 1747–8 | —; V/2 |

# *Personalia*

**Abel,** Christian Ferdinand (1682–1761) was a bass viol player in the court orchestra at Cöthen from about 1715, and thus during Bach's period as *Kapellmeister* there. Bach was godfather to one of Abel's daughters, Sophia Charlotta, in 1720, and may have written his three bass viol sonatas sonatas (BWV 1027–9) for him. Abel's son Carl Friedrich (1723–87) also played the bass viol. He was a member of the Dresden court orchestra from *c.* 1743 to *c.* 1758, and later became an associate of Bach's youngest son Johann Christian in London, where they collaborated in an important series of public concerts.

**Agricola,** Johann Friedrich (1720–74), a composer and writer, was a pupil of Bach in Leipzig (1738–41). He then moved to Berlin, where he served Frederick the Great as court composer. He collaborated with C. P. E. Bach in writing the valuable Obituary of J. S. Bach published by Mizler in 1754.

**Ahle,** Johann Rudolph (1625–73) and his son Johann Georg (1651–1706) preceded Bach as organists at the Blasiuskirche, Mühlhausen. Both were composers. J. R. Ahle's many hymn tunes include *Liebster Jesu, wir sind hier* and *Es ist genug*, both used in well-known works by Bach.

**Albinoni,** Tomaso Giovanni (1671–1751) was an Italian composer important, along with Vivaldi, in the development of the solo concerto in Venice. Bach used some of his music as teaching material and based keyboard fugues (BWV 946, 950–1) on themes from Albinoni's trio sonatas Op. 1 (1694).

**Altnickol,** Johann Christoph (1719–59) was a pupil of Bach and from 1744 assisted him as a bass singer in the Leipzig churches, and also as a copyist. In 1748 he was organist for a short time at Niederwiesa in Silesia, and then from 20 July at Naumburg, where he remained until his death. In 1749 he married Bach's daughter Elisabeth.

**Bach,** Carl Philipp Emanuel (1714–88) was the fifth child of J. S. Bach and his first wife, Maria Barbara. He studied law at Leipzig University and, from September 1734, at Frankfurt an der Oder. Between 1738 and 1768 he served Frederick the Great as harpsichordist, and was then Kantor and music director at Hamburg until his death. He married in 1744 and had three children, the last of whom, named Johann Sebastian after his grandfather, became an artist. Emanuel Bach inherited about a third of his father's musical works, some of which he performed in Hamburg. His own compositions, especially the keyboard works, symphonies, concertos, and chamber music, are of supreme importance in the formation of the late eighteenth-century Classical style, and his *Versuch über die wahre Art das Clavier zu spielen* (Essay on the True Art of Playing Keyboard Instruments, 1753–62) is a valuable source of information about performing practices of the period.

**Bach,** Johann Christian (1735–82) was the last son of J. S. Bach and his second wife, Anna Magdalena. After his father's death in 1750 he went to live with his elder brother, Emanuel, in Berlin, and in 1755 he broke with family traditions by going to Italy, becoming a Roman Catholic, and composing operas. He was made organist at Milan Cathedral in 1760 but left Italy two years later to settle in London, where he wrote operas for the King's Theatre, served as music master to Queen Charlotte, and collaborated with C. F. Abel in promoting orchestral concerts. He married the singer Cecilia Grassi in 1773. His music is still not as well known as it deserves to be, but he has long been recognized as a master of the *galant* style and as an important precursor of Mozart, whom he knew in London in 1764–5.

**Bach,** Wilhelm Friedemann (1710–84), the eldest son of J. S. Bach and his first wife, Maria Barbara, was educated at the Thomasschule and at Leipzig university. In 1733 he was appointed organist at the Sophienkirche, Dresden, and in 1746 he went to Halle as organist and music director at the Liebfrauenkirche. A few months after his father's death he married, but he became increasingly unsettled, and in 1764 he resigned his post and earned a precarious living by teaching and performing. His last ten years were spent in Berlin, where he suffered poverty and ill-health. In the opinion of many, Friedemann inherited more of his father's genius than any of his brothers, and in 1750 he received the largest share of his father's manuscripts. His failure to make the best use of the former is a matter for regret, but his careless custody of the latter must have robbed the world of numerous masterpieces.

**Birnbaum,** Johann Abraham (1702–48) taught rhetoric at Leipzig university. He was a good keyboard player, became friendly with Bach, and was the latter's principal spokesman in the controversy engendered by Scheibe's criticism of Bach's music in 1737.

**Böhm,** Georg (1661–1733) was born at Hohenkirchen, near Ohrdruf. He attended Jena university, spent some time in Hamburg, and succeeded Christian Flor (1626–97) as organist of the Johanniskirche, Lüneburg, where he remained until his death. His organ music, especially the chorale settings, exercised a profound influence on Bach, who may have been his pupil in Lüneburg.

**Buxtehude,** Dietrich (*c.* 1637–1707) succeeded Franz Tunder as organist of the Marienkirche, Lübeck, in July 1668 and in the following month married one of Tunder's daughters. He remained at the Marienkirche for the rest of his life, organizing there a famous series of evening concerts (*Abendmusiken*), which Bach attended in 1705. Buxtehude's organ music and church compositions constitute one of the most potent influences on the formation of Bach's musical style.

**Corelli,** Arcangelo (1653–1713) was born at Fusignano, trained at Bologna, and employed from 1675 (or earlier) in Rome, where he enjoyed the patronage of Queen Christina of Sweden, Cardinal Pamphili, and Cardinal Ottoboni. His surviving works are entirely instrumental and few in number (four volumes of trio sonatas and one each of solo violin sonatas and *concerti grossi*, besides a few others unpublished during his lifetime), but their popularity and dissemination were out of all proportion to their number. Bach's Fugue in B minor for organ (BWV579) uses a subject taken from Corelli's Trio Sonata Op. 3 No. 4, and the Italian's influence is perceptible in several other Bach words.

**Couperin,** François (1668–1733), known as 'le grand', was the most important French composer of the generation preceding Bach. He was harpsichordist to King Louis XIV, composed over 200 pieces for the instrument, and published a famous treatise, *L'art de toucher le clavecin* (1716), on how to play it. His other music includes Latin motets, French songs, and chamber compositions. Bach owned some of his music and held it in high esteem.

**Dieupart,** Charles (d. *c.* 1740) was a French composer, violinist, and harpsichordist. The *Six suittes* (1701) that Bach copied in 1713 were dedicated to the Countess of Sandwich, an English lady who was Dieupart's pupil in France. Shortly after these were published Dieupart went to London, where he apparently spent the rest of his life.

**Fasch,** Johann Friedrich (1688–1758) attended the Thomasschule and the university in Leipzig and in 1708 founded the second *collegium musicum* there. He was appointed court *Kapellmeister* at Zerbst in 1722 and competed with Bach for the post of Thomaskantor in Leipzig. His voluminous output included twelve cantata cycles (over 700 works) and almost

100 orchestral suites, some of which Bach transcribed for his own *collegium musicum* in the 1730s.

**Fischer,** Johann Caspar Ferdinand (?*c.* 1670–1746) was from 1695 at the latest *Kapellmeister* to Ludwig Wilhelm, Margrave of Baden. His influence on Bach's keyboard music is not confined to the *Ariadne musica* (1702), an important forerunner of the *Well-tempered Clavier.*

**Franck,** Salomo (1659–1725) studied law at Jena university and at Leipzig. He was at Arnstadt shortly before Bach went there and from 1701 was employed as secretary, librarian, and poet at the Weimar court. His several volumes of cantata texts include about twenty known to have been set by Bach.

**Frescobaldi,** Girolamo (1583–1643) was active in many Italian cities, but especially in Rome, where his patrons included the cardinals Aldobrandini and Barberini. His influence on Bach can be traced not only in the *Fiori musicali* (1635), which Bach owned, but through his famous pupil Froberger (see next entry) and possibly Kerll.

**Froberger,** Johann Jacob (1616–67) studied with Frescobaldi in Rome (1637–40/41) and was for many years court organist to Emperor Ferdinand III in Vienna. He did much to establish a German keyboard style and played an important role in the formation of the classical suite of dance movements. C. P. E. Bach included Froberger among the composers whose music his father had studied.

**Goldberg,** Johann Gottlieb (1727–56) may have studied with Bach at Leipzig in 1742–3, at which time he was harpsichordist to Count Keyserlingk in Dresden. In 1751 he was appointed chamber musician to Count Heinrich von Brühl, in which post he remained until his death, from consumption, at the age of twenty-nine. His church cantatas are strongly influenced by Bach's, while much of his other music is more *galant* in style. A trio sonata for two violins and continue by Goldberg was once attributed to Bach (BWV1037).

**Görner,** Johann Gottlieb (1697–1778) was educated at the Thomasschule and at Leipzig university. He was organist at the Paulinerkirche there from 1716, at the Nikolaikirche from 1721, and at the Thomaskirche from 1729, and during the years 1723–56 he was in charge of the *collegium musicum* that Fasch had founded. Although he came into dispute with Bach during the early years of the latter's cantorate at Leipzig, the two men seem to have been on amicable terms afterwards, and when Bach died Görner served as guardian to his younger children.

**Graupner,** Christoph (1683–1760) attended the Thomasschule in Leipzig and after a short period of study at Leipzig university went to Hamburg and then to Darmstadt, where he was appointed *Kapellmeister* in 1712. After competing successfully for the cantorate at Leipzig in 1722–3, he remained at Darmstadt, with an increased salary, until his death. His huge output included operas (all dating from before 1720), over 1,400 church cantatas, and a great deal of orchestral and chamber music.

**Grigny,** Nicolas de (1672–1703) was born at Rheims and became organist at the cathedral there. His only known music is the *Premier livre d'orgue* (1699), which Bach copied out in 1713. He was probably one of the 'good and old Frenchman' whose music Bach is said to have studied in his youth.

**Handel,** Georg Frideric (1685–1759) was born in Halle in the same year as Bach, but his career followed very different paths. He studied for a short time at the university in Halle and then joined Keiser's opera orchestra at Hamburg. A decisive step towards realizing his ambition to be an opera composer was taken in 1706 when he went to Italy 'with a view to improvement' (as his first biographer, John Mainwaring, put it). But his reputation was consolidated in London, where he settled in 1712 and remained for the rest of his life. Public apathy, professional rivalry, and the unpredictability of some of the singers he had to work with finally led him to give up opera in the 1730s and to turn to the oratorios which, for 200 years after his death, were mainly responsible for keeping his name before a wide public in England. Handel never married.

**Harrer,** Gottlob (1703–55) studied law at Leipzig university and may have been a pupil of Hasse in Italy. Before succeeding Bach as Thomaskantor he was for nearly twenty years in the service of Count Heinrich von Brühl in Dresden, where he composed Latin church music and a fair number of instrumental works.

**Hasse,** Johann Adolf (1699–1783) studied with Alessandro Scarlatti in Naples and married the Venetian mezzo-soprano Faustina Bordoni. He was *Kapellmeister* to the Elector of Saxony in Dresden for over thirty years and became one of the most admired and respected composers in Europe. It was to the detriment of his posthumous reputation that he cultivated with skill and artistry a genre (*opera seria*) that became moribund even in his own lifetime.

**Heinichen,** Johann David (1683–1729) attended the Thomasschule in Leipzig and studied at Leipzig university (1702–6). He wrote operas for Leipzig before 1710, and after a period in Venice and Rome (where he taught Bach's future patron, Prince Leopold of Anhalt-Cöthen) he was engaged as *Kapellmeister* to the Dresden court. He was the author of one of the most important Baroque treatises on music, *Der General-Bass in der Composition* (1728), and has sometimes been credited with the composition of the *Kleines harmonisches Labyrinth*, an organ work previously attributed to Bach (BWV591).

**Henrici,** Christian Friedrich, *see* 'Picander'.

**Hurlebusch,** Conrad Friedrich (*c.* 1696–1765) was a restless, lonely musician who failed to obtain several appointments and either declined or resigned many others before he finally settled down as organist at the Oude Kerk, Amsterdam, from 1743 until his death. He was the subject of several slanderous articles during his lifetime, and his posthumous reputation has not been helped by unjust and injurious interpretations often placed upon his behaviour when he visited Bach at Leipzig. Bach thought sufficiently highly of him to act as the Leipzig agent for some of Hurlebusch's printed music.

**Johann Ernst** (1696–1715), Prince of Weimar, was taught the keyboard by Bach's kinsman, J. G. Walther. The young prince was a gifted, though not fully developed, composer, and his Six Concertos Op. 1 were published by Telemann in 1718. Bach arranged two of them for harpsichord and two other concertos by Ernst for organ.

**Keiser,** Reinhard (1674–1739) was educated at the Thomasschule in Leipzig before making his name as an opera composer in Brunswick and Hamburg. A *St Mark Passion* which Bach performed at Leipzig was once attributed to Keiser, and Bach's own Passion settings may reflect Keiser's influence in certain particulars, for example in the dramatic use of accompanied recitative and arioso.

**Kerll,** Johann Caspar (1627–93) studied in Italy, possibly with Frescobaldi, and was appointed *Kapellmeister* at the electoral court of Munich in 1656. He resigned in 1673 and went to Vienna as organist at St Stephen's Cathedral. From 1677 he served as organist at the imperial court. He returned to Munich in 1684 and died there. His keyboard music, known to Bach and admired by him, includes toccatas, ricercares, and some descriptive pieces.

**Kirchhoff,** Gottfried (1685–1746) was a pupil of Zachow (Handel's teacher) and succeeded him in 1714 as organist at the Liebfrauenkirche, Halle (Bach having declined the post). He wrote mainly vocal and organ music for church use. One of his cantatas is to a text also set by Bach (BWV63).

**Kirnberger,** Johann Philipp (1721–83) was among the most gifted of Bach's pupils and sought to perpetuate Bach's teaching methods in his own treatises. He did much to promote Bach's music and was instrumental in securing publication of the chorale harmonizations. His own copies of Bach's works were preserved in the library of his patron Princess Anna Amalia. Kirnberger's own music is said to be correct but uninspired.

**Krebs,** Johann Ludwig (1713–80) was the son of the composer and organist Johann Tobias Krebs (1690–1762). Both were pupils of Bach, the younger Krebs being particularly well thought of by him. He served Bach as singer, organist, and copyist, and in 1750 he competed unsuccessfully for the post of Thomaskantor. His own music combines Bachian polyphony with features of the new *galant* style; it includes an organ fugue on the letters BACH. Both J. T. and J. L. Krebs have been suggested as possible composers of the eight short preludes and fugues for organ BWV 553–60.

**Krieger,** Johann Philipp (1649–1725) spent most of his life as *Kapellmeister* at the Weissenfels court, where Bach was an occasional visitor and where he held the title of *Kapellmeister von Haus aus* (1729–36). His works include over 2,000 church cantatas, some of which were among the first to adopt the reforms of Neumeister, who was also at Weissenfels for a time (1704–6).

**Kuhnau,** Johann (1660–1722) preceded Bach as Thomaskantor in Leipzig. He was something of a polymath: a practising lawyer, a proficient mathematician, a novelist, and a fine linguist. After serving as organist of the Thomaskirche from 1684, he was appointed Kantor in 1701. More of his church cantatas have been lost than survive, and he is remembered now chiefly for his keyboard music, especially the six programmatic *Biblical Sonatas* (1700). His nephew Johann Andreas Kuhnan (b. 1703) studied with Bach and was one of his principal copyists.

**Kusser,** Johann Sigismund (1660–1727) studied with Lully in Paris and was active at Brunswick, Hamburg, Stuttgart, and other German cities before going to London in 1704/5. From there he went in 1709 to Dublin, where he remained until his death. He wrote mainly operas and other stage works.

**Legrenzi,** Giovanni (1626–90) was active mainly in Ferrara (1656–65) and at Venice, where he was *maestro di coro* at the *Conservatorio dei Mendicanti* from *c.* 1671 and *maestro di cappella* at St Mark's from 1685 until his death. His works include operas, oratorios, church music, secular cantatas, and instrumental pieces. The theme on which Bach based his organ fugue BWV 574 has been identified as a much-altered version of one from Legrenzi's Trio Sonata Op. 2 No. 11.

**Marcello,** Alessandro (1684–1747) and his younger brother Benedetto (1686–1739) were both amateur composers of elevated rank (their father, Agostino Marcello, was a Venetian senator). Although Alessandro lived longer, Benedetto was the more prolific. As well as sacred music, oratorios, cantatas, concertos, and sonatas, he wrote a famous and amusing satire, *Il teatro alla moda* (*c.* 1720).

**Marchand,** Louis (1669–1732) possessed, along with an amazing keyboard technique, some less desirable personal attributes (including an inclination towards wife-beating) which make his ignominious retreat from the contest with Bach at Dresden in 1717 seem entirely in character. On his return to Paris he resumed his post as organist to the Cordeliers and devoted much of his time to teaching (his wife having by then separated from him).

**Marpurg,** Friedrich Wilhelm (1718–95), the German theorist, was a devoted admirer of Bach's music. As well as writing the preface for a new issue of the *Art of Fugue* in 1752, he proposed Bach's polyphony as a model in his treatise on fugue (*Abhandlung von der Fuge*, 1753–4), and his other writings contain frequent and valuable references to the composer.

**Mattheson,** Johann (1681–1764) spent most of his life at Hamburg, where he sang tenor in the opera, enjoyed the friendship of Handel, and later served the English ambassador as secretary and diplomat. He married an English woman, Catharina Jennings, in 1709. His compositions included many operas and oratorios, but posterity has valued him for his critical writings, which include historical and biographical material of unique importance besides a good deal of polemical material.

**Mizler,** Lorenz Christoph (1711–78) attended the Gymnasium at Ansbach, where his teachers included. J. M. Gesner. He enrolled at Leipzig university at the same time (1731) that Gesner went there as Rektor of the Thomasschule. Along with Count Giacomo de Lucchesini, Mizler founded the Correspondierende Sozietät der Musicalischen Wissenschaften (Corresponding Society of the Musical Sciences) in 1738 and published a great deal of important material in the *Musicalische Bibliothek*, which became the society's official journal. The society enrolled nineteen members (including Bach), Leopold Mozart declining an invitation to become its twentieth in 1755.

**Muffat,** Georg (1653–1704) was a German composer of French birth and Scottish ancestry. He studied with Lully in Paris and visited Rome, where he heard and admired the concertos of Corelli. From 1690 until his death he was *Kapellmeister* to Johann Philipp of Lamberg, Bishop of Passau. He did much to popularize French and Italian musical styles in Germany. His son Gottlieb (1690–1770) was no less important a composer of keyboard music.

**Neumeister,** Erdmann (1671–1756) was a student of theology and literature, and then *magister*, at Leipzig university. From 1715 until his retirement in 1755 he was head pastor at the Jacobikirche, Hamburg. His nine cycles of cantata texts played a crucial role in establishing a new type of church cantata which included the frankly operatic forms of recitative and da capo aria as important constituents. The five texts set by Bach come from two cycles written for the Eisenach court and published in 1711 and 1714.

**Pachelbel,** Johann (1653–1706) was born at Nuremberg. He was deputy organist at St Stephen's Cathedral, Vienna, and then organist at the Eisenach court and from 1678 at the Predigerkirche, Erfurt, where his pupils included Bach's eldest brother Johann Christoph. In 1690 he moved to Stuttgart and then to Gotha before taking up his final appointment at St Sebald's Church, Nuremberg. He was among the most important composers of organ music before Bach.

**'Picander'** was the pen-name of Christian Friedrich Henrici (1700–64), Bach's librettist at Leipzig. He studied law at Wittenberg and from 1720 worked in Leipzig as a writer, tutor, and post-office administrator. He supplied the texts for Bach's *St Matthew* and *St Mark* Passions, and for many of his secular and occasional cantatas. Whether or not Bach composed a complete Picander cycle of church cantatas in 1728–9 has not yet been firmly established.

**Pisendel,** Johann Georg (1687–1755) was a member of the court orchestra at Ansbach, where he studied the violin with Torelli. He made Bach's acquaintance at Weimar in 1790, and no doubt renewed it many times after 1712 when he joined the court orchestra in Dresden. He succeeded Volumier as *Konzertmeister* there in 1728.

**Poglietti,** Alessandro (d. 1683), an Italian composer, was employed from 1661 at the Austrian court in Vienna, where he was treated with particular favour by Emperor Leopold I. His keyboard works, for which he is best known, include both ricercares and descriptive pieces.

**Quantz,** Johann Joachim (1697–1773), the son of a blacksmith, became the greatest flute player of his time. He was in the service of the elector of Saxony from 1718 to 1741 and then moved to Berlin, where his privileged position at the court of Frederick the Great brought him a basic salary three times as much as Bach received altogether at Leipzig. Prominent among his compositions are the 300 flute concertos, while the interest and importance of his treatise *Versuch einer Anweisung die Flöte traversiere zu spielen* (1752) extend beyond flute technique.

**Raison,** André (d. 1719) was organist at the abbey of Ste Geneviève and at the a college of the Jacobins de St Jacques in Paris. He published two books of liturgical organ music (1688 and 1714), the first containing a valuable preface as well as the *Trio en passacaille* often invoked in discussions of Bach's organ Passacaglia.

**Reincken,** Johann Adam (1643–1722) lived and worked for a time at Deventer in the Netherlands. The researches of Ulf Grapenthin have cast doubt on his longevity (he is usually said to have lived to the age of ninety-nine). He died in Hamburg, where he had been organist at the Catharinenkirche since 1663 (he was assistant organist there for five years before that). His organ improvisations attracted Bach from Lüneburg, but his surviving works are disappointingly few.

**Rolle,** Christian Friedrich (1681–1751) was town Kantor at Quedlinburg from 1709 until 1721, when he went to Magdeburg as Kantor of the Johanniskirche. His works included at least five Passions and some chamber music. His son Johannes Heinrich (1716–85) succeeded him at Magdeburg and became an important oratorio composer.

**Scheibe,** Johann Adolph (1708–76) was the son of the organ builder Johann Scheibe (c. 1680–1748). He was educated at Leipzig university, where he was strongly influenced by the reformist views of J. C. Gottsched. After several unsuccessful attempts between 1729 and 1736 to secure a post as organist, he established himself in Hamburg as a critic and composer, and from 1740 was active in Denmark, where he died. His criticism of Bach's music, published in 1737, is balanced elsewhere in his writings by an unfeigned admiration for the composer.

**Schott,** Georg Balthasar (1686–1736), organist of the Neukirche, Leipzig, from 1720, was one of the contestants for the post of Thomaskantor in 1722–3. When he left Leipzig for Gotha in 1729 he handed over to Bach the directorship of the *collegium musicum* which he had held since 1720.

**Schütz,** Heinrich (1585–1672) was, from the age of ten, a choirboy at the court of Landgrave Moritz of Hessen-Kassel, who later arranged for him to study with Giovanni Gabrieli in Venice. Shortly after his return to Germany in 1613 he went to Dresden, where he served as *Kapellmeister* to the elector of Saxony. Except for frequent and sometimes prolonged absences, he remained there for the rest of his long life. Schütz excelled in most vocal genres, and in 1627 composed the first German opera, *Dafne*. His motets and Passions are important both in their own right and as precursors of Bach's.

**Silbermann,** Gottfried (1683–1753) came from a family of organ builders and worked for a time with his elder brother, Andreas, in Strasbourg before settling in Freiberg in 1711. He built all the major organs in Dresden as well as other important ones in Freiberg, Rötha, Zittau, and elsewhere. He also made clavichords and some of the earliest grand pianos.

**Sorge,** Georg Andreas (1703–78) was court and town organist at Lobenstein in Thuringia from 1722 until his death. He made his name as a composer of keyboard music (including three fugues on the letters BACH) and as a writer of treatises on music. In 1747 he was elected the fifteenth member of Mizler's Corresponding Society of the Musical Sciences.

**Sporck,** Franz Anton (1662–1738) was a Bohemian count, resident at Lysá nad Labem. He was largely responsible for introducing the horn (which he had encountered on a visit to Versailles) into Bohemia and Austria, and he was also a keen promoter of opera, both at his residence in Kuks and in Prague. A connection with Bach is indicated by a note on the autograph score of the D major Sanctus (BWV232$^{\text{III}}$): 'the parts are in Bohemia with Count Sporck'. The two men may have become acquainted through Picander, who dedicated to Count Sporck his *Sammlung erbaulicher Gedancken* (1725).

**Telemann,** Georg Philipp (1681–1767) studied at the university of Leipzig, where he also founded a *collegium musicum* among the students and directed the Leipzig Opera. From 1708 to 1712 he was at the Eisenach court, and it was probably there that he first met Bach. He was godfather to Bach's son Carl Philipp Emanuel in 1714. After nearly ten years as

*Kapellmeister* at the Barfüsserkirche, Frankfurt, he went in 1721 to Hamburg as Kantor of the Johanneum and musical director of the city's main churches. Telemann was an indefatigable composer, publisher, writer, concert promoter, and administrator. His surviving compositions include operas, oratorios, well over 1,000 cantatas, and numerous examples of every type of orchestral and chamber music.

**Vivaldi,** Antonio (1678–1741) taught at the Ospedale della Pietà in Venice, and it was for that institution that many of his 500 or more concertos were written. They established the three-movement (fast–slow–fast) form of the solo concerto and the ritornello structure of the outer movements. Bach transcribed some of them at Weimar and his own stylistic development as a composer was profoundly affected by them.

**Volumier,** Jean Baptiste (*c.* 1670–1728), despite his French-sounding name, was of Flemish origin and probably born in Spain. He was a violinist and dancing-master at the electoral court in Berlin, and in 1708 moved to the Saxon court at Dresden, where he was promoted to *Konzertmeister* the following year. Nothing survives of the ballets and violin music he is known to have written.

**Walther,** Johann Gottfried (1684–1748) became organist at the Stadtkirche, Weimar, in 1707. Before that a period of study and travel had brought him into contact with several musicians, notably Werckmeister, who helped to shape his musical thinking. At Weimar he taught the young Prince Johann Ernst and, like Bach, arranged concertos for him. He also wrote some excellent organ music of his own. Spitta took the modest length of the Bach article in Walther's famous *Musicalisches Lexicon* (1732) to indicate an estrangement between the two men; others have, explained it as the work of the local censor, recalling the circumstances of Bach's 'dismissal'. But there is no reason why Walther before 1732 should have valued Bach's music any more highly than did most of his contemporaries and even after 1732 Bach acted as a sales agent for the *Lexicon* in Leipzig.

**Weiss,** Silvius Leopold (1686–1750), born in Breslau, was one of the finest lutenists of his day. He spent some years in Italy, and in 1717 joined the *Kapelle* of the Saxon court at Dresden. He travelled widely, including at least once (in 1739) to Leipzig, when he visited Bach. Bach's Trio for violin and keyboard in A major (BWV1025) has been shown to be an arrangement of a lute sonata by Weiss (see *Bach Jahrbach*, lxxix [1993], pp. 47–67).

**Werckmeister,** Andreas (1645–1706) held posts as organist successively at Hasselfelde, near Blankenburg (1664), Quedlinburg (1675), and Halberstadt (1696). More important than his organ works are his writings, particularly those dealing with the tuning of keyboard instruments and with musical hermeneutics.

# APPENDIX D

# Select Bibliography

This bibliography is intended as a guide to the more important studies of Bach and his music generally available in bookshops and libraries. It has been designed primarily for English-language readers, but important non-English writings are not excluded. Indeed, many of them are indispensable.

## 1 Bibliographies and Research Guides

The most comprehensive Bach bibliography available is probably that maintained on the Internet by Yo Tomita at Queen's University, Belfast. Its address is:

http://www.music.qub.ac.uk/~tomita/bachbib

The following may also be consulted for guidance through the vast and ever-growing literature on the subject:

Blankenburg, Walter, 'Zwölf Jahre Bachforschung', *Acta musicologica*, xxxvii (1965), 95–158.
—— 'Die Bachforschung seit etwa 1965' I, *Acta musicologica* l (1978), 93–154; II, ibid., liv (1982), 162–207; III, ibid., lv (1983), 1–58.
Breig, Werner, Bibliography to article on J. S. Bach in L. Finscher (ed.), *Die Musik in Geschichte und Gegenwart*, 2nd ed.: *Personenteil*, i (Kassel and Stuttgart, 1999), cols. 1518–35.
Godman, Stanley, 'A Classified Index of Bach Articles (including Literature from 1935 to 1951', *Music Book (Hinrichsen's Musical Year Book)*, vii (1952), 392–403.
Jones, Richard, Bibliography to article on J. S. Bach in S. Sadie (ed.), *The New Grove Dictionary of Music and Musicians* (London, 1980), i, pp. 836–40; reprinted with additions in *The New Groove Bach Family* (London, 1983), 215–37, and in *Die Bach-Familie* (Stuttgart and Weimar, 1993), 225–86.
Melamed, Daniel R., and Michael Marissen, *An Introduction to Bach Studies* (New York, 1998).
Robertson, Alec, *Bach: a Biography, with a Survey of Books, Editions and Recordings* (London, 1977).
Wolff, Christoph (ed.), *Bach-Bibliographie* (Berlin and Kassel, 1985) [a reprint, with supplement and index, of bibliographies originally included in the *Bach-Jahrbuch*, 1905–84].

Extensive and classified bibliographies are contained also in Alberto Basso's *Frau Musika* (see Section 3, below).

## 2 Catalogues and Source Material

*Bach-Dokumente*, ed. Werner Neumann and Hans-Joachim Schulze, i, *Schriftstücke von der Hand Johann Sebastian Bachs* (Kassel and Leipzig, 1963); ii, *Fremdschriftliche und gedruckte Dokumente zur Lebensgeschichte Johann Sebastian Bachs 1685–1750* (Kassel and Leipzig, 1969); iii, *Dokumente zum Nachwirken Johann Sebastian Bachs 1750–1800* (Kassel and Leipzig, 1972); iv, *Bilddokumente zur Lebensgeschichte Johann Sebastian Bachs* (Kassel and Leipzig, 1978).

David, Hans T., and Arthur Mendel, *The Bach Reader* (New York and London 1945; 2nd ed., 1966).; revised and enlarged by C. Wolff as *The New Bach Reader* (New York, 1998)

Herz, Gerhard, *Bach-Quellen in Amerika/Bach Sources in America* (Kassel, 1984).

Kast, Paul, *Die Bach-Handschriften der Berliner Staatsbibliothek (Tübinger Bach-Studien, ii–iii)* (Trossingen, 1958).

Kinsky, Georg, *Die Originalausgaben der Werke Johann Sebastian Bachs* (Vienna, 1937).

McAll, May DeForest, *Melodic Index to the Works of Johann Sebastian Bach* (New York, 1962).

Neumann, Werner (ed.), *Sämtliche von Johann Sebastian Bach vertonte Texte* (Leipzig, 1974).

Schmieder, Wolfgang, *Thematisch-systematisches Verzeichnis der musikalischen Werke Johann Sebastian Bachs: Bach-Werke-Verzeichnis* (Leipzig, 1950; 2nd ed., 1990); *Kleine Ausgabe*, ed. A. Dürr, Y. Kobayashi, and K. Beisswenger (Wiesbaden, 1998).

Schulze, Hans-Joachim (ed.), *Johann Sebastian Bach: Leben und Werk in Dokumenten* (Leipzig, 1975).

Schulze, Hans-Joachim, and Christoph Wolff, *Bach Compendium: Analytisch-bibliographisches Repertorium der Werke Johann Sebastian Bachs* (Leipzig and Dresden, 1985–).

## 3 General Surveys: Life and Works

Basso, Alberto, *Frau Musika: la vita e le opere di J. S. Bach* (Turin, 1979–83).

Beisswenger, Kirsten, *Johann Sebastian Bachs Notenbibliothek* (Kassel, 1992).

Blume, Friedrich, *Two Centuries of Bach* (London, 1950; German original, 1947).

Boyd, Malcolm (ed.), *Oxford Composer Companions: J. S. Bach* (London, 1999).

Brainard, Paul, and Ray Robinson, *A Bach Tribute: Essays in Honor of William H. Scheide* (Kassel, 1993).

Butt, John, *Bach Interpretation: Articulation Marks in the Primary Sources of J. S. Bach* (Cambridge, 1990).

Butt, John (ed.), *The Cambridge Companion to Bach* (Cambridge, 1997).

Chiapusso, Jan, *Bach's World* (Bloomington and London, 1968).

Dadelsen, Georg von, *Beiträge zur Chronologie der Werke Johann Sebastian Bachs (Tübinger Bach-Studien, iv–v)* (Trossingen, 1958).

David, Archibald T., *Bach and Handel: the Consummation of the Baroque in Music* (Cambridge, Massachusetts, 1951).

Dickinson, A. E. F., *The Art of J. S. Bach* (London, 1936; 2nd ed., 1950).

——*Bach's Fugal Works* (London, 1956).

Dreyfus, Laurence, *Bach's Continuo Group* (Cambridge, Massachusetts, 1987).

Emery, Walter, *Bach's Ornaments* (London, 1953).

Forkel, Johann Nikolaus, *Ueber Johann Sebastian Bachs Leben Kunst und Kunstwerke* (Leipzig, 1802; facsimile, Berlin, 1966; English translation, 1820; English translation, ed. C. S. Terry, London, 1920).

Franklin, Don O. (ed.), *Bach Studies* (Cambridge, 1989).

Geck, Martin, *Bach-Interpretationen* (Göttingen, 1969).

Geiringer, Karl and Irene, *The Bach Family* (London, 1954; 2nd ed., 1977).

—— *Johann Sebastian Bach: the Culmination of an Era* (New York, 1966).

Gurlitt, Wilibald, *J. S. Bach: der Meister und sein Werk* (Berlin, 1936; 5th ed., 1980; English translation, 1957).

Herz, Gerhard, *Essays on J. S. Bach* (Ann Arbor, 1985).

*Kalendarium zur Lebensgeschichte Johann Sebastian Bachs* (Bach-Archiv Leipzig, 1970; 2nd ed., 1979).

Kock, Hermann, *Genealogisches Lexikon der Familie Bach* (Gotha, 1995).

Küster, Konrad, *Der junge Bach* (Stuttgart, 1996).

Leaver, Robin, *Bach's Theological Library: a Critical Bibliography* (Neuhausen-Stuttgart, 1983).

Little, Meredith, and Natalie Jenne, *Dance and the Music of J. S. Bach* (Bloomington, 1991).

Marshall, Robert Lewis, *The Compositional Process of J. S. Bach* (Princeton, 1972).

—— *The Music of Johann Sebastian Bach: the Sources, the Style, the Significance* (New York, 1989).

Melamed, Daniel R. (ed.), *Bach Studies 2* (Cambridge, 1995).

Mellers, Wilfrid, *Bach and the Dance of God* (London, 1980).

Neumann, Frederick, *Ornamentation in Baroque and Post-Baroque Music, with Special Emphasis on J. S. Bach* (Princeton, 1978).

Neumann, Werner, *Bach and his World* (London, 1961; German original, 1960).

Parry, C. Hubert H., *Johann Sebastian Bach* (London, 1909; 2nd ed., 1930).

Pirro, André, *Johann-Sebastian Bach* (Paris, 1906; English translation, 1957).

Schering, Arnold, *Johann Sebastian Bach und das Musikleben Leipzigs im 18. Jahrhundert* (Leipzig, 1941).

Schweitzer, Albert, *J. S. Bach* (London, 1911; German version, 1908; French original, 1905).

Schwendowius, Barbara, and Wolfgang Dömling, *Johann Sebastian Bach: Life, Times, Influence* (Kassel, 1977; German original, 1976).

Smend, Friedrich, *J. S. Bach bei seinem Namen gerufen* (Kassel, 1950).

—— *Bach in Köthen* (Berlin, 1951; English translation, 1985).

Spitta, Philipp, *Johann Sebastian Bach* (London, 1884–5; German original, 1873–80).

Stauffer, G. B. (ed.), *Bach Perspectives*, ii (Lincoln, Nebraska, 1996).

Stiller, Günther, *Johann Sebastian Bach und das Leipziger gottesdienstliche Leben seiner Zeit* (Berlin, 1970; English translation, 1984).

Stinson, Russell, *The Bach Manuscripts of Johann Peter Kellner and his Circle* (Durham, North Carolina, and London, 1989).

—— (ed.), *Bach Perspectives*, i (Lincoln, Nebraska, 1995).

Tatlow, Ruth, *Bach and the Riddle of the Number Alphabet* (Cambridge, 1991).

Terry, Charles Sanford, *Bach: a Biography* (London, 1928; 6th ed., 1967).

—— *Bach's Orchestra* (London, 1932; 4th ed., 1966).

—— *The Music of Bach: an Introduction* (London, 1933).

Weaver, Robert L. and others (ed.), *Essays on the Music of J. S. Bach and Other Divers Subjects: a Tribute to Gerhard Herz* (Louisville, 1981).

Williams, Peter (ed.), *Bach, Handel, Scarlatti: Tercentenary Essays* (Cambridge, 1985).

Wolff, Christoph, *Der stile antico in der Musik Johann Sebastian Bachs* (Wiesbaden, 1968).

—— *Bach: Essays on his Life and Music* (Cambridge, Massachusetts, 1991).

—— *Johann Sebastian Bach: The Learned Musician* (New York, 2000).

Young, Percy M., *The Bachs 1500–1850* (London, 1970).

## 4 Vocal Works

Blankenburg, Walter, *Einführung in Bachs h-moll Messe* (Kassel, 1959; 3rd ed., 1973).

Butt, John, *Bach: Mass in B minor* (Cambridge, 1991).

Chafe, Eric, *Tonal Allegory in the Vocal Music of J. S. Bach* (Berkeley, 1991).

Crist, Stephen A., *Aria Forms in the Vocal Works of J. S. Bach, 1714–1724* (dissertation, Brandeis University, 1988).

Daw, Stephen, *The Music of Johann Sebastian Bach: the Choral Works* (Rutherford, Madison, Teaneck, 1981).

Day, James, *The Literary Background to Bach's Cantatas* (London, 1961).

Dürr, Alfred, *Die Johannes-Passion von Johann Sebastian Bach* (Kassel, 1988).

—— *Die Kantaten von Johann Sebastian Bach* (Kassel, 1971; 5th ed. [with cantata texts], 1985).

—— *Zur Chronologie der Leipziger Vokalwerke* (Kassel, 1976).

Marissen, Michael, *Lutheranism, Anti-Judaism, and Bach's St. John Passion* (New York, 1998).

Melamed, Daniel R., *J. S. Bach and the German Motet* (Cambridge, 1995).

Neumann, Werner, *Handbuch der Kantaten Joh. Seb. Bachs* (Leipzig, 1947; 4th ed. 1971; English translation, 1947).

Schering, Arnold, *Johann Sebastian Bachs Leipziger Kirchenmusik* (Leipzig, 1936; 2nd ed., 1954).

Smallman, Basil, *The Background of Passion Music: J. S. Bach and his Predecessors* (London, 1957; 2nd ed., 1970).

Stauffer, George, *Bach: Mass in B minor* (New York, 1997).

Steinitz, Paul, *Bach's Passions* (London, 1979).

Terry, Charles Sanford, *Bach's Chorales* (Cambridge, 1915–21).

—— *Joh. Seb. Bach: Cantata Texts, Sacred and Secular* (London, 1926).

Wolff, Christoph, *The World of the Bach Cantatas* (New York, 1995).

## 5 Instrumental and Theoretical Works

Boyd, Malcolm, *Bach: the Brandenburg Concertos* (Cambridge, 1993).

Butler, Gregory, *Bach's Clavier-Übung III: the Making of a Print* (Durham, North Carolina, and London, 1990).

Carrell, Norman, *Bach's Brandenburg Concertos* (London, 1963).

David, Hans T., *J. S. Bach's Musical Offering: History, Interpretation and Analysis* (New York, 1945).

Dreyfus, Laurence, *Bach and the Patterns of Invention* (Cambridge, Massachusetts, 1996).

Grace, Harvey, *The Organ Works of Bach* (London, 1922).

Humphreys, David, *The Esoteric Structure of Bach's Clavierübung III* (Cardiff, 1983).

Keller, Hermann, *Die Klavier-Werke Bachs* (Leipzig, 1950).

Marissen, Michael, *The Social and Religious Designs of J. S. Bach's Brandenburg Concertos* (Princeton, 1995).

Poulin, Pamela L. (ed.), *J. S. Bach's Precepts and Principles for Playing the Thorough-Bass or Accompanying in Four Parts, Leipzig, 1738* (Oxford, 1994).

Schulenberg, David, *The Keyboard Music of J. S. Bach* (New York, 1992).

Stauffer, George, and Ernest May (eds.), *J. S. Bach as Organist: his Instruments, Music and Performance Practices* (London, 1986).

Tomita, Yo, *J. S. Bach's 'Das Wohltemperierte Clavier II': a Critical Commentary* (Leeds, 1993–5).

Tovey, Donald Francis, *A Companion to the Art of Fugue* (London, 1931).

Vogt, Hans, *Johann Sebastian Bach's Chamber Music* (Portland, Oregon, 1988; German original, 1981).

Wiemer, Wolfgang, *Die wiederhergestellte Ordnung in Johann Sebastian Bachs Kunst der Fuge* (Wiesbaden, 1977).

Williams, Peter, *Bach Organ Music* (London, 1972).

—— *The Organ Music of J. S. Bach*, i,ii (Cambridge, 1980), iii (Cambridge, 1984).

## 6 Periodicals etc.

To list every important article on Bach in periodicals, journals, *Festschriften* and conference reports would require far more space than is available here. Two journals devoted specifically to Bach studies are:

*Bach-Jahrbuch*, published by the Neue Bach-Gesellschaft, Leipzig, since 1904 (vol. 50 [1963–4] contains an index to the preceding volumes).
*Bach*, published half-yearly (formerly quarterly) by the Riemenschneider Bach Institute, Baldwin-Wallace College, Ohio, since 1970.

Several important periodical articles have been cited in footnotes to the present study. Others may be located through the following:

*The Music Index* (Detroit, 1949–).
*RILM Abstracts* (1967–).

Indispensable for tracing relevant articles in *Festschriften* and conference reports are:

Gerboth, Walter, *An Index to Musical Festschriften* (London, 1969).
Tyrrell, John, and Rosemary Wise, *A Guide to International Congress Reports in Musicology* (London, 1979).

# General Index

# Index of Bach's Works